PRAISE FOR
PROFILES IN MURDER

"I am seldom ⸻ agel's seminar. . . . Thi⸻s that will shock you wit⸻ prepared. You will learn ⸻g than you hoped for. Vor⸻smerizing. This is not a te⸻aching you; *he is the real thing.*"

—Ann Rule, author of
The Stranger Beside Me and *Bitter Harvest*

"A frank, no-holds-barred chronicle of violence and death in all its brutally shocking, graphic details. Russell Vorpagel delivers his message with astonishing candor. . . . He gives a clear, penetrating glimpse into the minds of sick, depraved, deranged killers involved in serial murders, sexual crimes, and celebrity violence."

—Frank M. Jordan, former mayor and
chief of police, city and county of San Francisco

"This is rip-roaring biography that reads like fiction."
—*Booklist*

"Russ Vorpagel was a legend in the FBI. This book is about that legend. It is as exciting as the man himself. Here is the art of profiling—the psychological autopsy of a murder—laid out before you like a series of FBI reports. I invite you to join the most intriguing account of profiling you are ever likely to read."

—Robert Ressler, author of
Whoever Fights Monsters

"This book is real. . . . You will ask yourself, 'Where is this going?' at the same time you will find yourself unable to set it down. For years to come you will find this book in the offices of homicide investigators and prosecuting attorneys throughout the world in death investigations. This investigating tool is long overdue."

—J. Fred Bowman, former chairman, criminology
department, Yuba Community College

PROFILES IN MURDER

AN FBI LEGEND DISSECTS KILLERS AND THEIR CRIMES

RUSSELL VORPAGEL

as told to
JOSEPH HARRINGTON

A DELL BOOK

A Dell Book
Published by
Dell Publishing
A division of Random House, Inc.
1540 Broadway
New York, New York 10036

Cover design by Robert Santora

Dell books may be purchased for business or promotional use or for special sales. For information please write to: Special Markets Department, Random House, Inc., 1540 Broadway, New York, N.Y. 10036.

Dell® is a registered trademark of Random House, Inc., and the colophon is a trademark of Random House, Inc.

ISBN: 0-440-23552-9

Reprinted by arrangement with Perseus Books

Printed in the United States of America

Published simultaneously in Canada

January 2001

10 9 8 7 6 5 4 3 2 1

OPM

To my mother, Gladys, who said, "Be a master of ceremonies"; to my father, Ervin Vorpagel, who said, "Be a sailor or a policeman"; and to my beloved wife of forty-eight years, Nancy.

CONTENTS

FOREWORD

A few years ago, I was invited to present a seminar to a group of law enforcement professionals in Walla Walla, Washington. After my presentation was finished, I joined the students for the next seminar. The presenter was Russell Vorpagel, a former special agent of the FBI. To say that I had my eyes opened would be an understatement—Vorpagel was a dynamic teacher, a man of vast experience in dealing with the criminal—and often deranged—mind. As a onetime police officer myself and an author of true crime books for twenty-five years, I am seldom shocked. I was shocked by Russ Vorpagel's seminar, but I left that auditorium in Walla Walla armed with information and insights I had never before encountered.

Profiles in Murder is a book that will make readers feel as if they are sitting in a darkened auditorium somewhere in America, hearing things that they could never have imagined. Russ Vorpagel and a handful of special agents had the vision years ago to develop a new kind of detective work, techniques that did not *replace* the time-honored "seat-of-the-pants" knowledge that great working cops have, but, rather, added to it. Profiling aberrant human minds makes so much sense that it is amazing no one ever defined the concept before. Profiling uses known facts and moves on to deductive reasoning. A simple procedure? Perhaps. But in the hands of those FBI agents and superior detectives who employ profiling, it is an almost mystic process. They can winnow out the killer from a mass of suspects.

This book will show you, the students, a series of real cases that will shock you with their depravity and their cruelty, so be prepared. However, at the same time, you will learn more about the actual art of profiling than you hoped. Vorpagel's instructive techniques are mesmerizing. This is not a television or movie detective who is teaching you; he is the real thing.

I have often wondered what killers think when they learn just how much their trackers discerned about them. If they had known, would they have carried out their crimes? Tragically, they probably would not have been deterred. There is some comfort to be taken, however, in picturing a caged murderer who contemplates the profilers who smiled inwardly as they said a silent "Gotcha!"

Profiles in Murder will take its place beside Robert Ressler's *Whoever Fights Monsters*, Robert Keppel's *Signature Killers*, John Douglas's *Mindhunters*, and, I hope, some of my own books that discuss the inner workings and Achilles' heels of the most dangerous criminals of our time.

ANN RULE

This is a book about the art of profiling—the psychological autopsy of a murder.

This book will not make you a profiling expert; but it will help you understand what goes on in the minds of sexual perverts and serial killers. It is important to recognize the clues that give the telltale signs that say it is time to call in the professional—the FBI profiler.

RUSS VORPAGEL

ACKNOWLEDGMENTS

The author would like to thank the following people:
Author Ann Rule for writing the Foreword.

Author and former FBI Agent Robert Ressler for writing the Introduction.

San Francisco Deputy Police Chief Diarmund Philpott for suggesting that Russ Vorpagel had a story to tell.

Attorney Doug Vigil, of the Turner Branch Law Firm, for his cooperation and help in the Randy Force Case in Albuquerque, New Mexico.

Attorney Bill Wagner, senior partner of the firm of Wagner, Cunningham, Vaughan & McLaughlin in Tampa, Florida, for his help in providing information on Vorpagel's testimony in the Jake Horton case.

Author Robert Burger for active participation in structuring the story line and editing.

Historian Steve Cotrell for his research involving the Jake Horton case.

Script doctor Tucker Spolter for his analysis of story flow.

Police Chief Fred Bowman for all the years he worked with me as an instructor in homicide.

FBI Agent Jack Shed for the countless hours we spent creating criminology curriculums.

FBI Supervisory Special Agent Roy Hazelwood for his experiences while investigating sex crimes.

FBI Agent Ken Lanning for helping me on scores of bombing/homicide cases in California.

FBI Assistant Director Bob Doran for getting me transferred to the Behavioral Science Unit.

FBI Deputy Assistant Director Jim McKensie for standing beside me during the entire Bell fiasco.

FBI Supervisory Special Agent Dave Kriskovcich for introducing me into criminal education in Central and South America.

FBI Special Agent in charge of California's Sacramento office Jack Reed for encouraging me to teach death investigation throughout the entire country and federal park services.

Milwaukee Police Inspector George Fuhr for stimulating my initial hunger for law enforcement work.

Retired FBI Agent William Hagerty, now Director of Criminal Training for the Institute of Police Training and Management, University of Northern Florida, for getting me involved in the Jake Horton case.

Police Chief Dennis La Piane for introducing me to Ann Rule.

Joe Harrington, without whom this book would never have been written.

And to the many law enforcement departments across the United States that gave us access to their transcripts and files in the dozens of cases used as examples in this book.

INTRODUCTION

The first sentence of my book about serial killers, *Whoever Fights Monsters*, is: "Russ Vorpagel was a legend in the FBI."

This book is about that legend. It is as exciting as the man himself.

Here is the art of profiling—the psychological autopsy of a murder—laid out before you like a series of FBI reports. What does the crime scene tell us about the mindset of the perpetrator? And what does that mindset tell us about the habits and the appearance and the background of the killer?

This approach to criminology was broadly hinted at by Edgar Allan Poe, but its full psychological component did not come to the fore until the Mad Bomber case of 1939–1946 in New York. Along with myself and a few others at FBI headquarters in the 1970s, Russ formalized this technique in our Behavioral Science Unit. The popular book and movie *The Silence of the Lambs* brought this work to public attention. Profiling, in serial-killer cases, is today one of the most powerful tools that law enforcement possesses. At the FBI alone, hundreds of cases of this type benefit each year from the art of profiling.

Russ shows the strong similarities between cases that have attracted intense media coverage—such as the Unabomber, O. J. Simpson, Jeffrey Dahmer—with lesser known events that are just as frightening, but received only local media attention and happen all the time.

This is not a book about Russ Vorpagel, but about an important tool of criminology. It is based on the classes he has conducted for police officers all over the country and in many parts of the world. It was natural to structure the book along these lines, to put you, the reader, in the front row of the classroom. His coauthors have been in that room many times and have written the book from their vantage point. I invite you to join in the most intriguing account of profiling you are ever likely to read.

ROBERT RESSLER

THE THIN BLUE LINE

Russell Vorpagel glanced at his roster—twenty-eight students, some detectives, some DA's, some pathologists, and a few coroners—all wanting to improve their knowledge in the field of death investigation.

Vorpagel had opened the first three days of his two-week class in exactly the same way for the past twenty years. He had stumbled on the presentation by accident. He had heard the poem years earlier in an English class. In a flash of inspiration, he realized how it could be used to send a powerful message to law enforcement agents.

He turned off the lights and turned on the slide projector. The first slide was of a field of poppies.

In a voice filled with strong emotion, he began, "The following poem was written by Lieutenant Colonel John McCrae in 1915. He was a physician, a volunteer at the front. The Lieutenant Colonel died in Number 14 General Hospital, British Expeditionary Force, on January 28, 1918."

Vorpagel saw the looks on his pupils' faces. They were puzzled, as they should have been. He said, "When you buy a red poppy on Memorial Day, it is in commemoration of the thousands of fine men who died and were immortalized by McCrae's beautiful poem."

Russ paused, then recited the verses written over seventy years before, accompanied by an appropriate slide.

> In Flanders field the poppies grow,
> Between the crosses, row on row,
> That mark our place; and in the sky,
> The larks, still bravely singing, fly
> Scarce heard amid the guns below.

Some of the students shuffled in their seats.

Vorpagel knew what they were thinking: what did this have to do with death investigation? He clicked the button and a picture of Arlington Cemetery appeared on the huge white screen. Here he showed dozens of slides of dead bodies.

He recited, in a low, husky voice,

> We are the dead. Short days ago
> We lived, felt dawn, saw sunset glow,
> Loved and were loved, and now we lie
>   In Flanders field.
> Take up our quarrel with the foe,
> To you from failing hands we throw
> The torch; be yours to hold on high,
> If ye break faith with us who die,
> We shall not sleep, though poppies grow,
>   In Flanders field.

Vorpagel paused. It inevitably happened in every class. Someone would ask the question.

A student asked, "What does a poem written about World War I have to do with murder investigation?"

Vorpagel hit the slide button one more time. He heard the intake of breath from his students.

"This," he said, "is a photo of the abdomen of La Bianca, one of the Charles Manson victims. Don't ever think, not for an instant, that you, and all your fellow officers across the country who make up that incredibly thin blue line, are not engaged in a war." Approximately 25,000 murders a year equals almost 2 million dead since World War I.

CHAPTER ONE

KILLING WAYS

Profiling the repeat murderer," Russell Vorpagel told his class, "can be compared to a doctor's predictions regarding a patient's progress in a disease."

The class was composed of twenty-eight men and women, all linked in one way or another to the criminal justice system. After showing them his opening slides accompanied by the words of "In Flanders Field," it was time to teach them about the repeat killers, perverts, and bombers.

"Serial killers have a disease," Vorpagel continued. "If a doctor is told that his new patient first showed signs of increasing fatigue, then rapid heartbeat when trying to go to sleep at night, and finally blurred vision, one next logical step is to test for a thyroid condition. If a criminal profiler is told that a teenager is a bed wetter, plays with matches, and tortures animals, he can predict the potential for future sociopathic homicides. It's not magic, it's logic."

Vorpagel had taught in warehouses, in police academies, and in military armories all his life. Teaching used to be one of the assignments of the Federal Bureau of Investigation countrywide. But now, because of financial cutbacks, this mandate was only continued at Quantico, FBI headquarters in Virginia. Retired FBI agents were taking up the slack.

Now in his seventy-first year, Vorpagel was in robust condition. He was six-two and a half. He had a mane of hair and an unkempt beard that contrasted, jarringly, with his precise diction. The beard could not disguise a cleft under his right cheekbone, a trace of scar tissue. Nor did he choose to cover up, with a long-sleeved shirt, the dragon tattooed down his left shoulder to his forearm.

After a week and a half of lectures, his students had gotten used to all this, even to the stomach-turning procession of slides that illustrated each subject: Hostage Negotiation, Differential Diagnosis of Death, Forensic Anthropology, Interrogation, Legal Search and Seizure.

He studied the faces of his students and wondered how they would react to this, his final act, the last three days of the two-week course of horrors.

Vorpagel said, "For the last three days of lectures, we will look at something challenging: profiling the criminal's mind. In the past few years, many people have jumped on the bandwagon and have tried to enter this field.

"Even television has engaged in showing profiling—of course, every case is solved in an hour."

He studied his students' faces. These men and women knew from the street that nothing is that easy.

Vorpagel continued, "The FBI had a program in the Behavioral Science Unit, where we would take four police officers a year from the outside, each with a minimum of a psychology degree and five years of field experience. They would spend one year at Quantico. This school lasted for ten years, and then a couple of students became so stressed out they committed suicide. That was the end of the project. Now, only FBI agents attend the program."

The Latino woman in the second row and the Asian woman seated next to her looked skeptical. The dour, pale-faced man in the third row, sullen, either unshaven or swarthy, narrowed his eyes. The youngest member of the classroom, sitting in the last row, sat up a little straighter.

Vorpagel said, "If it takes a year and a specialized college degree to even grasp the concept, why do I include this subject in my lectures? Because, even a smattering of knowledge, learned from sample cases, can give you the warning signs. Those case histories that mean 'call in an expert.' When you arrive at a homicide scene, you know you'll need fingerprint experts, blood experts, DNA experts. But not every homicide case needs profiling. And the FBI does not have the manpower. I teach these lessons so you, the front line troops, can recognize the signs and know when to use them."

Vorpagel continued, "In profiling we try to determine what goes on in the mind of the criminal. Why is this so unusual? In a job interview, we 'size up' our applicants and in sports, we try to 'feel out' the competition with preliminary parries."

The students fidgeted in their seats as he paused for a reaction. A few, the two women in the second row, the dour man in the third row, the intensely alert young African-American in the fourth row, met his eyes.

He glanced at his attendance roster, moving his finger over the names and job descriptions: the Latino woman, Ava, California Department of Corrections; the pale-faced man, Gary, a lawyer with the Sacramento District Attorney's Office; the Asian woman, Shui, a public defender from Fresno; the young African-American man, Marcus, a San Francisco patrolman.

Vorpagel sized up the man in the fourth row. Too young to be an investigative officer. He's a rookie.

He continued, "Edgar Allan Poe, in 'The Murders in the Rue Morgue,' dealt with predicting future acts in reviewing the past behavior of a criminal. He had his nineteenth-century character solve the murders by profiling. He found that the perpetrator of the grisly killings was an escaped orangutan."

Gary, the pale-faced lawyer with the air of a mortician, raised his hand. Long, white fingers and knuckles, accentuated under the neon lights, asked for acknowledgment. "Are you saying," the question came dirge-like, "that you could have deciphered that the killer was an ape?"

"No, an orangutan. Not a gibbon, not a gorilla, not a chimpanzee. Hair fibers left at the scene, the Rue Morgue, made it absolutely conclusive as to the heritage of the perpetrator."

Marcus raised his hand, a bemused smile on his dark face. "Was the art of forensics advanced enough during Poe's era to differentiate between the hair of a simian and a human?"

Good question, Vorpagel thought, and I don't have a clue.

"Or," Marcus continued, "was it just the intuitive

hunch of a brilliant author of what was to come in police procedure?"

The answer came from the second question. "No, it had to be an orangutan. Just as serial killers pick the spectacular, Poe did also. The story would not have had the impact if the killer was just an ape. Drab, colorless, mundane. But an orangutan gave it spice, life, vigor. The various minds of the sociopath act in the same way—they want a statement, they want individuality, they want identity."

Vorpagel paused, then said, "To establish patterns, the FBI did something. We instituted the Behavioral Science Unit to study as many mass and serial murderers and recidivistic rapists as possible. Hundreds of case histories were compiled through interviews in the prison system and from police departments throughout the country."

Gary said, "I've learned a bit about that FBI study. The story I heard said you and a few other agents worked *sub rosa* to set up that unit."

"Our work was viewed, back in the seventies, as being close to soothsaying. If I predicted that the killer was a midteenager who lived within viewing of the crime scene and it turned out that the perpetrator was a dirty old transient, then the Bureau would have been embarrassed."

"Same old political bull," Ava said.

Vorpagel said, "Maybe not. The basic psychology is still not accepted by a lot of educated people. Yet the prisoners we talked to were cooperative. They were quite truthful once they had their appeals denied and no longer needed to con their social workers, defense attorneys, and juries."

Shui said, "That's pretty cynical."

"Maybe, for a defense attorney like yourself. But I conducted many of these interviews. Mine was not a cynical observation; it was a fact. The convicted prisoners told it from their own points of view. My colleagues and I made appropriate checks of the facts. We explored fantasies and rituals. We asked about childhood, family, family activities, dating habits, sex habits, work habits, hobbies, fears, frights, goals, ideals, dreams. A pattern began to emerge in the personality of a crime and its scene . . ."

Gary interrupted, "Is it really a branch of criminology?"

"Each branch of criminal investigation was once something else. The key word here is *patterns*. Patterns become a mold—a casting—into which you pour the 'facts' from a crime scene. Without enough information, the casting is incomplete. With incorrect or conflicting information, the picture is useless."

Marcus asked, "Can you give us an example?"

Vorpagel answered, "I'll give you two. One brief and very famous, the other obscure, but more in depth. The first—the Unabomber circus and trial—had a very personal meaning for me. FBI headquarters in Sacramento requested I do the first profile on this mad bomber, after his first three attacks. I suggested, among many other things, that he was probably very good at physics but not at chemistry, because of the quality and flaws in his devices."

"Based on?" Shui asked.

"He used homemade black powder, timed to go off by an altimeter on an American Airlines plane.

Good mechanics, poor explosive. Not enough brisance, or shattering power. So the power just did a slow burn."

"I remember when Kaczynski pled guilty to the killings."

Vorpagel said, "Just another deadly felon trying to avoid the death penalty."

"I've read about how . . ."

"Books have already been written about the Kaczynski case, just as so many have been written about Ted Bundy, Edward Kemper III, and all the others, the John Wayne Gacys and the Wayne Williamses of this world."

Shui said, "Those are the ones that made the news."

"Exactly. And if you want to study the famous, buy those books. I deal with what is happening every day all over this country. Your next-door neighbor, your barber, your boyfriend—there are ticking time bombs out there. Over 2 percent of the population of the United States has been classified as suffering a major mental disorder, Also Known As psychotics. One-half of 1 percent of the psychotics are considered to be dangerous to themselves or to others.

"In 1979, the American Psychiatric Association [APA] changed the terminology of the word *psychopath* into two new words: *sociopath* and *antisocial*. The reason for this was that 'psyche' relates to the mind, and 'path' relates to illness. The APA classified the 'psychopath' not as psychotic but as antisocial because his characteristics were not considered a major mental illness.

"Something occasionally triggers psychotics into

action. They kill, they mutilate, they destroy. Your chances are fairly good of running into the types of cases I am going to present to you, like the following case, typical of hundreds. It is very short compared to some of the ones I'll give you over the next three days."

The body of a twenty-two-year-old white female was found in a makeshift dump in a mountainous region by a man who was on a nature walk. The local coroner was not inexperienced, just new to this type of crime.

He bent over the table and examined the corpse. His voice shook as he talked into the overhead microphone: "There are indications of multiple blunt injuries to the head, face, and jaw resulting in a massive, transverse, basal skull fracture. Multiple sawed or carved wounds, some apparently made postmortem, reveal both nipples avulsed by a dull instrument, irregularly arranged margins just outside the areola areas, as if each nipple had been grasped, pulled up, and sliced off by a rapid back-and-forth cutting motion."

The young coroner turned from the mutilated body. He wiped his forehead with a handkerchief and looked up at the case's investigating police officer. The man's craggy face was unchanged, despite the presence of such carnage. He said, "An avulsed nipple was found near the body of the victim."

The coroner turned back to his work. His voice came out low as he continued, "A huge nonbloody laceration extends from the lumen of the vagina backward, upward and to the right completely transecting the rectovaginal structures to the extent that when fully spread apart this allowed the cervix uteri to be viewed between the buttocks."

• • •

Vorpagel turned off the classroom lights and turned on the projector. A colored slide appeared on the screen. It was a picture of the crime scene and the victim. It was sickeningly vivid. He continued relentlessly to show slide after slide. Different angles of the corpse appeared. The wounds, the organs, the blood, the terror on the victim's face—all were shown.

Vorpagel asked, "What are your conclusions?"

Most heads were bent forward. With the exception of the two women in the second row, the pale-faced man in the third, and the rookie, Vorpagel could not see anyone's eyes.

Hard-core my ass, he thought. We all feel—we all identify—with the horror, no matter how many times we see it, hear it, smell it, taste it.

He repeated, "Conclusions?"

Shui said, "Do you have to be so graphic? I mean, the exact details and the slides?"

"I know defense attorneys don't like crime scene photos shown to juries. This is not a courtroom. This is a classroom. I deal in reality, so I use slides to make the crime scenes come alive."

Vorpagel paused, then asked, "Now, conclusions?"

Marcus said, "There are several patterns of criminal brutality noted in your sample. Some offenders rape, mutilate, then murder. Others murder, then mutilate. In the case cited, the mutilation happened after death—the nonbloody laceration—and it acted as a defeminization of specific body areas."

"Wrong," Vorpagel said. "The act of defeminization is an attempt by the perpetrator, who has an intense fear and loathing of women, to believe in his mind that this is no longer a threatening female. For example, after death, both breasts are cut off and a stick or similar-shaped object shoved in the vagina, representing a penis. You can break this into three categories: one—curiosity, only one breast is cut to see what's inside, and the stick is placed gently into the vagina to test its depth; two—defeminization, which I've just described; and three—torture, a vicious assault while the victim is still alive. The first two are psychotics, the last, the sociopath. The sociopath performs these sort of acts while the victim is alive and conscious."

Vorpagel studied the rookie. "Any other thoughts?"

Marcus plunged on. "One nipple was missing from the scene of the crime. The perp was a trophy-taker."

Not bad, Vorpagel thought, for a rookie. He said, "The perp *was* a trophy-taker. That's how we caught him. He left a crime signature as clear as any fingerprint. A pattern was identified, linked, projected, and the man was caught."

"What was the pattern?"

"The killer repeated in a ritualistic manner, and in a sadistic fantasy. A pattern of dates and times emerged."

"Could you elaborate on how you caught him?"

"He was a hospital ambulance driver. He would kidnap his female victims from the parking lot of a restaurant, take them to another location, mutilate, rape, then murder them. Then he would make an anonymous phone call to the police, reporting that he had seen a body. He would then wait to receive the call from the police for an ambulance to be sent. He would drive the ambulance with the body back to the hospital, during which time he would watch people's reactions. A profile was done, a trap set, he was caught."

Marcus said, "The murderer was obviously orchestrating the entire scene so he could relive his fantasy."

"Exactly. When he was arrested, we found a secret life and props that allowed a continual reliving of events. We found women's underwear in the man's closet. We found young boys' clothing, women's high-heeled shoes. Photos of the victims were there, both before and after death. Newspaper clippings describing the events were found on the wall of his apartment. We also discovered that he had a preoccupation with pornography, an emphasis on S&M, bondage, and discipline. The lab discovered masturbation fantasies involving pictures of Nazi officers."

Vorpagel paused, not for dramatic effect but to observe. For years, he had used this particular case in his lecture, not because it was more grisly than any of the others that he had investigated.

It wasn't.

His career was sprinkled with a liberal dosage of horror, like the Sacramento Vampire—a man who, while being interviewed by the prison psychiatrist, hurled himself through a wire-meshed window, ran across a manicured lawn, grabbed a bird, and bit its head off—then drank its blood, just as he had drunk his victims' blood.

The ambulance driver, his fetishes, his fantasies, were actually run-of-the-mill stuff among serial killers. The particulars, the S&M, the Nazis, the photos, added an element that almost screamed for a disgusted reaction from both men and women.

Vorpagel saw the revulsion in most of his students'

faces. Ava had her jaw clenched. The eyes of Gary, the pale-faced prosecutor, held a look of avid, horrified interest.

Shui, Russ thought, is staring at me with an unflinching gaze.

He glanced to the last row. Marcus's eyelids were half closed. His cheek muscles were clearly tight.

Vorpagel thought, I wonder what he's doing in a class almost exclusively filled with men and women whose jobs are directly related to homicide? He's too young to be involved in anything besides patrol work.

Vorpagel glanced at his watch—the period had sped by. "That's it for today. The next three days, we will study actual cases involving murder."

"Like what?" Ava asked.

"The rich and the famous. The poor and the infamous. A vampire. A pedophiliac and murdering barber. A jilted bomber. Profiling that worked; and profiling that didn't."

His students stood.

Marcus waited patiently for the room to empty.

Vorpagel asked, "Can I help you?"

"When I joined the force, I didn't want to walk a beat the rest of my life."

"You wanted . . . ?"

"To investigate homicides."

"And that's why you're taking this course."

"One reason. Another is you were recommended to me by my commanding officer, who mentioned you've been involved in over a thousand death investigations. You were there in the very beginning in helping to create the FBI's serial-killer profiling."

"And you're hopeful that I'm a good enough teacher to impart some of that knowledge to you."

"That, and . . ." The young cop shrugged, "and curiosity. My commander mentioned that something happened between you and the Rastafarians."

"Ultraextremist branch of the Rastafarians."

"Something that made you famous in the FBI."

Vorpagel shoved his notes into his briefcase. "Ancient history."

"Not that ancient. I heard it happened just before you retired."

"What did you hear?"

The rookie pointed to the small scar under Vorpagel's right eye. "That you're the luckiest man alive."

Vorpagel said, "You'd be better off concentrating on the work at hand. The past's the past."

Marcus grinned, "If I get an A in your course, will you tell me what happened between you and the Rastafarians?"

"*If* you get an A. Get a good night's sleep. Tomorrow's cases are on a man who used artwork to stalk a terrified woman, a couple of examples of big and small errors made in profiling, and a rampaging vampire."

BLOOD LINES

The twenty-eight men and women in the classroom watched Vorpagel set up his projector and insert his slides.

The ex-FBI agent shuffled the papers on the dais. He found what he was looking for and read, "There are basically two types of crime scenes: organized and disorganized. Subtitles under these are altered and unaltered. First, let's examine the altered crime scene."

Gary asked, "Are you talking about concealed crime?"

"No. The organized crime scene does not mean that the crime itself has been concealed. Rather, there is a sense of organization aimed at deterring detection. The offender takes precautions against discovery of himself. Few, if any, weapons or fingerprints are found. The crime appears to be deliberate, calculated, and preplanned. Investigators find little evidence to work with in developing a profile of the subject. The offender has stalked, abducted, abused, and murdered the victim—all with cold, calculating premeditation."

Ava, from the Department of Corrections, said, "Like a Mafia hit."

"Exactly. This morning, we will examine the second type, the disorganized crime scene. The first impression of the disorganized crime scene is that the crime was committed suddenly and with no action for deterring detection."

"Meaning?" Marcus asked.

"There is great disarray and disorganization."

"Can you give an example?"

"The weapon is often present at the scene. No attempt has been made to conceal the body. There is usually a great deal of evidence to use in the investigation."

"I assume," Marcus said, "that this type lends itself to profiling the most."

"Exactly."

"Can you give an example using an actual case?"

"Of course. That's how I teach. The following case helped establish the validity of profiling with the higher powers in the FBI."

"Involving?" Shui asked.

"It started with a shortage of beds."

"And led to?"

"To a sort of cannibalism you saw in the Jeffrey Dahmer case. All of you have heard of that one. I'd like you to look at the similarities and differences with this one."

Vorpagel took a deep breath. He loved dredging up the ability he learned in college as a thespian when he told the class his case studies. He created vivid dramatization of the cases. He acted out the dialogue. He internalized the thoughts of both the victims and the perpetrator. The recreation of the victim's thoughts came from talking to the victim's relatives.

He'd been asked many times how he knew what someone was thinking.

It's easy, Vorpagel thought, they told me.

"We need the bed." The psychiatrist plopped his file on the table and threw his hands in the air. "There are all kinds of incapacitated patients who should be in here. But not this one."

A man in a three-piece suit agreed with a loud sigh. "As the conservator, I feel it's in the best interest of his estate."

"Estate, hell!" a female voice boomed from the back of the room. She was a nurse, dressed in crisp whites. "You don't know what's going on. He's tearing the heads off birds."

A male nurse tried to intervene. "Please, we're dealing with personal opinions. But I will say that the staff is united on this. They're mad as hell."

The psychiatrist persisted. "My report is that Richard is responding to medication."

"He's also," the loud nurse broke in, "biting the heads off birds." She looked out the window at a playground across the street. It was alive with children of various ages, some graceful, some awkward.

The chief psychiatrist insisted, "He's controlled, even calm, during my counseling sessions."

"He's still smearing blood on his shirt," the female nurse said firmly.

"Where's he getting the blood?"

"Probably from birds with no heads."

The second psychiatrist pointed again to his records. "Richard is in control of himself."

"The guy got in here in the first place for trying to shoot a rabbit's blood into his arm."

"He's not doing that anymore."

"No, he's drinking it now. Two nurse's aides have quit because of this maniac. There isn't a patient in the place that will share a room with him. Even the nut cases are afraid of him."

"I've warned you about using derogatory language when referring to our patients."

"Okay, but the inmates have nicknamed him 'Dracula.' Even the patients recognize a paranoid schizophrenic, with persecution delusions, when they see one."

"When did you become a psychiatrist?"

"I'm just a nurse. But you don't have to be Freud to know there's something wrong with a guy who thinks his own blood's turning into powder."

"He hasn't spoken about that for months."

"Maybe not to you. I talked to him yesterday. He explained in great detail how a rabbit he had eaten had drunk battery acid. And now that acid was eating him from the inside."

"That's old history. Richard has assured me that he realizes he was wrong about the battery acid."

"His mother wants Richard released," added the lawyer for the conservatorship.

"This morning," the male nurse said, "he followed me down the hallways, insisting that I take his blood pressure. I did—it was normal. Richard kept insisting that I did it wrong, that he had no blood pressure."

The psychiatrist said, "His mother has agreed to have him released in her custody."

Richard's lawyer opened a file, studied it, then said, "Richard is not a schizophrenic. He has taken LSD. These reports are recent—August—and they indicate he's afflicted with toxic psychosis—from his use of LSD. He is not a mental patient, in my view; rather, he suffers from a curable condition brought on by his massive use of drugs."

"You're just trying to save the state the expense of his hospitalization."

"That's one of my job descriptions."

"What if he escalates?" the female nurse asked, and pointed at the playground across the street. "What if he hurts someone?"

"I find that highly improbable," the psychiatrist said. "He views his situation realistically. He interacts now in a reasonable manner. I'm signing the release form, and that's final."

The male nurse whirled and strode to the door. He turned and said, "The guy's a ticking time bomb."

The female nurse added, "Maybe I shouldn't argue. At least, when the bomb goes off, it won't be here."

The next day, Richard Trenton Chase walked out of the psychiatric ward.

A few months later, the insistent ringing of Vorpagel's telephone, demanding to be answered, finally pierced his sleep. He looked at the clock on the end table: 11:48 P.M.

He lifted the phone, immediately recognizing the voice of a Sacramento deputy sheriff, Fred Homen.

"We have a bad one, far beyond a normal homicide. We are just now transporting the body to the morgue. I think you should attend."

Vorpagel drove to the morgue. The autopsy was just about to begin. The pathologist adjusted the overhead microphone, cleared his throat, and began explaining each part of the proceedings.

Vorpagel watched for a few moments, then buttonholed Deputy Sheriff Ray Biondi. The homicide inspector, who had been assigned to the case, reprised what he knew.

"David Wallin, a teamster, came home earlier, at five that evening. He found his wife, Terry, dead. Her abdomen was gutted. She was three-months pregnant."

Vorpagel studied the crime scene photos and asked, "Is this a trail of blood on the carpet?"

"Yes, the victim was hauled from the front room to the bedroom. She was shot twice—.22 shells were found on the carpet"—Biondi pointed out the location "—then moved to the bed for the postmortem. . . ."

"Desecration?" Vorpagel completed.

Biondi nodded. "See the blood on the carpet, with the smaller circles around it? The lab hasn't a clue what caused them."

Vorpagel studied the photos and shook his head. "Neither have I, except that you're right, she was obviously dragged. Look at the smeared blood going down the hall."

"There was blood on the bathroom floor, and in the sink."

Vorpagel's mind raced ahead as he heard the pathologist intone in a monotone, "The intestine is protruding from the wound. The left nipple has been sliced open."

Vorpagel picked up another photo. "What's that?"

Biondi said, "That's a yogurt cup. It contained blood."

"There was blood *in* the cup?"

"Yes. The blood was also smeared on the outside. No usable prints."

Vorpagel thought, a yogurt cup? Filled with blood? What sort of maniac's loose now? He asked, "Were lip prints on the cup?"

"You mean like lipstick?"

"No. But if you drink blood out of a cup you're bound to get some on your mouth—and then transfer some of it back onto the cup."

"I'll ask the lab. Look at the photograph. The blood on the lip of the cup is smeared, almost like it was . . ."

"Like a wine glass when a woman wipes her lipstick off."

The pathologist began the methodical verbal dissection of the corpse on the table. He could use his knife only after every scratch was duly noted and photographed.

Vorpagel said to Biondi, "I assume you want me in on this for a profile?"

"Yes."

"Bob Ressler and I have talked of doing two independent behavioral profiles, with no consultation, and then comparing the findings. Kind of a scientific test— on the battlefield."

"From a cop's point of view, there's only one big question mark."

"The husband?"

"Yes, he claims he left for work at seven this morning. He's got an alibi for lunch—a sandwich truck at the terminal. The coroner has fixed the time of death before noon."

"How so?" Vorpagel asked.

"The body at home was partially undressed, by an open door, and eviscerated."

"All allowing the body's warmth to escape faster."

"Yes."

"Then, I assume the corpse was taken to the morgue and placed on a cold slab."

"You got it."

"So the time of death is wide open."

"Yeah. The husband is always the first one to suspect. Did you talk to him?"

"I've never seen a guy so broken up."

"I've seen guys cry their eyes out, epitome of bereavement, then learned they'd done it."

"I don't think so," Vorpagel said, "not in this case."

The pathologist droned on. "There are two slugs in the skull, from their size, I would say, .22's. There is fecal matter in the mouth."

The criminologist added, "I've scanned the body with ultraviolet light; there is no evidence of semen."

The pathologist said, "The incision is six inches deep. The force of the entry split the breast plate and sternum."

Vorpagel said, "Degradation of the victim." A slide of the victim showed her legs spread and her privates exposed.

He pointed at another slide. Terry Wallin's kidneys had been removed, then carefully placed under the liver.

"I saw that," Biondi said. "I asked the doctor to give a professional opinion of the ability of the surgical procedure—amateur or professional."

"Smart. Conclusion?"

"Amateur, but he believes the killer has experimented with carving up animals, to practice."

"An amateur with experience. I'll read the rest of the report. Give me a day."

"Then you're thinking the same way I am."

"Which is?"

"That this guy's got all the markings of a repeater."

The Sacramento Sheriff's Department hit the bricks. Door-to-door interviews were conducted. Several people had seen a man in the neighborhood on the day of the Wallin murder. He was dirty, unshaven, wearing a soiled orange parka.

Three days passed. Nothing further—except that a woman in the neighborhood found her cat eviscerated. Then, a dog was picked up by the pound a half-mile away. His guts had been surgically removed.

On Friday, Vorpagel was in his office when a phone call came from Biondi. "There's been another murder, multiple this time, but it looks like the same thing as Monday night."

Vorpagel drove to the location on Merrywood Drive. He had no trouble finding it: Police cars ringed the area. He had to park two blocks away.

He worked his way through the crowd, spotted the county homicide inspector, and ducked under the yellow tape. He noticed that the police officer was visibly shaken. He asked, "How bad?"

"Bad. Brutal. Barbaric."

Vorpagel followed him into the house. His job was to observe, take the overview. Plenty of competent men were gathering evidence, snapping photographs, looking stunned.

He organized his thoughts. Logical, he warned himself, stay logical. There is a dead man, face down, in the front room. There appears to be a bullet hole next to his left ear.

Vorpagel watched the lab team lift two .22 cartridges, unspent, off the carpet.

Unspent? Nervousness maybe? Dropped while trying to reload?

The lab crew tagged a used shell and placed it into a plastic bag.

Vorpagel studied the body again. The legs were crossed at the ankles. There was no postmortem lividity noticeable.

Was the body moved? Turned over? As the crossed ankles indicated? And if so, why?

Vorpagel bent and examined the entry hole. The gun had been fired at extremely close range—almost a contact wound.

He studied the body again. The head was pointed into the living room. The feet extended into the hallway entry. If the man had been facing the other way, before being shot and rolled over, then he'd been going toward the entry, not away.

But the bullet hole is behind the ear.

Did that mean the assailant was in the living room?

The dead man might have come home, entered his living room, seen the intruder, whirled to escape, and been shot.

No—didn't work. The body would have fallen the other way. The body fell into the living room, not into the hallway.

Maybe he wasn't turned over.

Maybe his ankles just got twisted together.

Vorpagel studied the position of the body. It didn't look right. But the body could have been turned over—after death.

Recreate the scene, he told himself. Two possibilities. One, the man enters his house, starts to walk into the living room, and is shot behind the ear. He falls forward, turning as he does, and lies face up. The murderer rolls him over, entangling his ankles. Or two, the man hears someone at the door and . . .

Of course, he thought, the murderer just walked in and surprised him. The door must have been unlocked—as it was in the Wallin killing.

Now, Vorpagel thought, getting into it, I'm the killer. I open the door, I see the man, the man turns to flee, and I shoot him behind the left ear. He falls—face up.

Why do I roll him over?

I'm looking into his lifeless eyes. I know he's dead.

If he had fallen face down, I might roll him over to check his eyes—to see if he's alive. But why roll him over when I'm staring into his face?

Maybe, Vorpagel thought, I don't want to look at his eyes. Maybe I don't want to see that I've killed him. This body wasn't mutilated like Terry Wallin's body. Just a clean, surgical kill.

Why did Biondi want me in on this? Then he remembered, the inspector had said "multiple kills."

The homicide inspector waved at him from the end of the hall. The man's face was ashen.

Vorpagel walked down the hall. He passed a bathroom and glanced inside. The bathtub was full of bloodied water. The sink was smeared with blood.

He walked the few remaining feet into the master bedroom. A woman's naked body was sprawled on the bed, her feet touching the floor. There was a bullet wound under her right eye. She had been gutted just as ruthlessly, and in the same manner, as Terry Wallin.

Vorpagel felt the revulsion rise from his stomach to his mouth and mind. He grappled with it, got it under control, and forced it back down, to that place where so many other terrible crime scenes lay hidden. Once there, the thoughts would only emerge, as they did so often, at four o'clock in the morning, when he would wake up, sweating, panting, and trembling. Once again, he would have to force those demon memories back into the hidden recess where they lay dormant—most of the time.

There was a butcher knife by her head. Another blood-stained knife lay on the floor.

Biondi said, "Here." The inspector pointed at something at the end of the bed. His face was no longer ashen; it was filled with red rage.

Vorpagel went to the end of the bed. A small boy, five, six, maybe seven, lay crumpled. He also had died from a head shot.

This body did not appear to be mutilated, beyond the desecration of stealing a full life from one so young.

Stay distant, Vorpagel warned himself, stay distant. He studied the body again. Had it been moved? A strange thought hit him as he remembered Gary Cooper in the movie *Beau Geste*. The French Foreign

Legion recruit had wanted to die like a Viking, on a burning ship with a dog at his feet.

Was this some sort of macabre reenactment of a twisted ritual in the murderer's mind?

Biondi said, "The deceased's car is missing. So is the dead man's wallet. His name was Daniel J. Meridith. The woman on the bed was Evelyn Miroth; her son was named Jason."

Vorpagel saw a crib in the corner. He looked inside: There was a slug on the mattress. There was also blood and brain matter.

A baby? Vorpagel thought. Then, where is it? He and the officer searched the room. No baby.

A sickening thought entered his mind. Why take the baby if it was dead? And if it wasn't, what kind of awful events awaited it in the hands of someone who could do this?

The case had just taken on more urgency, not just because it was inevitable that the murderer would strike again, but because the baby might be alive.

He asked Biondi the baby's name. He didn't know. Evelyn had been baby-sitting the child.

Vorpagel thought, a friend drops by—and is shot dead. A baby is left to be watched, and is either dead or being tortured.

He stood in the hallway. He heard the lab technician, who was in the bathroom, say, "Yep, this tests out as blood."

Vorpagel looked at the scarlet water shimmering in the bathtub from the overhead light.

The technician continued, "There's bits of brain in the water, plus feces."

A horrendous thought swept over Vorpagel. He

stepped into the bathroom and stared down at the scarlet water. Was the baby here? He felt his throat constrict. He asked the technician.

"Nope. That's the first thing I did, probe around the bottom of the tub. I can tell you, I won't be eating well for a long time. Or making love to my wife."

Vorpagel knew what he meant. The grisly sights they were forced to see affected people the same way. Withdrawal from loved ones, nightmares, even horrific daydreams.

He went back to the bedroom door. He heard a homicide investigator say into a tape recorder, "There are multiple wounds all over the corpse. They appear to be, with the exception of the bullet hole under the eye, caused by a knife."

Biondi ran down the hallway. "We just found the friend's missing station wagon. It was stolen from Miroth's driveway. It's parked only a few blocks from here; the door was open, the keys in the ignition."

"Prints?"

"The lab's dusting right now. This guy's disorganized enough to have left some."

"The lab hasn't found any here yet."

"You suspect gloves?"

Vorpagel nodded.

"Damn, then there won't be any fingerprints in the car." Biondi added, "I found out the name of the baby—Michael Ferriera. He was Evelyn's nephew; he was two months short of two years old." The Sacramento Sheriff's homicide inspector's face was flushed, his anger apparent. "Why did this maniac take the baby?"

Vorpagel thought, twenty-two months wasn't much of a life span. He realized that he was thinking of the baby in the past tense. Am I unconsciously hoping the baby is dead? Am I afraid of what might be inflicted on it if it's still alive?

No, he decided, I'm not. This guy has to be caught immediately, for the baby's sake. Maybe this butcher woke up after he saw that he had hurt a baby. Maybe he took the baby to tend to it, to care for it, to help it.

Dear God, I hope so.

He surveyed the scene once more. Set a thief to catch a thief, he thought. No way can I think like this guy.

Vorpagel went to his office. He prepared a profile, then called the Sacramento Sheriff's office. Ray Biondi arrived, read the profile, and shook his head. "I'm amazed."

"At what?"

"Not amazed, flabbergasted. Fred Homen, without telling me, sent all the data on this case to Quantico. Bob Ressler also did a profile." Biondi handed over a piece of paper.

It was a detailed yet concise profile of the suspected killer. As Vorpagel read the document he became more and more absorbed. He read:

White male, aged 27 years; thin, undernourished appearance. Residence will be extremely slovenly and unkempt and evidence of the crime will be found in the residence. History of mental illness, and will have been involved in use of drugs. Will be a loner who does not associate with either males or females, and will probably spend a great deal of time in his own home, where he lives alone. Unemployed. Possibly receives some form of disability money. If residing with anyone, it would be his parents; however, this is unlikely. No prior military record; high school or college dropout. Probably suffering from one or more forms of paranoid psychosis. Lives within a mile. Aware of houses in the area. Not too disabled to drive or use an automatic pistol. Weird looking. Disheveled.

Vorpagel checked his own notes. The profile, with a few exceptions, matched his own.

Why did Bob suspect the perp was undernourished? What did I miss?

He knew why his counterpart had come to most of his conclusions. The interviews they had done for the past five years with convicted psychotics revealed that this type of crime—an unorganized, brutal, blitzkrieg attack, with no logical motive—was done by a seriously mentally disturbed person. Such a person began displaying his insanity in his late teens. Then, it took about a decade to percolate—often through various forms of treatment—before exploding into action.

The white male was easy. These kinds of crimes were almost always between members of the same race. And only males displayed such vicious anger.

The living alone, the filthy appearance and dirty living conditions all followed from the idea that the killer was a disorganized schizophrenic. People suffering from this condition do not care what they look like. They do not care what kind of squalor they live in. And, unless they can find a companion who is also disorganized or paranoid, they live by themselves.

The same illness prevented military service. It prevented holding a job.

But why thin? Vorpagel wondered.

He called Ressler in Quantico and explained about the two independent profiles being done.

Ressler asked, "So how did we match up?"

"Almost identical."

"Almost?"

"I wrote that the perpetrator probably lived within a few hundred yards of the abandoned station wagon, in government subsidized housing."

"Anything else?"

"Why did you suspect thin?"

"You agree with the disorganized or paranoid schizo assessment?"

"I do."

"I've read texts written by the psychiatrists Kretchmer and Sheldon. Both believe that this type of illness has a direct correlation to body size and temperament."

"I've read Sheldon, or at least some of his work. But that was formulated fifty years ago."

"I have another reason."

"Which is?"

"Off the record?"

"No, I'm running to the *Sacramento Bee* as fast as I can and filing the story."

Ressler said, "Did you notice the concentric circles on the carpet?"

"Of course."

"And the yogurt cup containing blood?"

"Saw the photo."

"People who drink blood can't have a very good diet."

Vorpagel thought, the assailant will strike again, and soon. The police had time, but not much time to catch the killer. They had to amass their resources, their manpower, their information, part of which was the two profiles.

The men in the Behavioral Science Unit of the FBI, founded only a few years before as an offshoot of the Special Operations and Research Section (SOARS), realized that profiling doesn't capture the culprit. It was a tool—just as forensics, dusting for fingerprints, and good plain observation were tools.

Bob Ressler had worked in SOARS dealing with the psychological manifestations of hostage negotiators. This field eventually split off, but the manifestations of mental illness became a separate course at the Academy, taught by the new Behavioral Science Unit.

Vorpagel was teaching Death Investigation and how to handle mentally disturbed suspects.

The FBI had been sending agents from the SOARS and the Behavioral Science Unit to Vorpagel's class for a couple of years.

Vorpagel first met Ressler at one of these classes.

The two men's profiles would help in a mathematical way. It would narrow the search. It would save time.

And with the kind of explosion of unmerciful violence shown in this case, it could be expected that the murderer would not suddenly change his behavior.

It was indeed a race against the clock.

The Sacramento Sheriff's Department went after the "Vampire," so-called by the press, with everything they had. The ballistics in both cases were linked to a third killing, a drive-by shooting that took the life of Ambrose Griffin. This happened on December 29, weeks before the butchering of Terry Wallin.

Vorpagel updated his profile and teletyped it to Quantico.

Within an hour, Ressler fired his opinion back. They mirrored each other. None of their earlier assessments had changed; rather, they'd become reinforced.

What both men agreed on now was that because the murderer had walked to the scene, then drove away, but only a short distance, he lived in the neighborhood. Terry Wallin's house was less than a mile from Evelyn Miroth's.

Both men had come to the same conclusions about the murderer's killing spree beginning with animals. They both agreed that it was possible that the murderer was also the perpetrator of a series of fetish burglaries that had hit the area over the past few months. These type crimes, usually the theft of female undergarments, or any object such as shoes, bras, "turn the perpetrator on." These objects are frequently used in masturbatory activity.

The police concentrated their efforts based on the profiles. People within a mile radius from the killings were asked if they knew anyone fitting the FBI's profile.

One woman told the police, "That sounds like Richard. He asked me for a puppy. He said he liked pets."

Another woman added, "He got a dog and a cat from me. My husband and I wondered about it, because we never saw the dog or cat after he took them."

The man referred to as Richard was Richard Trenton Chase. The police report released to the press contained information from his mother to the effect that her son was recently released from a mental institution and had lived with her until he had killed the family dog. She threw him out. She had paid her unemployed son's rent on his apartment from money that came from the State Disability Insurance Fund.

Police staked out the apartment.

The police also made a composite drawing of the strange man seen in the neighborhood—the man in the orange parka.

A woman who had been a classmate of the suspected killer passed a police car and saw the flyer, with the composite on it. It was a startlingly close depiction of a man she identified as Richard Trenton Chase.

The police checked with the manager and got Chase's room number. They approached the apartment. They knew that inside was a possible killer, perhaps armed with one or more guns. They knew they could kick in the door without a search warrant because the "Rescue Doctrine," the missing baby, eliminated the need for a search warrant. They used a ruse: "We're checking on the voting list. We want to know if you're registered or not to vote."

There was a shuffling inside, but no one answered the door. The deputies then said in a loud voice, "I guess nobody's home." They stomped away from his doorway and waited around the corner of the building.

After approximately ten minutes, Chase opened the door. He was carrying a large cardboard box and wearing a shoulder holster.

He tried to run. They cuffed him. He was searched.

The police found Daniel Meridith's wallet in his back pocket. In the apartment, there were a dozen or more dog and cat collars and leashes. A box was filled with bloody rags, which eventually were found to be the missing baby's blood type.

The apartment was filthy. Three blenders had blood caked inside of them. The refrigerator contained either canine or feline meat.

On one wall were two colored charts of the human circulatory system. A machete in a drawer tested positive for the baby's blood.

Lying on a table was a Nazi swastika.

A calendar on the wall marked the day Terry Wallin died in large block letters: simply the word *Today*. The day of the family's murder was similarly marked. And on the calendar were forty-four more days with the same word branding them.

The baby wasn't in the apartment.

Chase was taken into custody. In an interrogation room, Vorpagel asked, "Did you do it?"

"Yes."

"Why?"

"I did nothing wrong."

"People are dead. Why?"

"I had to kill them to save my life."

What? Vorpagel thought. This guy is claiming a case of necessity? Cases of necessity, under the California Penal Code, state that if a person commits an act that would be a crime, but does so to save his or someone else's life, the culpability of the actor is removed.

Vorpagel asked, "How did killing these people save your life?"

"I needed their blood."

"Why?"

"To replace my own."

"What's wrong with yours?"

"It's turning to sand."

"When did this start?"

"My mother was poisoning me."

"Why?"

"Because I'm Jewish. And the American Nazi party told her that if she didn't kill me, they would kill her."

"What was she using to kill you?"

"Soap dish poison."

"What's that?"

"The goo in the bottom of the soap dish from the soap laying there. That's why I started killing animals."

"Why did you start killing people?"

"I was bit by a rabbit."

"That made you angry at people?"

"No. The rabbit had eaten battery acid. The acid got into my blood. My blood was turning to sand."

When Vorpagel, along with two deputies, again interrogated Chase about the baby, his response was "What baby?"

"There was a baby in that house."

"What baby?"

"Didn't you see the crib?"

"No."

"The crib with an expended projectile in it. The crib with blood in it. The crib with bone fragments and brain tissue in it. That baby."

• • •

Vorpagel called Ressler and filled him in.

"I just learned the Sacramento Sheriff's office did a computer background run on Chase. Richard Trenton Chase turned up on a Nevada police file, in Reno. He had been arrested, found sitting on a rock, naked, with blood smeared all over his body. A bucket of blood and two rifles and a pistol were found in his car."

"They let him go?"

"The blood in the bucket came from a cow."

"Police departments all over the West are going to start looking at every strange unsolved case on file. What about the baby?"

Vorpagel answered, "Chase hasn't talked about the baby, although the Sheriff's Department did an excellent job of grilling him."

Chase was interrogated again. He was asked, "Where would you think someone would have gotten rid of a baby?"

"In the river."

Divers checked the Sacramento and American rivers with no success.

A few days later, Chase was asked, "What other ideas do you have about what may have happened to that baby?"

"Probably dumped along some trail in the mountains."

Scores of off-duty police officers and firemen voluntarily conducted searches in five local counties without success.

The baby was found one month later. It had been stuffed into a fast-food carton and discarded in the backyard of the rectory under fire-escape stairs.

The baby had been gutted and beheaded.

Richard Trenton Chase was convicted the following year.

Ressler called Vorpagel after the verdict. He asked, "Did they find him insane?"

"No. I think the jury thought, like just about everybody else involved, that Chase was insane. But they were afraid that if he went to a mental institution, someday he'd be freed again. And everyone, including the jury, shuddered at the thought."

Richard Trenton Chase received the death sentence. He never went to the gas chamber.

Three years later, on Christmas Eve, he overdosed on pills he had been stockpiling for months. He died the same day.

Vorpagel glanced up from his file at the silent members of his homicide class. He turned off the lights in the classroom and ran through a series of slides depicting the crime scenes involved with the Vampire of Sacramento.

He turned the lights on and said, "This case came up very early, at almost the inception of the Behavioral Science Unit. It went a long way in getting funding for further research from the Bureau."

Marcus raised his hand. "What did the profiling achieve?"

"It narrowed the search for the police."

"But it didn't prevent the second family's slaughter by Chase."

"Profiling isn't magic. It doesn't give an investigator a crystal ball that points to the precise location of the criminal. Neither does most police procedure. We all know from past cases that most of police work involves eliminating people. Profiling helps to narrow the search. In the Dahmer case, did you see anything surprisingly different from the Vampire of Sacramento? Besides the obvious data that both were cannibals."

Marcus answered, "Dahmer was a reasonably organized killer."

"Exactly. And Richard Trenton Chase is still used in classrooms as one of the most disorganized murderers on file. What else links the Vampire case to Dahmer?"

Ava said, "Both died in prison."

Vorpagel nodded. "One by his own hand, one by the hands of his fellow inmates."

Marcus asked, "Both you and Ressler put down twenty-seven as the age. How old was Chase?"

"Twenty-seven. But let me add, both Ressler and I were surprised we'd hit the mark. Usually we'd put down twenty-five to thirty. For some reason I still don't understand, we both independently put down a specific year rather than a span of years. Gut hunch? Luck? Who knows?"

He studied his notes. "I want to go over several cases that illustrate the point that profiling may eventually become a science, but is more an art."

"Meaning?"

"If you're not careful, it's easy to make a serious mistake."

FALSE DIRECTIONS IN DEATH

The Richard Trenton Chase case," Vorpagel said, "went a long way in establishing the credibility of profiling."

Gary said, "That's the first time I've heard of a real vampire case."

"They are rare. Yet, at almost the same time as the Chase case, another man with bloody habits was captured."

"Another vampire?" Marcus asked.

"A joker named Crutchley started a rampage in West Virginia that ended in Florida. He was small in stature. Married. Had an engineering degree. No prior felony arrests. He was entirely the opposite of Chase. He had kidnapped his victim, chained her to the pipe behind the commode, and every day took her into the bedroom, tied her to the bed, injected a tube in her arm, and drank her blood while raping her."

"And you did a profile that helped capture him?" Shui asked.

"Nope. One of his potential victims knew something about plumbing. Her adrenaline level must have gone through the roof because, with her bare hands, she managed to unscrew the sewer pipe she was handcuffed to. She escaped and later identified her attacker. I only mentioned this case to show you that no matter how bizarre you may think a case you're working on is, there's another one out there that's even stranger. Chase was only more infamous."

Vorpagel turned to the blackboard. "The following disclaimer was placed in the files of every profile the Behavioral Science Unit prepared." He wrote in a broad hand: "It should be noted that the attached analysis is not a substitute for a thorough and well-planned investigation and should not be considered all inclusive. The information provided is based upon reviewing, analyzing, and researching criminal cases similar to the case submitted by the requesting agency. The final analysis is based upon the probabilities, noting, however, that no two criminal acts or criminal personalities are exactly alike, and therefore the offender at times may not always fit the profile in every category."

Gary said, "Talk about covering your butt!"

"Spoken like a prosecutor."

Shui said, "Speaking as a public defender, I'd second the prosecutor's comment. And it would be one of the first times in my life I did so."

Vorpagel grinned as he brushed chalk dust off his hands. "Profiling is not magic, it's art. You paint a picture of what you think the personality of the suspect will be. But some real whoppers were made, both big and small. Especially in the early days. But, even with the mistakes, we were on to something. Émile Zola said it best: 'What matters the false directions in life if a few fervent and luminous hours give meaning to a lifetime.' "

Ava asked, "How about an example of a big mistake?"

"Examples are how I teach. One big case was called the Trailside Killer. Northern California was held in terror for almost a year before the serial killer was captured. If Richard Trenton Chase is a classic example of a disorganized psychotic, then the following is just the reverse. Here, the killer was methodically brutal in the organized way he selected and murdered his victims."

"How?"

"He haunted Mount Tamalpais and that section of Marin County. Plus he made extended hunting trips for victims as far south as the Santa Cruz mountains. On one Saturday, four bodies were discovered just off Sky Trail on Mount Wittenburg in the Point Reyes National Seashore. A few days later, a phone caller claiming responsibility for the killings called the Marin Sheriff's Department. He was so irate about mistakes in the newspapers that he called three times in less than a half an hour. The taped transmissions of the phone calls were turned over by Sheriff's Captain Robert Gaddini to a team of consulting criminal psychologists. Their interpretations of the caller: He acts like a spoiled child."

Marcus interrupted by raising his hand. "As you've already told us that this case involves a big mistake, I suppose it's that the criminal turned out to be a sophisticated adult."

"No, he did act like a spoiled child. Of the four bodies initially found, two were nude women in a remote ravine. Both had been raped, then killed. A half-mile away, two more bodies, badly decomposed, of a murdered young couple were found."

Ava asked, "And then the Behavioral Science Unit was called in?"

"Yes. The unit did a profile. The killer was obviously organized: lying in wait for his victims, planning his attack, having an escape route. The killer also did not want to be discovered—hiding the bodies in remote areas. We gave a general psychological description: organized antisocial, has job, probably blue-collar, twenty-five to thirty. Does not want to get caught, but does want his crimes reported accurately. His tantrums on the phone were over misrepresentations of the crime scenes. We all know that this misdirection when giving press releases is routinely done by law enforcement to separate the false confessors from the real killer.

"For instance, in Los Angeles, in the seventies, bodies were found in parks and Salvation Army or YMCA dorms with their throats cut. Eight people, in writing, confessed to these killings. None of these false confessors knew about certain clues discovered at each crime scene. Salt circles were poured around the victims' bare feet or shoes to capture their souls for eternity. Keeping back evidence saves many hours of police work following false trails given by false confessors seeking publicity."

"So," Shui asked, "what broke the case? And how did the profile help? And did he get the death penalty?"

"Spoken like a defense attorney. A witness came forth; a young woman named Sharon claimed she had seen a man slightly obscured by the bushes. She was placed under hypnosis. She described a Caucasian male, medium build, with dark hair. She placed his age at around fifty."

"Fifty?" Ava said. "I thought you said that the . . ."

"I did. A composite drawing was made. A suspect was arrested. Another witness, named Steven, who'd been wounded, came forward. His college girlfriend, Ellen, had been raped and killed in the Santa Cruz mountains. He identified the suspect. The suspect, David Joseph Carpenter, was a printer in San Francisco."

"The profile was partially right—" Marcus said, "blue collar."

Vorpagel grinned at his class. "We were just a bit off. David Carpenter was fifty-two. We were off on the age by more than two decades. However, like any science or art form, it was a learning experience. Here's what we discovered: Time spent in an institution such as a mental hospital or prison can arrest a person's psychological growth, freezing it as it were. Most killers who follow Carpenter's pattern start their murdering ways between twenty-five and thirty. That's what our profile suggested. But Carpenter had spent over two decades in an institution. After that case, we told the police to add on institutional years served to any suspect's age."

Ava asked, "If that's true, how can we ever let such people out; no matter how old they are?"

"Exactly. Yet we do. Too bad cops aren't probation officers. Cops understand recidivism far more than psychologists, psychiatrists, and probation officers."

Gary said, "So the Behavioral Science Unit learned to add institutional time? It's a science and it changed?"

"Sure, why not? Consider adipose tissue and how its view has changed forensically."

Marcus asked, "What's adipose?"

"Adipose is the waxy fat built up when a body is in water or on damp ground. Once it was thought it took four to six weeks for the chemical reaction to occur. Then, a surfer and his board were bitten and killed by a great white shark off the California coast near Carmel. The shark took a huge chunk out of the man's torso. The body was found six days later, and it was in advanced stages of adipose! Pathologists learned that the chemical reaction is accelerated if the interior of the body is exposed to sea water."

"But how about an example from a murder?" Marcus asked.

"Sure. The following happened in Modesto."

A two-year-old's body was found in a sitting position, leaning up against an orchard tree. An autopsy was done. The coroner examined the body and turned to the detective. "I thought you said this child has been missing for six weeks."

"She has been. The mother filed a missing person's report six weeks ago. We interrogated a live-in boyfriend, but came up with nothing."

The coroner turned back to the small form on the examining table. "This child was found in the open, yet the body has not mummified."

"Meaning?"

"It's summer. The body would have mummified very quickly in this heat. Plus, look at the skin. There's no evidence of insect or animal damage."

"What is there evidence of?"

"Adipose tissue. This baby's been in water, and for almost the entire six weeks. I need to check something under a microscope."

The coroner prepared a slide and carefully placed a sample tissue under the microscope. "Just as I suspected. There are algae on the skin."

"That's it!"

"What's it?"

"I know what the live-in boyfriend does for a living."

"What?"

"He works in a bait shop."

Vorpagel waved a file. "The boyfriend confessed. After killing the baby, which had been annoying him with its crying, he hid the tiny corpse in an unused fish tank at work."

Shui asked, "Why did he put the corpse in water?"

"To hide it. So that, at a later date, he could dispose of it. He waited until the police hunt died down and then got rid of the baby."

"Out in the open? In an orchard. In plain sight?"

"I'd have used that," Shui said, "as part of his defense."

"Any straw to clutch at," Gary said. "Right, public defender?"

"That's my job."

Vorpagel said, "He put the body in an orchard. In plain sight. I didn't say he was brilliant. Again, another small piece was added to the knowledge of forensics: Do tests to determine what kind of water caused the chemical reaction. During the course of my lectures, I will give you small problems involving whether a death was a suicide, an accident, or a murder. Try this one, about a violent boyfriend."

The farmer usually took the main road to town but the weather was extremely balmy and his arthritis wasn't bothering him. It felt good to be alive. He decided to take the gravel backroad and enjoy the scenery.

As he rounded a curve, he saw a car parked sideways across the road. The passenger door was open. The farmer got out of his truck and walked toward the vehicle. He saw a woman's head, with long flowing black hair, lying on the front seat.

The farmer didn't go any closer. Shielding his eyes from the overhead sun, he studied the surrounding terrain. Up a slope, on a nearby embankment, he saw what appeared to be the headless body of a woman.

The farmer sped into town and notified the Sheriff's Department.

A radio call went out. Two sheriffs simultaneously responded from different directions and arrived at the scene at precisely the same moment. Seeing each other, the two deputy sheriffs stopped approximately a hundred feet on either side of the parked car. They approached the scene carefully. What the farmer had thought was a severed head in the front seat turned out to be a model's wig holder and black wig.

The two deputies went to the embankment and examined the female corpse. There were scraps of plastic, like those used in making a dry cleaner's garment bag, clinging to her face. She had been crushed to death against the embankment and died of exposure, shock, and scalding, when the radiator boiled over.

In the trunk of the vehicle, they found a hose with

bits of the same plastic stuck on one end and black electrical tape on the other. The exhaust pipe had bits of black tape and melted rubber from the hose stuck on the end.

In the car were six different suicide notes.

The older deputy said, "See the tire marks?"

The younger deputy stared at the ground. There was a clearly visible set of tire imprints in the dirt. The imprints ran up the hill and ended on either side of the dead woman.

The two men did a crime scene search. Near the car, they found more plastic shreds hanging from a clump of weeds in the stickers.

"What do you think?" the younger deputy asked.

"I thought suicide, but run over yourself?"

Vorpagel studied his class and repeated the questions, "How do you run over yourself? That's what we were asked. We did a psychological autopsy on the woman and found she had just broken up from a tumultuous and violent relationship. So murder, accident, or suicide?"

Ava said, "We don't get many hit and runs in the Department of Corrections."

Vorpagel smiled, "Yet you have an opinion?"

"Absolutely. I agree with the deputy sheriff at the scene: You can't commit suicide by driving over yourself. Unless the car rolls over you going downhill. But you did say the body was up a slope, next to an embankment."

"That I did."

"Up a slope means it's impossible to run over yourself."

"Then that leaves murder or accident."

Marcus said, "I vote for murder. You stated that the boyfriend was violent. That they'd just severed a relationship."

Gary said, "What about the six suicide notes? And who ever heard of anyone writing six suicide notes?"

"Do what I do," Vorpagel said. "Try to recreate the scene with the known facts. If it was murder, what happened?"

Gary said, "Isn't that a waste of time? What good does it do to fantasize about . . ."

"Every good investigator uses his imagination. Over and over again, in this class, I will either tell you what the perpetrator was thinking or what can be deduced that the victim was thinking. This isn't magic, I've talked to the bad guys."

Marcus said, "Let me take a crack at a reenactment."

The couple met for breakfast, one last-ditch attempt at a reconciliation. The woman kept repeating, "I'm going to kill myself. I have nothing to live for."

The man kept silent, studying his hands.

The woman began writing suicide notes. After she finished each, she showed them to him and said, "See, I really mean it."

"I don't believe you."

"Then come and watch."

The couple drove out to the deserted road. The man watched as the woman took a hose from the trunk. Using electrical tape, she attached one end to the exhaust pipe. She removed a plastic garment protector and, defiantly, placed it over her head.

The man continued to wear a smug smile.

The woman turned on the car's engine. She ran the hose under the plastic and ran more electrical tape around her neck. Then she lay on the ground.

Still the man remained motionless, doing nothing.

Carbon monoxide fumes filled the bag. The woman began to thrash on the ground. The plastic around her head ripped as it came in contact with the stickers on the weeds.

The woman breathed in oxygen and cleared her head.

"You bastard," she screamed. "You rotten bastard. You would have let me die. Right before your eyes!"

"I knew you didn't have the guts to go through with it."

"What? I almost died. You saw. I was almost unconscious. You saw and did nothing. Bastard."

"Knock it off or I'll teach you another lesson."

Marcus finished his reenactment: "The woman continued to taunt the man. The man became enraged. He got in the car. The woman ran. In the car, he followed her up the hill and crushed her against the embankment."

Vorpagel nodded.

"You agree?" asked Marcus.

"No, just nodding because a lot of what you said makes sense."

"A lot?"

Vorpagel asked the class, "What's wrong with his logic?" The class thought for a few moments. Then Ava said, "The car was found a hundred feet from the body. Down the hill. Yet the weeds with the plastic were found near the body. So the attempted suicide happened up the hill, not near the road."

"Which means?"

"The car had to be up the hill also when she ran the hose to the exhaust. If the boyfriend was there, got angry, and started to chase her, wouldn't she run down the hill?"

"Maybe," Marcus said. "But maybe he remained outwardly calm. Maybe she was on the driver's side of the car and he opened the passenger door and gestured to her to get in. Then, he just waited until she walked in front of the car and accelerated."

Vorpagel waited for someone else to comment, then said, "Is that it? Is that all you would do at this crime scene? If that's all, then you would have arrested the boyfriend and got egg all over your face."

"Why?"

"He had an air-tight alibi."

"So what really happened?"

"Accident."

"She accidentally ran over herself?"

"Exactly. Marcus was right on the money for a while. Except the boyfriend wasn't there; he was at work at a machine shop with half a dozen fellow employees. The woman tried to commit suicide, but the weeds tore open the bag. After her head cleared and she realized how close she'd come to death, she removed the plastic, replaced the hose in the trunk of the car, and walked in front of the car and . . ."

"And what?" Marcus said hotly. "The car magically ran over her?"

"When we became involved in this case," Vorpagel continued calmly, "we suggested to the Sheriff's Department that a mechanical check be run on the car, asking specifically that they measure the amount of fuel in the tank and the mechanical status of the transmission. This was done. It was learned that the car's gas tank was empty and the engine had a faulty transmission clutch. She had the car in neutral while trying to kill herself. The clutch slipped into low gear at precisely the moment she was in front of the car. The car lurched forward and crushed her against the embankment. The car continued running, but as anyone knows, some vehicles need more fuel to keep running than what's fed by an accelerator pedal with no foot on it. The car idled, backed up, then the clutch engaged again. The car continued this repetition, lurching its way down the hill in fits and starts until it wedged sideways on the road, where the engine continued to run until the fuel ran out."

"I'm embarrassed," Marcus said.

"Don't be. I use this problem, and many others, to continually reinforce several concepts: Don't contaminate the crime scene, don't jump to conclusions, and think, think, think. The two deputy sheriffs did an impeccable job at preserving the crime scene. They were very careful not to disturb anything until it was photographed. There was only one set of tire tracks on the dirt road other than those of the victim's and the deputy's cars. We took the car out to the embankment and replicated the situation. The faulty clutch acted up again, the car slammed against the embankment and then lurched down the hill, creating identical markings on the ground."

Vorpagel opened his briefcase and removed another file. "Let's look at another profile with mistakes.

Another example of the learning curve. This is about a young girl who went to a dance."

Shui asked, "No male victims' examples in this class?"

"There are well over two thousand, four hundred female victims countrywide each year, victimized in sexual or abnormal situations. We call these stranger murders. Most male deaths are not sexually motivated and do not require the in-depth crime scene investigation that complex female murders do."

Vorpagel closed his eyes. He visualized the case he was about to tell.

Many times he had wondered what had gone through the young victim's mind on the way to her last breath. He had talked to her friends, her family, her teachers, and slowly a picture of the dead girl's personality and thought process developed.

The rural high school dance wasn't formal; most of the teenagers wore cut-offs and Keds. The disc jockey music was mostly soft rock with occasional heavy metal tossed in for balance.

The dance was held at the hall of a local grange. Instead of chairs, bales of hay were scattered along the walls as seats.

Sarah, the personification of a wallflower, stood in the corner. Even though overweight and pimply, she still had a certain quality, an inner beauty waiting to emerge.

No one asked her to dance.

None of her fellow female students talked to her. They clustered in familiar cliques or gathered around the table spread with punch and cookies. Some girls flirted and were asked to dance; others already had their steady boyfriends staked out.

Sarah had been through this ritual before, at every dance. Only one boy ever asked her to dance, and he had graduated the year before: Tom, a local ranch hand.

Sarah usually handled her social rejection stoically, but tonight her period had started. She was in pain and queasy.

Her father had told her that, with time, the baby fat would disappear and Cinderella would emerge.

"Look at each boy, Sarah," her dad advised. "Stare them down, make them look away. When your maturity appears, they'll remember. They'll remember the Ugly Duckling. They'll remember their snide jokes. They'll ask you out."

Sarah carefully sent her stare from teenage boy to teenage boy. I can't wait, she thought.

When Sarah walked to the buffet table, the crowd parted in an unconscious act of social separation.

I don't need them, Sarah thought, none of them.

She wished she knew how to drive. She would have left the dance in a New York minute. But, at sixteen, she still didn't have a driver's license.

She had to wait for the bus, as if still in grammar school.

The last dance was announced. Everyone danced—even some girls with each other—except Sarah.

Outside, couples walked to their cars.

Sarah stood in the darkness alone.

Her body was found the next day. She had been stabbed nineteen times, both in front and in back, her throat cut. Her body was positioned as if she were sleeping.

The police photographer took the usual grim pictures. A knife was found—four-inch blade. It was closed and only a few feet from the body.

There was no evidence of a struggle. Sarah's clothes were scattered about the scene. She still had on her slip. The body appeared to be sleeping; there was no degradation or exposure of private parts, only the knife wounds.

The police interviewed everyone who attended the dance.

They narrowed their case down to two suspects: Tom, the boy who had danced with Sarah a few times the year before, and the bus driver, Frank.

The police picked up Tom. He was interrogated. He was asked if he would agree to a polygraph. Tom agreed and was hooked up to the appropriate wires and gauges that ran the lie detector.

The police asked, "Your name is?"

"Tom."

Background questions established graph patterns: pulse, heartbeat, perspiration. Then, the interrogator asked, "Did you know Sarah?"

"Yes."

"How did you know her?"

"From school."

"Are you older than she was?"

"Two years."

"You ever hit her?"

"Of course not."

"Did you wait for her the night she died?"

"No."

"I think you laid in wait."

"No."

"You removed her clothes."

"No."

"You attacked her."

"No."

"You stabbed her nineteen times."

"No, I didn't."

"You slit her throat."

"No."

The detective removed a knife from a manila envelope.

"This is your knife."

"Never seen it before."

"Did you kill Sarah?"

"No. Why don't you harass the bus driver?"

The polygraph was studied. Tom passed. The results weren't even marginal. The bus driver was brought in for questioning. He also agreed to take the polygraph.

His background was researched; then, he was asked the same questions. "Did you know Sarah?"

"Yes."

"How did you know her?"

"From driving her to and from school."

"How much older are you than Sarah?"

"Enough to be her grandfather."

"Ever hit her?"

"What is this?"

"You dropped off the last student and then went back and waited for Sarah."

"Why do you think that?"

"Only a few people knew that Sarah usually walked home from a dance. You, the girl who lives next door to Sarah, and Tom."

"So?"

"Tom's passed the poly. The girl next door has an alibi from her parents. That leaves you."

"I went right home."

"Live alone, do you?"

"Yes."

"You drove back down the road toward Sarah."

"No, I didn't."

"You parked the bus. Then you laid in wait."

"I tell you I didn't."

"You removed her clothes."

"No, no."

"You attacked her."

"Ridiculous."

"You stabbed her nineteen times."

"Nineteen times? That's . . . That's . . ."

"You slit her throat."

"Why slit her throat after stabbing her nineteen times?"

The detective removed a knife from a manila envelope. "This is your knife."

"Don't own a knife."

"Never owned a knife?"

"No."

"Ever in the military."

"Infantry."

"They give you a bayonet?"

"Yeah, I had a bayonet."

"Then you owned a knife."

"No, I didn't. The Army owned everything."

"Ever kill anyone. Firefight. That sort of thing?"

"Never saw action."

"Do you like teenage girls?"

"I'm fifty-four."

"Do you like teenage girls?"

"I help them out. Give them advice."

"Did you ever give Sarah advice?"

"Yes. She was overweight and felt bad about it. I tried to boost her morale."

"While you were boosting her morale, did you ever ask her to take her clothes off?"

"What?"

"While you were boosting her morale, did you rip her clothes off?"

"I never touched her."

"While you were boosting her morale, did you discover she was having her period?"

"You're crazy."

"While you were boosting her morale, did you stab her nineteen times?"

"I . . . I . . ."

"While you were boosting her morale, did you slit her throat?"

"No more questions."

The bus driver also passed the poly, but only marginally. The local District Attorney had a policy of never prosecuting if a suspect passed a poly.

Russ Vorpagel looked up from his notes. The class returned his gaze expectantly. He said, "One year later, we were contacted and . . ."

"A year later?" Gary interrupted. "What could you possibly do after a year?"

Shui added, "What could you possibly do that wouldn't be challenged by a defense attorney?"

"Being contacted that late was usual in the early years of profiling. We were allowed to profile only after all reasonable leads had been exhausted. It was a stupid rule, which we were able to change after a few years."

Marcus asked, "How do you go about solving a case when the clues are a year old?"

"We requested photos of the area where the girl had been found. We made a psychological autopsy of the victim. The photos at the scene showed the victim had been carried several hundred feet from the actual scene of the killing. There were no drag marks. The scene was a 'necker's point' in an old orchard, where the kids would sometimes gather for a little petting. So, class, what are your thoughts?"

Shui said, "If she'd been dragged and dumped, I would have guessed it meant the killer wanted to delay her body's discovery."

Gary added, "But she was carried and placed on the ground, and it appears to have been done gently. Not just dumped. Same as the clothes being folded so neatly. But how can you stab somebody nineteen times, slit their throat, then treat the body so reverently?"

"Exactly," Vorpagel said. "We at the Bureau called this psychic erasure or *restitution*. It's an attempt on the part of the perpetrator to assuage his mind and make up for his actions. This is not seen in sociopaths, or in psychotics, but almost exclusively in obsessive-compulsive personalities. The photos showed that the victim had been carried, placed gently on the leaves, in a comfortable position, as if a parent had carried a small child to bed after it had fallen asleep. Her legs were not spread to expose privates in an attempt to degrade or shock."

Ava asked, "What was your profile?"

"Not yet. What about the knife?"

"It was found near the body."

"Found how?"

Gary answered, "Closed."

"Which means?"

"An educated guess would be that it was not hurled aside after the butchery. I venture that it was closed deliberately and then accidentally dropped and forgotten while the killer placed the body and the clothes."

"What about the clothes?"

"As you said, just further psychic undoing."

Vorpagel opened a file and said, "The autopsy showed that the victim was in her cycle. Her hymen was intact; she had not been raped. The blood on the body and the clothes indicated that the victim was first struck, becoming unconscious, and her clothing removed in sequence. Not in a frenzy, not torn, but removed in layers. When the pad was discovered, the perpetrator became incensed, and impotent, and in a frenzy repeatedly stabbed her, front and back . . . and finished by slashing her throat."

Vorpagel closed the file and continued, "What happens now? What to do? He carried the victim to the edge of a berm and positioned the body. What he had done was now a shock, a horror, to him. His mind was already trying to make restitution, to convince himself that what happened didn't happen."

Vorpagel went to the blackboard and wrote as he spoke, "Our profile: She went willingly into the area.

The killer was someone she knew and lived in the same area."

Marcus said, "And you learned all that from the police report."

"Never saw the police report, until after the case was solved, only the photos and the autopsy."

"That's unconscionable," Shui said. "No matter what you came up with, I'd attack it as coming from a faulty premise."

"Whatever," Vorpagel said. "We based our opinion that she went willingly on evidence found in the photos. No drag marks. No signs of a struggle in the undergrowth. No broken branches. No clothing torn. Sometimes we only got partial material to make a profile. And nobody, as far as I know, was ever convicted from a profile. The Behavioral Science Unit was developed to aid the police by narrowing their search. It was never meant to convict. That's for the evidence."

Marcus asked, "When did you learn that the police . . ."

"Only later did we learn that the police had narrowed it down to Tom and the bus driver. Our profile further proposed that the killer was probably three years her senior, not a macho man, rather somewhat of a wimp. He worked locally, probably involved in the butchering of hogs or sheep, or cattle. He had graduated from high school, in the lower 10 percent of his class. He was quiet and shy and uncommunicative. A wallflower, like the girl."

Vorpagel continued reading his profile, "The killer does not have a car. After the incident, he may even have initiated the search for the victim, and might have been the one to find the body. After things quiet down, he will probably leave the area, joining the military."

"Why?"

"We know this type of personality follows a certain route, and joining the military to leave the area is one of them. Joining the military gives a person a legitimate reason to leave town without suspicion."

Marcus said, "And your profile fingered?"

"Obviously, the closest match was Tom, the boyfriend. We sent our report on to the police chief. He answered back that the profile was a very near fit to Tom, but he had passed the polygraph. We insisted that this was their man. The police chief told us that Tom had joined the military and was, coincidentally, home on his first year's leave. We continued to insist. The police chief had Tom picked up again. He agreed to take the polygraph. And he passed again!"

"So your profile was wrong," Shui said, with some satisfaction.

"We questioned the way the two polygraphs were handled, but to no avail."

"So you were wrong and this is another example of a mistaken . . ."

"You're correct. This is an example of mistakes. A year later, the town got a new District Attorney. This man had no problem prosecuting someone who passed a poly if the evidence warranted it. He reread old files and appointed a new lieutenant of detectives to the Sarah case. He reread our profile and went to Norfolk, where the suspect was stationed. He interrogated Tom.

"Tom, frustrated, finally blurted, 'You guys just don't give up, do you.' Then he confessed."

"So the mistakes were in the polygraph."

"Some people can control their heartbeat and blood pressure."

"I've run into that before," Gary said.

Vorpagel continued, "The poly is a tool, just like profiling. We made mistakes ourselves."

"What mistakes?"

"Tom was only two years older than the victim, not three. We guessed that he would most likely enter the Army; he chose the Navy."

"Not much of a mistake."

"Over a fifteen-year period, from 1978 to 1994, when the last study ended, the Behavioral Science Unit achieved a 92 percent accuracy rate. In the Tom and Sarah case, there were about fifteen characteristics given, and we were wrong on two. That's an accuracy rate of less than 90 percent. That's why I call this case a mistake."

"Do you have any other examples of mistakes?" Gary asked.

"Already told you about the Trailside Killer, David Carpenter. Our profile was off by over twenty years on his age. By the way, he has filed an appeal for a new trial."

"Based on what?"

"Carpenter still maintains his innocence. He was tried in Los Angeles for the two murders in Santa Cruz. He was found guilty. Then he was tried in Orange County for the five Marin murders. The female jury foreman, halfway through the six-month trial, told two friends over dinner, 'I'm not supposed to know this, but the defendant has been convicted of doing the same thing in another city.' "

"Wow!" Shui said as she wrote furiously in her notebook. "Talk about a solid basis for an appeal."

Vorpagel continued, "After Carpenter was found guilty in Orange County and received the death sentence, one of the foreman's dinner guests went to the Orange County District Attorney and told what the foreman had said."

Vorpagel stuffed a file back into his briefcase, looked around absentmindedly, then said, "Again, I can't emphasize enough, profiling eliminates subjects and may help point the law in the right way; it usually does nothing more."

"Usually?" Gary said.

"Usually."

"Meaning?"

"Sometimes a case comes up when profiling actually prevents the murder."

Marcus asked, "Can you be more specific?"

"Yes. I worked on a case once where a fantasy was leading to a possible murder. Some killers aren't spontaneous; they have to work themselves up to the crime. Building the fury inside of themselves to a boiling, murderous rage."

THE FANTASY

Vorpagel said, "The Chase case and David Joseph Carpenter offered two more opportunities to interview killers on death row. Since we started in the mid-1970s, the FBI has amassed overwhelming evidence that these murderers followed consistent patterns of behavior—and that their future actions could be predicted with a high degree of probability."

"How big was the team?" Marcus asked.

"At that time, in 1979, the Behavioral Science Unit of the FBI was broken up into various subdivisions. Bob Ressler, Anthony Rider, John Douglas, and myself did most of the profiling of serial killers. Rodger Davis and Swanson Carter dealt primarily in psychology. Jim Reese and John Minderman dealt with police stress. Robert Roy Hazelwood was head of the sex crimes. Dick Ault was involved in statistical analysis. And Larry Monroe was promoted, and Roger DePew took over as our unit chief."

Vorpagel emptied a folder of police reports,

handwritten letters, and transparencies onto his desk. He held up one of the slides and said, "This case involves the first time that I'm aware of that profiling helped *prevent* a possible murder. The Behavioral Science Unit was put to a new test in the Elaine case, not to catch a killer, but to prevent a murder. Not to prove an elusive scientific theory, but to end a deadly fantasy."

Elaine let the phone ring three times, then four, five. It had been a long day, and she didn't want another newspaper salesman calling when she was trying to fix dinner. But the ring was insistent.

"Yes?" she said.

"I hope I haven't caught you at a bad time," a cheery male voice said.

"Yes, you have. Is this important?"

"I think it is to you. You have been selected . . ."

"Stop right there. I don't take solicitations over the phone, and I'm sick and tired of come-ons."

Before she could disconnect, the voice assured her, "Please don't hang up—this is an offer to send you something without any strings attached. No salesmen. No follow-up. No obligations of any kind. We simply want to send you our product, and, if you agree, you may tell us how you like it."

"Well," she hesitated.

"This is the Warner Bra Company, we want to send . . ."

"Who?"

"Warner. We have a new line of bras we are test marketing. We have selected you at random for this product. No one will call you back. It's all up to you."

Elaine momentarily forgot her resolve—never to

buy anything or accept anything over the phone. And she didn't have the presence of mind, over the barrage of soothing phrases, to ask how she had been "selected at random."

"Look, I'm making dinner. Call me later and I'll let you know."

The following evening, the next phone call came. The man asked, "Have you made up your mind?"

"About what?"

"The Warner bra offer."

Elaine hesitated. Warner was a good company; their products weren't cheap. But there was something about the manner of the call, the persistence in the voice. She would have to give her address—and her bra size. It was all too personal. She blurted, "I'll have to ask my husband. Good-bye."

A week later, when no further calls came from the alleged Warner Bra representative, Elaine put the whole matter behind her. There are more and more freaky phone solicitations, she reminded herself. I said the right thing, bringing up my husband. But why did I lean on my husband to protect me? Why didn't I just say, "Buzz off"? If the guy had been real, he would have offered some ID. It's just too bizarre to think about. I won't tell my husband.

Six months later, the telephone rang at six-fifteen in the evening. Elaine let it ring as she stirred a gravy mix into the pan drippings. She finally picked up and heard a strangely familiar voice that she couldn't quite place.

"Thanks for your patience," the man said. "We *now* have approval from the home office to send you the Warner bras."

"What?"

"Don't you remember? We talked about your interest in Warner bras. I had to get approval to send you two samples. I'll put them in the mail today."

You have my address? she thought. My name? My bra size? She had mentioned a husband before. This time he was home. "Just a minute," she said.

Her husband was irate; he was sensitive to his wife's figure; he had heard whistles when they went out. He said hotly into the phone, "Send your credentials and then, and only then, send a free sample."

He forgot that no one had discussed name or address.

The next phone call came early the next evening. "Don't you know Warners is a big company. Do you want the free bras or not?"

"Buzz off," she said.

"All I wanted to do was give you some free merchandise, not screw you."

That night, when she told her husband about the last call, he suggested, "Elaine, let's get an unlisted number."

She agreed but realized the relatives, the friends from work, everyone they knew would all have to be given the new number and an explanation of why it was changed. She put off changing the phone number.

And all went well, for a while.

Then the package arrived. It had no return address. It was so carefully wrapped that Elaine assumed it was some sort of surprise from someone close. She carefully slit open the glossy paper and removed three identical pieces of drawing board, seven by ten inches.

When she saw what was drawn on them she froze.

Each board had an elaborate frame of a flowery design. The central depiction had a comic-book quality—stark, carefully shaded, exaggerated. The first showed a woman bound to a stake in panties and bra. Part of the bra was pulled down, exposing one breast's nipple, full and erect. One huge hand hovered near the bare bosom. The other hand held a knife. A carefully lettered caption followed the contours of the woman's body: It threatened what would come next in a typically pornographic style.

Her husband screamed, "My God! That's your face. This bastard has seen you!"

The pencil drawing was indeed a good resemblance of Elaine. The Providence Rhode Island Police Department responded immediately when Elaine's husband called.

The detective said, "This is a new twist. I don't think we should take this guy lightly."

Another officer held up one of the drawings and studied it closely. "Don't change your phone number. We have to catch this guy before he escalates."

This is embarrassing, Elaine thought. The drawings were very explicit. Police or not, these cops are men. What are they thinking? That I might have had some previous connection with this guy? A boyfriend on the side I'd rejected? There her body was, laid out in exquisitely shaded drawings for all to see. This man had never met her, and yet he had pictured her in her most private moments.

How was that possible?

I've never met the man.

And I never encouraged him. My husband knows this. I love my husband and two young children. This is an invasion of my home.

She thought about speaking, but decided not to. Any denial would appear fabricated. Anything said, misinterpreted, twisted.

Finally she thought of something she could say. It wasn't about herself. Maybe the police would find it significant. But it was her only hope to hang on to some semblance of her outrage.

She said, "See this postmark—November 13."

"Yes?"

"You can come to my home and look at last year's calendar. That's the same day he first called me."

Three nights later, the voice on the phone said, without preamble, "How did you like the drawings?"

Elaine put her hand over the phone. She thought, my God, we've got him! The police are here. She removed her hand from the phone and said, "Just a second." She waved to the inspector in the next room.

The inspector motioned to the policeman installing the wiretap. It had taken them three days to get there, police budgets being what they are, but they had picked a perfect time. The inspector whispered to Elaine, "Stall."

She said, "Ah—yes, I got the drawings."

"Then when do we meet?"

She hesitated.

"Bullshit!" he shouted over the phone, and the line went dead.

The inspector handed Elaine his card. "My guess is, he'll go underground. But, just in case, call me, day or night, if you ever hear from him again."

She thought she wouldn't.
She was wrong.

Vorpagel turned off the lights in the classroom and flashed the three slides containing the "art work" of Elaine on the screen.

"I must admit," Gary said, studying the pencil drawings, "when first hearing about profiling, I was very skeptical. It sounded like a fortune cookie or an astrology reading—broad enough to fit any circumstance."

"It works," Vorpagel said, "as long as it's seen as an aid. I've seen old-timers use gut hunches that came up with almost miraculous results."

"Can gut hunches be taught?" Marcus said.

"I try to get my students to avoid gut hunches and use logical thought. Sometimes, though, gut hunches are logical."

Using a pointer, Vorpagel highlighted the first drawing, aiming at the left hand hovering over Elaine's breast. "Notice the size difference between the two hands. The left is gigantic, the right minuscule. This is not a drawing error, everything else is in reasonable perspective."

Ava said, "There's additional sadism here, as if it were needed. See the exaggerated tightness of the ropes around her upraised arms, and the pained expression, actually terror, on her face?"

Vorpagel changed slides. The second "cartoon" extended the fantasy. A man with a shadowy face could be seen in profile sexually assaulting Elaine in a three-quarter view of the first scene. The helplessness of the victim was underlined, with the head thrown back and the face in a grimace.

Marcus asked, "Did you see a lot of this kind of stuff?"

"Not like this. This guy was creating his own pornography, and quite artistically. We see a lot of pornographic magazines—and some posed photo shots—in many murder and sexual attacks. But this was new to me."

The third cartoon took still another turn. Elaine's sexual response, vividly caught in detail, portrayed her writhing in ecstasy. The man drew himself wearing a black hood, and he was naked below the waist. Strangely, his body was small, childlike, though his penis was erect and prominent—ridiculously out of proportion to his body.

Vorpagel said, "Notice the knife is still turned away from the body. The hand that holds it is still small, delicate. Look at the tiny body of the attacker; it's all sign language."

Gary said, "But the size of the body might have been created to demonstrate the power of his masculinity. Look at the engorged organ—that's a threat, and a powerful one—of control, dominant."

"What about the tiny hand and knife?"

"The tiny hand holding the knife—yes, it is pointed away, but that might mean because she's cooperating. Look at her face in the third drawing; look at her body. It's obviously portrayed to show that she is in rapture. The sign language could be interpreted that the knife will stay pointed away if she cooperates."

"Not bad." Vorpagel said. "Who wants to continue the story?"

Marcus asked for the file, glanced at it, and paraphrased as he went through it. "The suspect called to get Elaine's reaction to his drawings. 'How'd you like the pictures?' he asked. Elaine was very disturbed by his blatant gall. She engaged him in conversation to keep him on the phone while the police ran a trace. He asked for a meeting, then hung up when she delayed. Why were the police there when he called?"

"Purely by coincidence, they were just in the act of setting up a wiretap. The caller must have sensed something because he didn't call again for a half a year."

Ava said, "The pattern is weird. It started out with a standard escalation, then tapered off. The suspect was cunning, and patient."

Vorpagel agreed. "After this six months of silence, Elaine again felt the trauma was over."

"But it wasn't."

"No, it wasn't; it was just beginning. The next call came out of the blue, like a Stephen King nightmare: The caller began describing Elaine's house, her picket fence, the front gate, the garden. The details poured out: the color of the drapes in her front room, the times and dates when she had come home early, the newspaper delivery at 4:00 A.M. But there was no mention of the husband or two children, all very much in evidence. Pretend you're back then; pretend it is happening now. Don't use past tense, use the present."

Marcus said, "I saw somewhere in the file that some phone calls came from White Plains, New York."

"Yes, even Chicago."

"Intermittent calls, some from a long distance."

Shui said, "I think he's on an expense account. He gets lonely away from home—and more emboldened. But he's got to live near the victim."

"I agree with living near the victim—how else

could he know her routine so well? But I take exception to the expense account."

"Why the objection to the expense account?"

"I don't rule it out; it's just he could be self-employed. Then, if he's married, he wouldn't want a record of the calls."

Shui said, "Come to think of it, he wouldn't want that even if he was on an expense account."

"Exactly."

Marcus asked, "Why is he so shrewd about the phone being traced, and so lax about letting us know that he's observed Elaine close up?"

"He wants to get caught. He's like the daughter who leaves birth-control pills on her dresser where the mother can see them."

"But why? I think he's an inadequate personality—just look at how puny he pictures most of himself in the third drawing. He must be sadistic, but well-educated. Those are clear from his MO."

"Look," Vorpagel said, "at the borders on the cartoons, look at the detail, look at the precision. He's tightly structured—not exactly a trait of an inadequate personality."

"But there's a deeper drive operating here."

"I'm the psychiatrist here; that's my territory."

"Just a younger man's view. I think he really believes he's going to seduce Elaine."

Vorpagel said, "There was another mailing. This one contained four cartoons. But these were different: The first three contained pornography cut out of magazines and glued to the cartoons. The fourth was very different: This one contained a real photograph carefully worked into the overall sketch."

Vorpagel put the slide in the projector. It was a photograph of a man wearing a hood and nothing else. He was in a state of sexual excitement.

Gary said, "I see why the FBI was worried this guy might be on the way to his first victim."

"Why?"

"The increasing anger. Notice how he draws the breasts as sagging in one case—then, like missile cones. There's nothing unusual about a breast fetish, but when it's this exaggerated, it's bad."

"What I don't understand is the photograph," Marcus said. "Why not continue with simple drawings? It's definitely safer."

Vorpagel answered, "He's delusional. He believes Elaine is going to come to him because of these erotic love notes. And because of his naked body."

"Even after repeated denials?"

"Denials have a way, with the sociopath, and sometimes even with a normal person, of being read more than one way."

Marcus persisted, "I think he's made a mistake. Look at the photo. The part of the room we can see looks like a typically drab motel or hotel room. Except the wallpaper in the background is distinctive. That shouldn't be too hard to trace—the letter was post-marked in Providence."

"That's exactly what I did. The local police had already started checking out hotel and motel rooms. Let me tell you how it actually went down."

The desk sergeant said, "One of the detectives knew the motel and he ID'ed the wallpaper. We blew the photo up and found a distinctive gash in the wallpaper in the background. We combed all sixty-eight rooms and found one that had a matching gash. We got the room number, then the matching registrations from the motel owner."

Vorpagel complimented the department on their fast work. "So now you've got a list of people to look into who rented that room for—how long back?"

"The chief wants us to go back two years."

"That's over seven hundred possible people."

"Yeah, there were only a few vacancies."

"Okay, seven hundred and thirty possible people minus the vacancies."

"And multiple use."

Vorpagel sighed. "You still have to check out hundreds and hundreds of possibilities."

"So? Leg work is our job."

"Let the Bureau do a profile on the suspect. A good profile would shorten the search considerably."

"We already know not to check grandmothers. Besides, I don't think we're going to need an FBI profile to nail down this one. Elaine received a surprise phone call and request from our Peeping Tom. He asked for a settlement. No more harassment if she would deliver two of her bras in a Macy's bag to the local Salvation Army Thrift Store and deposit them in the trash bin at the rear."

"What for?"

"He said he would pick them up."

"So you'll stake out the store . . ."

"And nail him," the desk sergeant finished.

Vorpagel wished him luck and thought, maybe not. The suspect had already eluded phone taps. Why would he walk blithely into a trap—a trap set up by himself?

Vorpagel studied the four most recent drawings sent to Elaine. Three were made up of cutouts that surrounded the cartoon drawings of Elaine.

And there's now another fantasy involved, Vorpagel realized. The voyeur was going to claim a ransom from his hostage—the hostage he held in fear with his phone calls and vicious drawings.

But instead of money in a gunnysack, what he asked for was two bras in a Macy's bag.

The next morning the Macy's bag was dropped off by Elaine at the downtown Salvation Army resale store. She opened the lid of the huge trash bin at the rear of the shop and tossed the bag onto the pile of garbage inside.

The Providence police kept their distance, but two detectives in plain clothes watched the large trash bin throughout the day and waited for the voyeur to appear. The employees of the Salvation Army store were told not to go near the trash receptacle.

By closing time, it seemed a lost cause. At seven in the evening, two more detectives were assigned to watch overnight. No one appeared.

The next morning, before garbage pickup, the trash bin was checked. The bras were gone! A few minutes later, a truck arrived and dropped off an empty trash bin, then took the full one away, as it did weekly.

Vorpagel phoned to find out what had happened. The detectives who had kept surveillance on the trash bin swore no one had approached it.

Vorpagel asked, "Did anybody rummage around in the bin, to see if someone was inside?"

"Why? We kept it in view for twenty hours. We

saw Elaine put the bag inside. No one came near it afterward."

"What if he got to the trash bin before Elaine did? Or any of you? Then hid inside, waited until dark, reached up and got the bag, then spread the garbage back over, hiding himself?"

"Spend twenty hours in a ton of garbage?"

"Why not?" Vorpagel said. "Does anyone else have a more logical solution than that he was taken away in the full trash bin?"

The next week Elaine found her bras in her mailbox. Lab tests revealed they had been soiled with semen.

The Providence Vice Squad commander called Vorpagel and said, "The 'Peeper' called Elaine this morning. He asked her how she liked his present and wouldn't she like to have the real thing."

Vorpagel asked the Commander, "Could you give me the exact words?"

"Why?" the Vice Squad man asked.

"Did he just ask? Or did he say what he was going to do?"

"I'll read it to you straight out of the report. He said, 'You're going to get the real thing between your legs instead of in your bra.'"

Vorpagel asked, "How is Elaine taking all of this?"

"She's hanging in there. Her husband is the one we have to watch. He's ready to booby-trap the whole perimeter of his house."

"Something is missing," Vorpagel said absentmindedly. "This guy's playing games with you cops. He's gloating now that he's outwitted you. But he hasn't filled out the profile of a paramilitary mind. He should have shown a gun in his drawings, or a grenade, or a uniform. Something . . ."

"My mistake," the Vice Squad commander said. "There was something else in the package of porno pages that I thought was accidental."

"Which was?"

"A full-page ad from a magazine—some company in Ohio: a catalog of Nazi memorabilia. Afrika Korps insignia, dress uniforms, that kind of junk."

Vorpagel said, "The last piece in the jigsaw. We'll work up a profile and get back to you. It should cut down considerably on the people you have to check out."

Vorpagel asked his class, "What are your thoughts? How would you use profiling to eliminate possible suspects?"

Shui said, "Forget about any females and couples who registered into that room."

"Obviously that should eliminate more than half. What else?"

Gary asked, "Why does he check into a local motel if he lives near Elaine?"

"Marital problems, perhaps."

"Why married?"

"If he wasn't married, why check into a motel? We know from Elaine's statement that this is no teenage prank. She stated that the voice was older, late twenties, early thirties. He doesn't want his wife to know. He goes on business trips—White Plains, Chicago—but he lives near Elaine. Every once in a while, he tells his wife he's going on a business trip, then checks into a nearby motel."

"Then," Marcus said, "if he's married, I'll bet he's in trouble with the relationship. And I'd further bet he's in trouble at work."

"Why?"

"He could control his sexual fixation if he had compensation elsewhere."

"Does he have kids?"

"Impossible to tell."

"Not really. Remember what we're doing. We make up a profile based on deduction. We give the police a list, the order in which to check out the potential suspects." Vorpagel held up the computer printout that contained the more than seven hundred guests who had checked into the room with the torn wallpaper. "We may not hit it on number one, but we are trying for percentages. We're not soothsayers. We're better described as oddsmakers."

Shui said, "I think he has kids. If he doesn't and he's as inadequate in his home life as we both believe, then she would have left him. If there were no kids."

"So," Vorpagel said, "we start with married because of checking into a local motel, and that leads to . . ."

"More than just kids," Shui said.

"Exactly," Marcus said. "From what we know about him, I'd wager that he was in the military, a strong hunch that he's a veteran."

"Why?"

"Because of the way he handled getting the bras from under the police observation."

"Exactly," Vorpagel said. "That wasn't spur of the moment. It was planned. The cartoon details tell us that he has concentration, that he is able to complete things with great precision. Anything else? Once he's caught, what about future danger?"

Marcus said, "He's bright enough to fight his battles verbally. Look at the brutal battle he's carried out against a thirty-two-year-old housewife."

Ava asked, "How do you think he met her?"

Vorpagel was always careful not to claim too much for psychological profiling—it sounded like looking at bumps on the cranium—or at predestination. He said, "We can never know why one person does something. We can only know why dozens, scores, hundreds, tend to do something."

"Then, just an educated guess on how they met?"

Vorpagel removed a paper from his briefcase and read, "He works for a large company, a nine-to-five job. He saw her coming home one day. She turned in a certain way. He clicked on a vision of a woman. But it was a 'woman' he could not have. Again, classic inadequacy. He followed her home, saw the fence, the flowers, the kids, and husband. Then his mind clicked again in a way we will never know. He was unable to seduce as a man, in a normal pursuit. So he chose the abnormal. He had to subdue her."

"What happened?"

"We began eliminating suspects. We called the motel's desk to get the clerk's memory of who was behind some of the names and license plates. When we were done, they had a primary possibility list containing two dozen men. The secondary list also had twenty-four. We teletyped the information to the Providence police and said that they would prepare a tertiary list if necessary. The culprit was the third man on the primary list."

"Was he a veteran?"

"Yes."

"How many of the hunches were correct?" Gary asked.

"Every one."

"What sentence did he get?"

"The man was charged with use of the mails to try to seduce. He was found guilty and plea-bargained a potential ten-year sentence down to a year in jail. Upon his release, he wrote two letters, one to the police officer in charge of the case, Captain Ricci, and the other to Elaine.

"Captain Ricci sent a copy of both letters to the Behavioral Science Unit of the FBI. The letters were read at the weekly group meeting held on Wednesday."

Using another slide, Vorpagel flashed the following on the screen. "In March of this year, I was arrested by detectives in your department and charged with making obscene phone calls and extortion—I was eventually sentenced to one year in prison with five years probation.

"At the time of my arrest, various belongings were confiscated from me and held as evidence. Part of this 'evidence' was a collection of pornography (if *Playboy* magazine can be considered truly pornographic). Since I never went to trial, it was not necessary for your department to hold any 'evidence'—my plea of 'nolo' was enough to get me sentenced.

"During my interrogation at the police station, we were introduced. I will never forget the arrogant, 'Holier than thou' attitude that you used against me, as if I were some kind of despicable pervert. The fact that the magazines were kept by your department illegally made me realize that you and your men are just like me. The only difference is that I recognize my problems and am doing what I can to solve them. In the meantime, I am sure that pictures from the collection grace the police station lockers, if not the walls of your own office or restrooms.

"You and I both know that reading magazines like that is not illegal, and we know the real reason for your keeping them. I have heard many reports from various people of personal items 'disappearing' from the station after being confiscated from arrested individuals.

"People have told me that I was very lucky to have my jewelry, money, and so forth returned to me intact—they said that was unusual for your department.

"Anyway, this whole experience has been a real eye-opener for me. I see now that many of the criminals' complaints of police dishonesty and corruption are not unfounded. John."

Gary said, "Talk about weird. John doesn't understand how ridiculous he sounds. I mean, what sort of logic claims that the police have to steal your copy of *Playboy*? It isn't like you can't buy them in almost every liquor store."

"You think that logic is warped?" Vorpagel said. "Listen to the letter he wrote Elaine." Another slide appeared on the screen. "Dear Elaine: By the time you get this letter I will have already been released from prison—paroled after serving only four months. There is no need to go rushing off to the police with this letter, since it is not like the others you have received from me. This letter is an attempt at an explanation for all the events that totally destroyed my life.

"It is impossible for me to apologize for my actions

because they were actions that I could not control, actions committed by a person I cannot recognize as myself. It should be obvious to any rational, thinking person that these acts could not have been carried out by someone who was thinking in a normal manner.

"You became the victim strictly by chance. Looking back at it, any woman who encouraged my phone calls as you did would have been the victim. It was my misfortune to call a woman who happened to be flattered and 'turned on' by this type of call.

"The point is, Elaine, that I'm getting help for my problem. Maybe you should be thinking about getting help, too. I still maintain that all you had to do was get your phone number unlisted and that would have been the end of it all. The fact that you did not do this makes everyone wonder what game you were playing.

"Anyway, that's all over with now. I am free again and will be trying to rebuild my life. By the way, you might be interested in knowing what our mutual game cost me. I lost a very good job with a company that I had worked for for seven years—I had an executive position with a Fortune 500 company and was on the way up. I almost lost my wife and three little children but they are staying with me and have vowed to see our future difficulties through with me. I have lost my good name and reputation—I'm sure you read the final newspaper account of my actions (in fact, you probably kept it and framed it!) and I'm sure you can imagine what many people think about me as a result. No matter that the account was more fiction than fact, it was printed, that's all that matters. The final blow is that I am now unemployed, with a family to support, and a mortgage to pay. In fact, we may lose the house in a couple of months if I cannot find a job. A criminal record will not make my employment any easier.

"You should also know that, despite the police allegations and your own vivid imagination, neither you or any member of your family was ever in danger of being harmed. I had no intentions in that regard. Whether you believe that or not makes no difference to me at all. I know myself now better than I ever did before and I know that I speak the truth.

"Well, no matter what you believe, it does not matter. Despite all that has happened, I have enough confidence in myself to know that I will rebuild my life again.

"I wonder if you can say the same?"

Ava said, "There is absolutely no remorse, and he's using every excuse of personal justification."

Vorpagel agreed. "John not only didn't feel remorse—he had transference of responsibility. It was Elaine's fault because she didn't get an unlisted number. Something she did not do at the request of the police. It was Elaine's fault because she sought to stop him, then have him thrown in jail for the maximum allowed. Elaine is the one who should seek counseling and whose life should be shattered."

Ava asked, "How are you sure that he would have tried to kill Elaine?"

"Never sure," Vorpagel answered, "just reasonably certain that this stalking would have continued to escalate."

"But," Ava said, "how do you know it would escalate to murder?"

"Look at the escalation of violence in the cartoons.

We have many examples in our society where this kind of escalation leads to attempted murder. Like Hinkley and his fascination with Jodie Foster. This type of paranoiac justifies everything he's doing. I'm afraid the Elaine stalker would have continued to build up his delusions until working himself to the point that the only way to make Elaine pay for her behavior was to teach her a lesson, namely, kill her. And that's our lesson for today."

The students stood, ready to leave.

Vorpagel interrupted them with a smile. "Not quite yet. The formal lesson's over, but I have a short problem for you before the day's session is finished."

The students quickly returned to their desks and Vorpagel continued. "I will give you an example of a crime involving cold, calculating premeditation. I became involved in an insurance case a few years ago. Two men held up a bank in Geronimo, Oklahoma. They killed the tellers, they killed the customers, they shot the guard. One female victim was shot in the head but survived. The bank robbers thought they had killed her. Then, the barbarians placed the muzzle of the revolver next to a six-week-old baby, whose mother they had also killed, and, according to the wounded woman, pulled the trigger. The gun malfunctioned. They pulled the trigger again, and the gun failed again to fire."

Gary said, "It wasn't the baby's time."

"Or God was feeling extra generous that day. The two bank robbers fled. They managed to elude capture until they were finally arrested in San Francisco. The wounded woman identified them. They were tried and received the death penalty."

"This seems pretty open and shut," Marcus said.

"The families of the executed bank employees and customers sued the bank."

"For what?"

"During the bank robbers' trial, both men claimed that they killed everyone to get rid of the witnesses. This was a last-ditch, desperate attempt by their lawyer to keep them off death row—with the twisted logic that their crime hadn't been vicious, just expedient. The families of the deceased claimed that if the bank had installed closed-circuit television, then there would have been no reason for the bank robbers to kill the witnesses."

Gary asked, "Is the safety device of closed-circuit TV the norm? In Oklahoma? In Geronimo?"

"Yes, it is."

Shui asked, "Do we have all the clues?"

"Yes."

"With only what you've given?"

"With only what I've given."

"Were the two bank robbers found insane?" Ava asked.

"No—I said they got the death penalty."

Shui said, "My first reaction, my gut hunch, was that the bank could have been found liable, whether there was any legitimacy to the claim or not."

Gary said, "I see this all the time. The jury wants to give something to the victims, because they feel sorry for them and want to give them something to ease the pain."

Marcus said, "But that shouldn't happen in a case that doesn't warrant it."

"So what's the answer?"

"The baby," Marcus said. "If they were trying to get

rid of eyewitnesses, they wouldn't have tried to kill a six-week-old baby."

"Exactly. They did try to kill everyone, including the baby, because the murders had nothing to do with witnesses; the killers just went on a murdering spree. This example has a point. All of you in this class are trained investigators. You have to take the time to stop and think about what is involved in each case you handle. This is part of what I'm trying to instill in you—to think, not to jump to conclusions. Don't accept the obvious. Look and think. I know how hard this is with the caseloads you're forced to handle. Just take those extra few precious moments to logically think things out rather than jumping to the most obvious conclusion. Strange as it may seem, there's a connection between Elaine and Jodie Foster and John Lennon and the Unabomber, and I might add, the cyberporn on the Internet. How do you think that Elaine's stalker fed his fantasies? In his day, on Nazi magazines. In our day . . ."

"Do you have any more puzzles?" Marcus asked.

"Sure, I'll have some more tomorrow. We'll start the day with a field problem involving a robbery and murder. Then, I'll give you a case study involving a personality not so different from the man who tormented Elaine for so long. Except this case, unfortunately, continued long enough for the man to whip himself into enough of a frenzy actually to kill."

"A woman?" Gary asked.

"No, a young boy."

THE REAL THING

For years, Vorpagel had pushed the FBI for more realistic types of training—more field problems. Book learning wasn't keeping pace with the real world. He could run through a lesson plan from memory. But a simulated crime scene often surprised even the teacher.

Vorpagel began recruiting actors for field exercises in the 1970s. His idea was to make the scene so realistic that, at one point or another, the students might believe that something had gone awry. They might think that they had stumbled onto a real robbery or murder. Sometimes, they were partially right.

For his actors, Vorpagel would go to the local community colleges where he was teaching, talk to the Drama department, and promise credit lines if his videotapes of the scenes were ever used in future training tapes. He had to borrow explosives. He had to use fake guns and water pistols for safety purposes.

Vorpagel drove his two volunteers to the site of the

field problem—a jewelry store, with a vacant back room, in a nearby Mother Lode village.

He described the roles to the volunteers.

"Who wants to be the shopkeeper?" he asked. "The other will play a robber."

The youngest actor immediately said he didn't want any part of being a robber in front of thirty lawmen, play-acting or not.

"Then you'll be the dead body of the shopkeeper—shot in the robbery."

"Hey, what kind of a role is that?" the young man protested.

"Playing a corpse is harder than playing Hamlet, in my opinion. You've got to keep deadly still, control every movement."

The second actor said he wanted to play the robber because he'd actually been caught as a thief the year before and did six months on a misdemeanor charge.

Vorpagel told him to wait in the car, then began to "prep" the shopkeeper.

The young actor took off his shirt. Vorpagel, using mortician's clay, carefully formed two tiny mounds in the center of the man's chest. He built up the two miniature volcanoes until they could not be distinguished from sucking chest wounds. Then he poured stage blood over the wounds. Finally, he handed the young actor contact lenses.

"What are these for?"

"These lenses will make your eyes look lifeless. Have you ever worn contact lenses?"

"Yes. You want me to stop blinking for three hours?"

"No, just for a minute. Just long enough for the investigators to see; then, my partner will close your eyelids."

"That's a relief."

Vorpagel removed a mannequin from the trunk of his car. The dummy was dressed as a deputy sheriff. The head had been deformed with a twelve-gauge shotgun blast. There was very little left of it.

Vorpagel reentered the vacant store. He told the actor turned victim, "Just lie over in the corner by the counter. Don't move. I'll put these red 'fizzies' in the wounds to simulate sucking chest wounds."

Vorpagel placed the mannequin by the door. Then he dropped various clues, mingled with garbage, around the store.

His class of twenty-eight law enforcement people arrived. They gathered in front of the jewelry shop.

Vorpagel introduced his partner, Jack Shedd. "Jack will act as control with the class. As control, Jack will give you the perimeters of the problem. I will act as control in the field of the class.

"This is the situation: A series of armed robberies has occurred locally at liquor stores. Two armed robbers are surprised by a deputy sheriff who entered the shop to buy cigarettes. The bad guys shoot and kill the officer. Then, they kill the shopkeeper. They take the safe with them and flee into the remote countryside surrounding us."

"They killed the officer." The anger was obvious in Marcus's voice.

"Yes, shot him in the face with a shotgun. This problem could involve a potential siege situation. Keeping that in mind, any suggestions?"

"Call the sharpshooters and whack 'em once they're found," Marcus suggested.

"What about the hostages?"

"What hostages?"

"Exactly. We don't know if they've taken hostages."

"Our guys can hit a dime at five hundred yards."

"Tell that to the bereaved relatives of shootouts that went wrong. It happens all the time.

"The idea is to save everyone: Hostages and hostage takers. They killed a deputy sheriff, and brutally. But the judge and jury and gas chamber fall under others' jurisdiction. Your job is to handle this situation properly without loss of life."

Vorpagel pointed at the store. "Inside is the crime scene. You are to find out what you can. Now go to work."

A command post was set up. A deputy sheriff was made the commander. He appointed a state trooper his immediate aide.

The law enforcement agents entered the building and began their search. Vorpagel left his partner, Jack Shedd, in charge.

Vorpagel opened his car door, joined the second actor, and drove twenty miles into the countryside. He parked and carefully emptied the trunk. He toted one hundred pounds of suet to a nearby knoll. He moved the safe next to the mound of fat. Then he hauled a ten-pound bag of cow intestines to the knoll and poured them over the suet.

Whistling between his teeth, Vorpagel placed a stick of dynamite under the suet and bovine intestines. He inserted a blasting cap, rolled out wire, hid behind a boulder, and hooked the wire to a battery. He closed the electrical connection and winced as the explosion echoed in the mountain air. The dust puffed up, then settled back to the now silent terrain.

He walked back to the safe, which was now lying on its side. He removed the door, which was covered with fat and intestines, and tossed it ten feet away. Then, he opened a plastic bag and threw thirty teeth he'd gotten from a dentist into what was left of the mound of suet.

He went back to the trunk of his car and got a two-pint bottle filled with stage blood. Using a sieve, he sprayed red drops around the semicircle of intestines, fat, and teeth, finally splashing about a pint over the center of the blasted safe. He returned to his car, removed two plastic hands, two plastic feet, and a wig. He placed one hand ten feet from the front of the safe, the other fifteen. He randomly did the same to the plastic feet. He poured lighter fluid on the wig, set it aflame, dropped it to the ground, and stomped on the smoldering hair. Then, he tossed the charred wig on the seared suet.

There was an acrid smell in the air.

He surveyed the scene, nodded in satisfaction, and went back to his car. He told the actor to follow him. They sat on a boulder.

The actor asked, "What were you doing?"

"You said you were arrested as a thief. You ever a safe cracker?"

"No."

"Then I guess you've never been on a crime scene when the safe cracker made a mistake with the dynamite." He pointed at the mess he'd just created. "That is the remains of one of the robbers."

The actor looked out at the fat, the red liquid, the intestines, the still-smoking wig, and the teeth. He shuddered.

Vorpagel thought, if my police students are any good, they should be headed here by now. Among other clues and red herrings left at the scene of the robbery was a notebook planted on the mannequin. It described the robbers. It also said that the suspects had a known hideout outside town.

The actor asked, "What am I supposed to be doing?"

"When the police come dashing in on the scene, stick a gun in my ear and yell, 'I want a helicopter and ten million bucks, and I want it right now. Any funny stuff and I'm killing this guy.' "

"Where's the gun?"

Vorpagel held up his hand and formed a pistol. He pointed at the prisoner and said, "Bang, bang."

"You're kidding."

"Unfortunately, I'm not. It would be nice to be able to use real equipment on these problems, but there's no budget."

"No budget? I just watched you use explosives. You blew up half a cow. The stench here is awful."

"You have to have some realism. It helps the law enforcement men and women get into it. I get friends to pitch in with donations every once in a while to buy equipment."

"Dynamite?"

"Sure. I know a guy who owns a mining company."

"A dummy with its head blown off? That's supposed to be realistic?"

"A mannequin wearing a sheriff's uniform. I guarantee you, every one of those law enforcement officers saw that dummy, but *didn't* see it. They saw a fallen comrade. They saw a funeral procession. They saw friends with tears streaking down their faces as they buried a fellow police officer who died tragically young. When they saw that mannequin, they saw an open grave, they saw the casket, they saw the lone piper on the hill—piping out the last moments of a fallen comrade."

The actor looked at the tension in Vorpagel's face. He said, "I was a petty thief. I never used a weapon. I've never hurt anybody."

Vorpagel put an arm around his shoulder. "How much time did you do?"

"Six months."

"What did you steal?"

The thief stared at his hands, his brow furrowed. He said, "A television set."

"Even if the television was first class, all the bells and whistles, it couldn't have cost more than three grand."

"Less."

"Even at three grand, six months work-farm time comes out to less than the minimum hourly wage."

The thirty students of the homicide course arrived a few minutes later and saw the blown safe and the carefully prepared remains. They saw the simulation of a man torn apart when he'd tried to blow the safe. They smelled the burnt flesh. A few of the officers got sick to their stomachs.

The former thief made a "pretend" gun with his fist and pointed his forefinger at Vorpagel's head.

From a distance of fifty feet, the students

surrounded the actor and his "hostage" and began trying to persuade him to give up. It took them four hours to talk the hostage taker into surrendering. Vorpagel had to feed him his lines, doubling the surrender time.

After the exercise, the class was debriefed. They returned to the classroom. Vorpagel asked what they learned.

Marcus said, "That you go for realism."

"I do. You have to be prepared for the real thing. There's nothing worse than an officer of the law getting sick at a crime scene. Unless it's in front of civilians. The stench, blood, the guts are to prepare you for the real thing."

Marcus asked, "Does it really?"

"Really what?"

"Prepare you for the real thing?"

"Partially. Nothing can duplicate the actual event of a first look at a homicide scene. Just as the cases I tell you about help you to do the most important thing in your chosen profession—to think. I'm now going to tell you the case of a murdering barber."

"And the purpose of this example?" Shui asked.

"His case is what can escalate from the sick mind of someone like the man John, who stalked Elaine. This case was the easiest to solve I was ever involved in. But it taught me the lesson that you have to listen carefully, even when the suspect is spilling his guts out to you. This case, coupled with another case, when I was a detective in Milwaukee, got me wondering about the mind of the killer. What causes a suspect to confess? Why do some suspects have a need to be caught? Why do others meticulously hide their crimes? And still others have a need to toy with the police? This case, in its own way, was my personal introduction to the idea of a psychological autopsy."

Vorpagel paused. He let his memory and imagination go into the past. He said, "A good investigator has to train himself to think like a criminal. He has to put his mind into that of the perpetrator. Many criminals have told me of their fantasies. This is part of profiling. I am now going to share, just as the killer shared with me, one of those fantasies."

It was already humid at 7:30 A.M. when Vorpagel arrived at his office. A man was waiting outside. He asked if Vorpagel was an FBI agent, then said, "I want to confess to murder."

Vorpagel called his partner, Dan Connors; confessions had to be corroborated by a second party.

The man was young, about thirty. His blond hair was already receding. His face was gaunt. He said, "I'm a barber. I'd like to talk to you about a murder I committed."

"Who?"

"A nine-year-old boy."

"Why?"

"Because I loved him."

In the beginning, when the barber was a junior in high school, back when the girls looked through him as if he were a window, back when even his own mother barely recognized, let alone acknowledged him, his first fantasy began.

He became infatuated one day with the eight-year-old boy who lived next door. Soon, he was going to the boy's house after school, playing big brother. That first fantasy, so many years and so many different fantasies before, involved seeing the little boy without his clothes on.

He planned meticulously. When he was ready, he entered the eight-year-old's backyard. He watered the plants. He let the turned soil around a rose bush become soaked. The water seeped into the ground, then ran in rivulets away from the colorfully blooming pink flowers.

He called to his eight-year-old friend. "Smell the roses."

The young friend leaned forward, held a gorgeous rose in his hand, and sniffed.

The older boy leaned forward, supposedly also to smell, and "accidentally" bumped against the boy.

The boy tumbled to the ground. His clothes, his face, his hands were covered in mud.

"You're filthy. We have to clean you up before your mother comes home."

The high school junior and the eight-year-old boy entered the house and went to the bathroom.

"Take those filthy clothes off," the older boy ordered, barely able to control the pitch of his excited voice.

The eight-year-old took off his clothes and stood in the bathtub.

The older boy turned on the shower and, using a bar of soap, fulfilled his first fantasy.

A new, strange emotion came over him. Wouldn't it be even more exciting to take complete control of the boy? To command him around? Then tell him to shut up?

To hurt him?

Even then, during the fulfillment of the first fantasy, the shadow of what was to come flitted just on the edges of his now pedophilic mind. He didn't recognize it, didn't analyze it—not then.

Later, he would realize that the murky thought was always there.

Wouldn't it be tremendously thrilling to kill the boy?

Fantasies remained only fantasies unless they were acted out—and that required planning.

How do you get near young boys?

He went to barber school. Part of the plan.

He applied for, and was accepted at, a boy's military school. Part of the plan.

He took his time. He introduced selected boys to child pornography. He talked: "I know how you're feeling. See, it's not unusual to have the emotions you're having at your age. See, others have them, too. They're normal. Everyone has experienced them."

He was caught by a watchful administrator. He was fired.

The military school, not wanting publicity, not wanting to get sued, gave him a glowing recommendation. The barber got a job at another military academy.

The next level of fantasy began. He would stand behind his barber's chair. He would study the boy whose hair he was cutting: the delicate male neck, the graceful curve of the throat, the thin developing shoulders.

Then, he would imagine wrapping the electric razor's cord around that neck. He imagined how the child would struggle. He imagined slacking off, letting enough air whistle into gasping lungs, enough air to hear a futile plea for life.

That fantasy remained a fantasy. The particulars changed. Instead of the razor's cord, he would put a plastic bag over the youth's head. He would watch the eyes bulge as the last oxygen in the bag was sucked into the small and failing lungs. He would watch the soundless begging, then the soundless screams.

Or—a gun.

Yes, a gun. A long-barreled revolver. The symbol of the Old West. The symbol of rugged independence in America. The symbol of the very essence of maleness.

He was caught molesting again. He was dismissed again. He moved on again, accumulating recommendation after recommendation from terrified principal after terrified principal.

The barber finally ran out of school opportunities. He bought a barber shop in a small town in Blount County, Alabama. He attended Little League games. In his shop, he set separate, lower prices for pubescent boys. He bought child pornography and shared it with them.

And he bought a gun. He bought fifty rounds of .25-caliber bullets for the automatic.

He sat in his room at night and rubbed gun oil over the metal surface of the gun. He buffed the ivory handle. He bought a can of Brasso cleaner, a solvent for copper. He polished each cartridge, each molded piece of protruding lead.

He stood behind his frayed armchair. He stuck the gun into the band of his pants. He concealed the weapon by tying the butcher apron he used at work around his waist.

Then he practiced with the scissors. He snipped his shining shears into the thin air above the frayed armchair. He imagined, by concentrating very carefully, the back of a young boy's head. The image appeared. He cut the hair. He talked about how the school's team was doing. He brought up girls and how difficult they could be until you got older. He talked about how hard it was to get sexual gratification when you were so young.

He talked about fantasies, probing closer, testing the water, sensing the boy's reactions: negative, tepid, lukewarm, hot. If he sensed curiosity, only then would he show the first picture—taken from a child pornography magazine.

"See," he said to the empty air over the frayed armchair, "see, it's completely natural."

The barber practiced. He pretended that the boy agreed. So many had in the past. But then, he pretended that instead of immediately gratifying the boy's curiosity and body, he would tie the boy up.

Then, he would threaten to kill the boy. He would show the polished gun. He would show the shiny bullets. He would make the boy do the things that were central in his fantasies. But he would not kill the first time—not yet.

Finally, he found the opportunity.

After he was finished with this, his first test, he told the boy that the reason he had shown him the gun was to remove any guilt the boy might feel afterward. "See, it's not your fault. See, I made you do it. But see, you really enjoyed it, didn't you? But if you tell anyone, if you destroy this gift I've given you of your first sexual rapture, then I will have to kill you."

Some of the boys never came back to the barber shop. Some of the boys did come back—for a time. None talked.

None even threatened to talk; they were either too embarrassed and ashamed or too frightened.

The barber's fantasies turned ever darker. He realized that a stark thought was always there: the ultimate thrill—to kill while engaged in the act of sex.

He began a new plan.

He bought an isolated cabin in the woods.

Then, he started to track his future, unknown, unwilling partner. He watched softball games. He studied the athletic young bodies: weighing, evaluating, rejecting. The first boy for this new fantasy had to be perfect.

It took him five weeks before he found what he was looking for. The boy had been out sick, but when he returned to baseball practice, the barber knew—this was the one.

He was perfect.

The barber gave the boy his card, complimented him on the Little League game he'd just helped win, and told him that he gave free introductory haircuts to special clients.

The boy came to his shop the next day.

The barber ran the comb through the nine-year-old boy's flaxen hair. As he did, he let the tips of his fingers brush against the soft, full strands. He felt a shiver run, like electricity, from the tips of his fingers. It had begun like this so many times, the gleaming shears, the state-of-the-art scissors clicking as he snipped a lock of hair here, a tress there, shaping, forming the wonderful, full, sensuous hair.

The fantasy began. His heartbeat accelerated. His blood pressure soared. Instead of carefully sculpting the hair, the barber imagined the scissors raised high, held with both hands, then coming down in a graceful half circle, and whizzing a hair's breadth past the carotid artery.

The nine-year-old eyes, terrified, alive, would never leave the weaving point of the scissors that circled, like a cobra, waiting to strike.

The boy would plead for his life.

The barber would ask, "And what will you do to have me spare you?"

The boy would answer, "Anything."

He again ran his fingers through the flaxen hair. Again, he felt the electricity spurting up his arm, then branching out: One conduit ran to his brain, a second to his heart, a third to his groin.

He felt the glow, the warmth, the burning desire for fulfillment of his new fantasy.

"Do you like to fish?" he asked the nine-year-old.

"I love it."

"I have a cabin in the mountains. Would you like to go there with me?"

"Is there fishing?"

"Yes. A stream runs behind my cabin. I've seen the trout flashing in the sunlight as they leap out of the cool water and catch the flies."

The barber inspected the flaxen hair, made a few minor last cuts, then brushed the slim neck and back of the boy, using the back of his hand. Was he right? Was this the time? Was this the right boy? For the ultimate fantasy. . . .

Gary asked, "I'm having trouble distinguishing between the barber, Meola's, fantasies and reality."

"That's the whole point. The man himself couldn't distinguish between his fantasies and reality." Vorpagel paused. Ava's hand was in the air. He acknowledged her.

"Do most ignored adolescent boys fixate on sex?"

"Yes. I've handled cases like this during my entire career. The ability to dominate and gain respect from someone older is prevalent in these type cases."

Vorpagel let his mind once again return to the past. He began to speak softly.

Vorpagel's partner, Connors, entered the interrogation room. Both agents took out their notepads. The man who wanted to confess appeared relieved.

Vorpagel began, "You spoke about a murder?"

"I did it. You've got to believe me."

"Whom did you kill? Where? Why?"

"A boy. A nine-year-old."

"Where?"

"Alabama."

Vorpagel placed a tape recorder on the table. "I'm going to make a record of this. Please begin with your name. And please be as specific as you can with places and dates."

"My name is Thomas Meola. I'm a barber. I've worked in military academies all across the country, since I was twenty. Now, I own a small barber shop in Blount County, Alabama. I've never been convicted of a crime. I've made a mistake. I got involved with a nine-year-old boy."

"How?"

"I watched him play in a softball game. After it was over, I asked if he wanted an ice-cream cone. Another boy, his friend, insisted he wanted to go along. They both got in my car."

"Both?"

"Yes. I became flustered. This wasn't part of my plan. I went to a gas station and asked if they wanted a Coke. I sent the other boy inside with some money. Then I sped off."

"Where?"

"To a cabin I own. During a sexual misadventure . . ."

Vorpagel erupted, "You mean sodomy, don't you?"

Meola stared at the floor. "I became terrified. The boy threatened to tell on me. I couldn't allow that. I panicked. I pulled a gun. I tried to scare him. I shot him in the side of the head because he resisted me."

Connors asked, "Why didn't you go to the local police or Sheriff's Department in Blount?"

"They'd send me to the State Penitentiary."

"So?"

"You don't know how bad the jails are in Alabama. Once the prisoners found out what I'd done, they'd kill me. I want to go to a Federal Penitentiary. I want my crime to remain unknown to the other prisoners."

Vorpagel thought, here's a man who wants to choose his prison. He asked, "Why didn't you go to the FBI office in Georgia?"

"I did. I went to Savannah. That was the day before yesterday. I confessed. They left me in the waiting room all morning. Then, they told me to go home. Then, I tried to turn myself in to the FBI in Atlanta. No good. Same result."

Connors nudged Vorpagel and motioned to the door.

In the hallway, Vorpagel said, "You think he's a nut? Or a publicity seeker?"

"If I've ever seen one."

"Call Blount County, and the state troopers in Alabama, and see if either of them has a dead-kid case. I'll continue to listen to his story."

For the next half-hour Vorpagel listened to a tale of rape spelled out in clinical detail. Meola had seduced young boys in military schools. After Little League games. On playgrounds. In his barber shop.

"I'd talk to the coaches," Meola said, "to find out who the best players were. I'd tell them, 'The coach thinks you're doing great, keep it up.' I'd invite them for a free haircut at my barber shop. I put a sign up in front of my shop: Haircuts—seventy-five cents, Special for Young Boys—fifty cents. I'd treat a special boy whose hair I was cutting to a Coke. I wasn't doing anything wrong. The boys enjoyed what I was doing. Someone has to introduce them to sex. Women can be so cruel. So demanding, so domineering."

Bile rising to his mouth, Vorpagel asked, "What happened with the last boy?"

"He was very special. I took him to my cabin."

Connors entered the interrogation room. He gave Vorpagel a note: Savannah called Blount County—No unsolved murders.

Vorpagel scribbled—There are too many details for him to be making this up. Then, he asked, "Mr. Meola, what happened after you arrived at the cabin?"

"At first, he was very nice. I gave him some candy bars and let him look at some of the pictures I keep in the cabin."

"Pictures?"

"You know, young boys, that kind of stuff. I wanted him not to feel guilty. There was nothing wrong with what we were going to do. Or who I'd already did it with. I showed him pictures of some of his fellow ball players. I mean, everybody was doing it."

"What happened next?"

"Erich became very nervous."

"Erich?" Vorpagel said in a hoarse voice.

"That was his name. He was nine." Then Meola told Vorpagel the boy's birthdate.

Vorpagel asked him to repeat the date, then felt a murderous rage fill his mind.

The barber continued, "I made him take off his clothes. Then he hit me. The scratches haven't healed yet. See where he clawed me?"

"Then what?"

"He said he was going to tell on me."

"Then?"

"No one had ever done that to me before. I shot him."

Vorpagel stared into the gaunt face. "How many times have you molested young boys?"

Meola itemized his tour of America's military academies.

Vorpagel had encountered these pathologies in psychology at the University of Wisconsin. Thoughts from his schooling resonated in him as he watched the barber spill out his perversion. Meola was a pedophile, but that did not indicate, in itself, a homosexual. There were many subclassifications: fixated, regressed, prepubescent. This type of person was described as inadequate. Adults were threats to him. Any attempt at an adult relationship was doomed to failure. He required a child as a sexual equal.

Vorpagel said in an even voice, "Give me facts that only the killer could know, and I promise you a conviction."

Meola described his cabin, the location, what the boy looked like, what position he played on the baseball team, where he buried the body.

Vorpagel said, "Connors, call Blount County."

"I already did—no kid murdered."

"Call again, except this time ask them if there's a missing child down there, not an unsolved murder."

Within an hour, a sheriff's party had found the cabin and the shallow grave of a boy named Erich.

Vorpagel charged Meola with UFAP—unlawful flight to avoid prosecution.

"Why not murder?" Meola asked.

"There's no federal statute against murder."

"What's unlawful flight?"

"A state law."

"What about kidnapping? That's a federal offense."

"No exchange of money," Vorpagel said, trying to keep the anger in his voice to a minimum. "No ransom demand. No state lines crossed. You're going to jail in Alabama."

Meola was taken away.

FBI Agent Connors asked, "Russ, what's the matter? You look like you're about to have a stroke."

"The entire time Meola was confessing, every time he used the name Erich, which is the name of my oldest son, I imagined my own son in the hands of this monster. Then, when he told me the age of his victim, I thought I was going to fling myself across the table and strangle the bastard."

"Why?"

"It's the same birthday as my second son."

Two weeks later, Meola was arraigned in the Blount County Courthouse. After a perfunctory plea of guilty, he was sentenced to life in the state prison.

It was hardly an investigative coup—the man confessed.

Vorpagel scanned the classroom, studying his students. He said, "This was the first time I got to see inside the mind of a killer."

Gary asked, "How did you know what he was thinking?"

"He told me. When questioning the barber during the original interrogation, I kept asking myself why? Why did he use a gun this time? Was he telling the truth when he said the boy tried to escape? I wondered how much of his confession was self-serving fantasy."

Marcus said, "You mean the I-couldn't-help-myself confession?"

"Exactly."

Ava said, "Planned murder, not fear, not spontaneous, unintentional murder."

"This was a case of a mental school for murder. A conscious effort to teach oneself to kill. Since then, I've seen it happen again and again. How do we interrupt the cycle? Where do we teach life and love, and reverence for other human beings?"

"It's not our job," Gary said, "to interrupt the cycle, only to . . ."

"I'm not speaking to you as professionals in law enforcement or criminal justice, but as human beings. How do we interrupt the fantasies we're all subject to, and keep them from becoming the real thing?"

Shui asked, "Why didn't the boy who was let off at the gas station tell anyone his friend was kidnapped? And who took him?"

"Fear, plain and simple. His dad had told him he'd tan his hide if he ever got into a car with a stranger. He'd gotten into a car with a stranger. Remember, these boys weren't even teenagers, just young lads."

Gary asked, "What happened to Meola?"

"He was sentenced to life imprisonment in Alabama, in 1962."

Almost ten years later Meola filed a writ of *coram nobis*, which claimed errors in his first trial. It was granted, and I and my oldest daughter, Jane, age 16, drove to Alabama for the trial. She had just gotten her license, and I needed another driver, as we were going to go to Wisconsin for a vacation after the trial.

The trial was to start in the afternoon in a typical rural deep south courthouse—American and Rebel flags, etc. First the judge had all rise and pledge allegiance to the flag, and stay standing to be sworn in on the case. One man sat down; he told the judge his case was for the morning, but he overslept. He was found in contempt and sent to jail. I was sure I would like this judge.

After all the preliminaries and qualifications were done, the defense attorney asked when I had given the suspect his Miranda warnings. I said he wasn't given any. Bedlam! He cried out for dismissal and the judge and prosecutor were horrified. Why was I not upset? Anybody? Some said noncustodial, others volunteered, but the best reason came through from me loud and clear. *There were no Miranda rights in 1962.*

The complaint was dismissed and Meola returned to prison.

Vorpagel shuffled the papers on the dais. "The next example I want to give you involves a different kind of profiling and a different kind of murder—yet with thematic parallels with what we've already seen. I know you've all heard of the Unabomber who used to terrorize people through the mail. The next case involves the exact same method and weapon. Only his motive was not to change society, only the person he loved."

FALSE POSITIVE

Vorpagel prepared his slides. He glanced around the room, picked up his briefcase, and said, "Before we begin the case of the jilted bomber, I have another puzzle for you to solve. These are the kinds of problems you will face out in the street. The answer is important because of the impact on other people's lives. Was the death murder? An accident? Suicide? The answer impacts on the living, tremendously. The following story happened here in Sacramento. But I've heard of cases like this happening all over the world."

A young male was arrested. It wasn't the first time. He'd always been busted for solicitation, and now he found himself in Elk Grove. Sacramento County had released the money to build a brand-new jail facility in Elk Grove. The walls still had vast spaces that were graffiti-free. The paint still smelled fresh. The concrete floors were free of urine stains.

The young jailer was a deputy sheriff. Sacramento

County made its newest deputy sheriffs, as policy and to get the feel of being a peace officer before hitting the street, spend a year as jailers.

The jailer looked at his rap sheet. "You've got suicidal tendencies."

The young man arched an eyebrow, puckered his lips, and said, "I'd die for you."

"The box marked 'alleged suicidal tendencies' is real. Just as is the box that reads alleged homosexual tendencies."

"Alleged? My dear boy . . ."

The jailer said, "Knock that crap off."

"Or what? You'll spank me?"

The jailer led the handcuffed prisoner down the hallway and into a prison section called general lockup. He put the man in a cell by himself. The cell to the left held four Mexicans, arrested after a drive-by shooting. The tank to the right held seven drunks.

As the jailer left, he heard the newest prisoner say, "Somebody back up against these bars and I'll give him the time of his life."

A few minutes later, the jailer heard shouting coming from the lockup area. He ran down the hallway.

A prisoner snarled, "We're going to kill him."

The four Mexicans were lined up against the bars. They were trying to reach the young man, who was cowering against the far wall. The drunks were lined up as far away from him as they could get.

The Mexican said, "He waved his thing at us. If I get close, I'm tearing it off. Put this *puta* somewhere else."

The jailer opened the cell door and led the prisoner down a hallway. The jailer said, "We have a new wing, hasn't even been opened up yet. I'm transferring you there. You'll be the first guest."

The young man's attitude was subdued. He kept his head down. His eyelids were squeezed into slits.

The jailer let him into the first cell on the right.

The prisoner was to be checked every fifteen to twenty minutes as a suicide risk.

Hours later, the Sacramento Sheriff's Office received the call. Two Internal Affairs investigators drove to the new prison facility. A sergeant let them in and said, "This looks bad, very bad."

"You mean suspicious?"

"Very suspicious."

"Call the medical examiner."

The two men from Internal Affairs (IA) went to the cell. The young man was lying on the floor. A bed sheet had been twisted into an impromptu noose. It was tied to a support board on the upper bunk, under a grill that was near the rear of the eight-by-ten cell. The other end of the sheet dangled off the bunk.

The jailer said, "When I checked in on him, I saw what he'd done. I lifted him up enough to get the loop from around his neck, then I tried to resuscitate him."

The older IA investigator said, "There's no ligature marks on the neck, just scratches, like someone manually strangling him and leaving nail prints."

The younger IA investigator said, "You get hanged, it leaves ligature marks. I know— I read about it in a class."

"Hanged? How could this guy get hanged? The noose is only five feet off the floor. All he had to do was stand up."

The older IA officer reached down and touched the dead man's jaw. "This guy's already in rigor."

The younger IA officer felt the dead man's face and neck. "He's cold to the touch."

The dead man was placed in a body bag and taken to the morgue. The pathologist of Sacramento county said that the death was due to suicide: strangulation from a soft ligature, not a cord, not a rope, but soft—like a bed sheet. That's why there were no ligature marks.

The body was turned over to the family. They didn't believe their son had committed suicide. He had bruises and abrasions on his face and forehead. There were scratch marks on his throat, and he had a broken nose.

They hired a pathologist from another county. He examined the body and said the man was manually strangled and beaten to death. He must have lain there a long time, because the body was cold to the touch. And it was impossible to be in rigor if he'd only been there twenty minutes. It was murder.

Vorpagel looked out at the students in his class and said, "I was called in by the County of Sacramento. They were being sued for negligence on their part for the security in the prison. The question that I was asked to look into was: Any possibility that the jailer was telling the truth?"

Ava said, "I'm familiar with this case, and its outcome, so I can't participate in this problem."

Vorpagel said, "Thank you for your honesty."

Marcus asked, "Do you have any pictures on this one?"

"No. I did get both reports and the pathologist's, which I summed up for you already. I solved this case by asking questions. I'll play everybody else, you students play me."

Shui said, "Obviously, it was suicide."

"Obviously? Why obviously?"

"Because you're looking very pleased with yourself, and that wouldn't be happening if the answer to this was that the pathologist's verdict was right. Therefore, the pathologist was right and the prisoner committed suicide."

"Nice train of logic. However, this is a puzzle. I didn't have my own reaction to solve it, just the clues I've told you."

"The clues look damning," Gary said. "But something jumped out at me. What was it? It had to do with direction."

Marcus said, "The marks on the throat. Vorpagel said vertical. Those weren't necessarily caused in a struggle. They could have been caused by the prisoner, fighting with the noose, trying to loosen it enough to escape."

"Correct," Vorpagel said.

Marcus said, "You never mentioned anyone doing a crime scene investigation. I assume the arresting officers . . ."

"The two IA investigators did nothing but take a few notes, touch the deceased a few times, and make a report. Neither had any training in death-scene investigation."

"They did touch the body and found it cold and in rigor. I'm not that familiar with how fast rigor comes on."

Vorpagel answered, "In postmortem rigidity, the small muscles show rigidity first, although rigidity is forming in the larger muscles all over the body. It's just more noticeable in the smaller muscles, such as the jaw and face and neck. However, there is a thing called cadaveric spasm, also known as instantaneous rigor. Most of the time, it's written up when someone shoots himself in the head with a gun, dies instantly, and cadaveric spasm acts on a muscle group that is in a state of tension at the time of death and the hand holds onto the gun. And so many cases have been resolved by the fingers having to be pried off the gun. So if a man is killed instantly, you couldn't—like so many television shows have erroneously shown—put a gun in his hand to make it look like a suicide."

The few coroners in the classroom nodded their heads.

Vorpagel continued, "To get by spontaneous rigor, you would have to have your intended victim holding the gun."

Gary said, "You've just explained why the jaw of the dead man was in rigor so soon. If he hung himself, his neck would act the same as a hand in a suicide by a gun."

"Exactly. The neck and jaw are in a state of extreme tension at the moment of death in a hanging. Mostly, this type of thing is found with handguns, although I know of one case where a woman jumped from a building holding her baby. The woman died instantly when her head hit the concrete, but her body cushioned the impact on the sidewalk. The baby lived. The mother's arms locked into instantaneous rigor. They had to be pried off the baby."

Marcus asked, "Is there a train of thought you use in cases?"

"Yes. What's the evidence? And where does it lead?"

"The bruises on the face did not indicate murder. The guard might have roughed the prisoner up—an atrocity, but not murder."

Gary said, "The most damning evidence is the body was cold. The body had also lost several degrees of temperature, something that usually takes two hours, not twenty minutes."

Shui asked, "But what could possibly accelerate the drop in temperature?"

Marcus asked, "The grill, was it an air-vent shaft?"

"Yes." Vorpagel smiled.

"Did the air vent deliver both hot and cold air?"

"Yes, it acted as a heater, or an air conditioner."

"Was the air conditioner on?"

"Very good."

"So that's how you solved it?"

"Not quite. The first thing I did was investigate the possibility of an accident."

"An accident? The man was found hanged."

"I checked on the past activities of the deceased. I wanted to learn if he was into autoerotic behavior. People into that particular activity sometimes die, and their deaths look like suicide. They stimulate themselves by placing their lives in danger. If any of you ever saw the movie *The Ruling Class*, you'll know what I mean. The English general, at the beginning of the movie, puts a satin, pink rope around his neck. He's wearing his uniform, with all its ribbons, above the waist. Below the waist he's wearing a pink ballet tutu—complete with slippers. This particular sexual exercise, to those who practice it, obviously, is very dangerous. One mistake and you hang. I will be giving you several other examples of this type of activity later on in the course. Again, problems of whether a death was suicide or accident."

A collective murmur went around the room: Most had never thought of an accident.

Vorpagel continued, "Except this wasn't an accident. The prisoner did kill himself, it was a suicide."

"The bruises?" Shui asked.

"Self-imposed. The blood marks on the wall of the cell and on the bunk, as well as the bruises on his face, were caused by his face banging up against the wall in his last desperate throes to try and free himself from the noose. It's not a pretty picture."

"No slides?"

"Not for this one. The prisoner is led to a new cell. It's noted that he was despondent. The jailer leaves and, spontaneously, the prisoner decides to end his life. He wraps the bed sheet into an impromptu noose, ties it to the bed beneath the air vent, and just bends at the shoulders. He falls off the upper bunk and the sheet tightens."

"Why didn't he just stand up?" Shui asked. "The IA officer said that was possible to do."

"Dying by hanging is dying by asphyxiation. The blood is cut off to the brain."

"Like drowning."

"Exactly. The suicide knelt on the top bunk. He bent forward. The sheet tightened. As the blood ceased to flow, the suicide fell off the bed. Then, in the last few moments of consciousness, he decides to live."

Shui said, "Again, why didn't he just stand up?"

"I think he did just that. He stands, and that's when, in absolute frantic terror, he claws at the cinched bed sheet. He fights desperately the last few moments of his life to live, slamming into the wall as he desperately tries to loosen the soft bed sheet. His legacy: He almost takes an innocent party with him. The young jailer was exonerated, his name cleared, his reputation restored."

Ava said, "I was working at a nearby prison when this happened. Everybody at the Department of Corrections was relieved when the young jailer was found innocent."

"Exactly. The results of this type of death don't just impact on the relatives. The ripples can spread out across the country. Look at the countrywide morale problem from the Rodney King beating." Vorpagel removed a file from his briefcase and said, "The next case presents certain unusual problems, especially in profiling. Or, more accurately, what happens when witnesses pass themselves off as experts when they have not received the proper training."

Vorpagel glanced at his notes, then continued, "The Behavioral Science Unit was developed to catch, and stop, a murderer. Conviction and punishment are left, as usual in police work, to someone else. And I must caution all you investigators to be aware of the state *you're* in."

Shui asked, "But why should the state *I'm* in affect the crime?"

"Were you out drinking the night before? Did you have a fight with your spouse before you went to work? Did your supervisor chew you out? The state of your mind, any investigative officer's mind, during the search can dramatically, if he or she lets it, change the view of the facts. Many of these interpretations may be described as 'gut feelings' but each, when properly evaluated, lends to accuracy, color, hue, and tint. In order to give some weight or credence to those interpretations, a pattern, a universality, has to be established."

"Universality? In murder?"

"Yes. And, unfortunately, the next case points out what happens when someone untrained tries to profile. It takes a year of intense education at Quantico even to get the drift of what it is all about. These few days I have with you are merely to give you a taste."

"What's this case about?"

"The following case started at a mining company in New Mexico. Its subject matter is very current: It's about a mad bomber, a guy who made a clever device, carefully disguised where he was mailing it from, and almost got away."

"Where's the security guard today?" the miner asked.

"Got a cold, off today."

Randy Forse shielded his eyes against the glaring overhead sun. He had worked at the Resources Mine, in San Mateo, New Mexico, for several years.

Today's the day, he thought. He had gotten the idea five weeks ago, while he was in a drift in the mine. He would mail Bonnie a bomb—just to hurt her.

Perhaps afterward he would be allowed to take care of her. But he needed to smuggle the explosives out. He carried his lunchbox to the magazine, a small red shed. He had every right to be there: He was an underground explosives expert.

The miners were scattered about the side of the hill, talking, sleeping, eating. Randy slipped in and removed two sticks of tovex, an explosive gel, and two number-eight blasting caps. He placed them in his lunchbox and left. That night, he nodded to the new security guard at the gate and was waved by. He had covered the items with Reynolds Wrap so the guard would miss it if he looked in his lunchbox at the gate.

He lived at home with his parents, in Grants, New Mexico. In mid-October, his mother and father left to go on vacation. Randy started making the bomb that day, in a shed at the rear of the property.

He was meticulous. He took two two-by-sixes, cut them into twelve-inch lengths, and hinged them together. He had to hollow out the wood with a chisel. He purchased a clasp, hinges, and stain. He sanded the two pieces of wood, then connected the hinges and clasp.

His brother, Jim, arrived and asked what he was making.

"A jewelry box for our niece. Check the circuit for me."

His brother checked the circuit. "What's this thing supposed to do?"

"It's a surprise."

Later, Randy went to his brother's house and borrowed a cookie box.

Back in his workshed, Randy carefully placed the two sticks of tovex inside the hollowed-out portion of the two-by-sixes. He placed two screws on each end of the tovex and tied the wire from screw to screw. He connected the other end of the wire to the blasting caps. Then, he wedged in the two caps. And, finally, he added a nine-volt battery.

He went to a hardware store and bought a toilet paper roller, a drill bit, perfboard, and two bolts. He drilled a hole through the cookie box, then through one of the two-by-sixes. He placed the perfboard in front of the battery and secured it with two bolts.

On October 22, he went to the airport and caught a plane to Las Vegas, taking components in his carry-on. The X ray machine did not alert the operator and Randy got through. There, he armed the device. He put the nine-volt battery beside the toilet roller, connected wires to the two bolts on one end, and the two blasting caps on the other end. He placed everything in the cookie box. Then, he inserted the drill bit through the holes he'd drilled as a safety precaution to prevent the battery from making the connection.

Randy took a cab to a post office. There, he removed the drill bit and wrapped the package. He addressed the cookie box to his ex-girlfriend, Bonnie Weatherby in New Mexico.

Bonnie had thrown him over for another man, whom she was going to marry. They already had a baby.

If she wouldn't marry Randy, she wasn't going to marry anyone.

He flew back to Albuquerque and went home.

The box was now armed. When the cookie box was opened, the toilet-roll spring would force open the two blocks of wood and allow a contact to close. Current from the battery would flow to the two blasting caps, and the tovex would explode.

On October 24, Rosa Torres picked up her mother, Nancy, and told her, "I have to run some errands." She showed her mother a yellow mail notice. "Bonnie asked me to pick this up for her at the post office."

The two women drove to the post office. Rosa got the package and put it on the seat between herself and her mother.

Her mother said, "It's from Las Vegas, from a publishing company."

Rosa dropped her mother off and went to Bonnie's home. She let her friend in, pointed at the package, and said, "A gift."

Bonnie's one-year-old daughter, Lorraine, was standing beside her. The two women went with the baby to the dining room.

Bonnie fussed over Lorraine and asked, "Rosa, would you mind opening the package for me?"

Bonnie Austin's next-door neighbor, Mrs. Verde, heard the sound of an explosion. She raced into the house and stood at the entrance to the dining room. It was a shambles, rubble scattered everywhere. Lorraine, holding a teddy bear, stood in the opposite doorway, the entrance to her bedroom. She was crying.

Rosa was sprawled on the floor. She was dead. The explosion had torn her flesh and scattered her blood.

Bonnie was slumped in a dining-room chair. She was seriously injured.

After an intense investigation by the FBI, a female postal clerk in Las Vegas was interviewed. She was on duty at the time the package was mailed and remembered, vaguely, something about a suspicious man who mailed a package. She agreed to be hypnotized. Under a trance, she said that a man about thirty-three years old brought in the cookie package.

She said the subject had brown hair and wore horn-rim glasses. The man was soft-spoken and nervous.

A sketch was drawn and faxed to the Grants police department. It looked like Randy Forse.

The police picked him up. They asked if he would agree to a polygraph. His answers indicated he was lying. A search warrant was issued. Material evidence was found.

Randy Forse confessed.

A civil action was initiated by the surviving victim's family, Forse's ex-girlfriend, Bonnie. The case was taken on by the law firm of Branch in Albuquerque, New Mexico.

Russ Vorpagel was called as an expert witness by Doug Vigil, a lawyer working for the firm of Branch. What was in question during Vorpagel's testimony was the accuracy of a psychological profile done by another ex-FBI man, whom Vorpagel code-named Klinger to protect the man's reputation.

Doug Vigil asked, "What do you think of Klinger's psychological profile?"

Vorpagel answered, "It's awful."

"Do you know Klinger?"

"Yes, I know Klinger. He's a friend of mine. I've worked with him. I've been asked to teach with him. I was asked to join the same Santa Rosa corporation that he taught for, but I declined."

"What's the problem with this psychological profile?"

• • •

Vorpagel paused, studied his students for a few moments, then said, "I am bringing up this case to show you the danger of profiling without sufficient background or education." He handed each member of his class Klinger's profile.

1. Education/intelligence: Most likely a high school dropout. Poor verbal skills . . . and dull-normal intelligence.
2. Socioeconomic status: middle class or lower middle class.
3. Lives alone or with someone.
4. In a female-dominated household.
5. Expect him to be thin, with poor muscle tone. But then, if he's heavy, he'll be soft and pudgy.
6. The subject tends to drive an old car, dirty and in poor repair.
7. Employment: unskilled labor, clerical work. Typically a busboy, fry cook, janitor, laborer, clerk, or bag boy.
8. A history of mental health problems.
9. Law enforcement history: Parking tickets, traffic offenses, residential burglary, and voyeurism when young.
10. The suspect is a loner, very few personal friends; all of them are male, and he's considered somewhat odd by his acquaintances.
11. An individual who becomes very dependent on the female; inadequate.
12. Takes little pride in his personal appearance.
13. Tends to brag to his male friends of sexual conquests that never happened.

14. He can be expected to attend the funeral and to visit the grave site.
15. If arrested and charged with the crime, he may attempt to take his own life when he's locked up.

Vorpagel allowed his students a few minutes to scan the contents, then asked, "What do you see in this profile?"

Gary answered, "Klinger has painted the picture of Randy Forse as what I would consider a classic disorganized personality. He deals with some sort of 'schizo' behavior, not 'schizophrenia' itself. But he's probably a schizoid, the way Klinger describes it."

Ava added, "I see Forse as an individual who is not anything that Klinger mentioned in his profile."

"Very good," Vorpagel said. "Klinger is describing the classic disorganized, which used to be called a 'simple schizophrenic.' And this guy is not a 'simple schizophrenic.' This man is intelligent. What evidence am I basing that conclusion on?"

Marcus said, "Forse is capable of planning ahead. He's capable of formulating a complex plan."

"Correct. Klinger's profile just dealt with what we used to call a 'simple schizophrenic.' "

Marcus asked, "How would you profile Randy Forse?"

"I was asked to do just that by the Branch law firm. Except the FBI has a policy not to profile anybody that is known. However, look at the facts without the knowledge of who the perpetrator is. Who would you study first?"

Ava blurted out, "The victim."

"Yes, you're right. We call this psychological autopsy. Were I to be given her history, her background, her marital status, her status in the community, her family relationship, her employment, her attitude toward law enforcement, her attitude toward morality, her basic religion, I would then determine that here was a victim who was not a random victim."

Shui asked, "Why does the victim's religion or morality make a difference? For that matter, why do any of these things you wanted to know make her an intentional victim as opposed to a random one?"

"We're not dealing with someone who was raped in the rear parking lot of a liquor store. This woman was sent a bomb. This definitely limits things. Who makes bombs? For one, terrorists. Was she the target of a terrorist? Was she a terrorist herself, and got blown up making a bomb? Did she work for a high-risk company: nuclear, CIA, political? Remember the Oklahoma City Federal Building bombing? McVeigh specifically chose a place as a target, not a specific person."

Shui said, "I see."

Vorpagel said, "Bonnie was none of those things. But she was a specific, targeted victim. The person who built this device was not a terrorist who was trying to interdict some corporation or business or firm or shop or store. It was sent to her home."

Shui said, "What's the next step in the profile?"

"Psychological. The person that did this is someone who had a very strong anger toward the target. The target was female, which leads to someone who probably was relatively inadequate with females. He had a relationship with this particular woman that has been broken off. Because of it, he feels completely lost. He feels that he is incompetent. He feels insecure. And therefore, out of anger, he's going to destroy that which first hurt him."

Marcus said, "That certainly limits the investigation."

"I can be even more specific. I would have guessed him to have been probably several years older, but not too many years older than the victim, because an individual of this nature usually is involved with people who are younger, who he had the ability to manipulate a little bit."

"Narrowing it even more."

Vorpagel nodded. "That's the point of profiling. And further, I would have said that he probably has a good job. He is relatively intelligent. He's capable of planning ahead, and, in this particular case, he had some knowledge of explosives. Plus, he's good with his hands."

Gary asked, "Based on what?"

"He's capable of building a relatively adequate device. He built a jewel box. He was aware of the fact that it would be lined. So we're talking about a man who is capable of getting along fine in life other than his feelings of loss because of his inability to maintain a particular relationship with a victim. That's how I would have described the person who built that bomb. Also, his ticket was bought for cash a month earlier under a false name."

Ava asked, "Would you go through Klinger's profile for us, please, and critique it, as you have said it was a— I think the word you used was 'awful'—psychological profile?"

Vorpagel picked up a copy of Klinger's profile and

read, "The profile states 'Education/intelligence: Most likely a high school dropout. Poor verbal skills . . . and dull-normal intelligence.' Why do any of you think I felt this was wrong?"

Shui answered, "He was certainly not stupid or he wouldn't have been able to plan and plot this particular activity."

"Exactly," Vorpagel agreed, then ran his finger to the next item on the profile. "Socioeconomic status. I'd agree with Klinger there. I'd also figure middle class or lower middle class."

Shui asked, "Why middle or lower class?"

"Simply the odds. Rich people don't blow each other up—at least not personally. They hire someone to do it—like T. Cullen Davis, who was indicted. The accusation: hiring a hit man to do in a judge."

Gary said, "I know that case. Davis supposedly shot his wife, killed his wife's daughter, and killed her boyfriend."

"That was cold, calculated rage, but it was not long-term planning. It was an eruption of emotions."

Shui said, "Was Davis ever convicted?"

"No. Profiling is based on statistics, on the odds. I am going to use the Davis case later to illustrate the use of profiling at a trial."

Gary nodded.

Vorpagel pointed at a line on the Klinger deposition and said, "This is one that I've always been astonished by in a profile. 'Lives alone or with someone.' What an inane statement."

Ava said, "A can't-miss comment, like must be a male or female."

"Exactly. Next, Klinger mentions 'in a female-dominated household.' Why do you think I disagreed with this statement?"

Ava answered, "The anger wasn't toward all females. No attempt to get even with all women. Just a particular victim."

"Again," Vorpagel said, "on the button. Next on the profile, his physical characteristics. 'Expect him to be thin, with poor muscle tone. But then if he's heavy, he'll be soft and pudgy.' "

Ava grinned, "The perp's a man or woman."

"Exactly, thin or fat."

Gary asked, "The statement has no meaning whatever?"

"No. What's Klinger talking about when he says, 'Expect him to be thin with poor muscle tone'? He's dealing with a particular type of individual that we used to call the simple schizophrenic—who does not have good health habits, good food habits, and many times is emaciated and scrawny. This is not what I would see in this particular person."

Vorpagel pointed at Klinger's profile and continued, "He says, 'The subject tends to drive an old car, dirty and in poor repair.' There's no indication that he would have a car like that. And because of the type of person that I think he is, he probably would have a car that might have been two or three years old, but not in disrepair."

Shui asked, "Where'd that logic come from?"

"The bomb he built. Randy Forse is handy with his hands and able to take care of things. He's meticulous, and meticulous people tend to be that way in everything they do."

"Why a two- or three-year-old car?"

"An educated guess, the same kind that Sherlock Holmes did all the time."

"Based on?"

"The odds. We know that the bomber could afford to go to a great extent to fulfill his murder. He flew to another city. He spent money on very elaborate wood for the jewel box. But he didn't fly to New York or Boston; he flew to a relatively nearby city, and one that offered very cheap fares to get there. This was not a man of unlimited means, but he was not broke either. So, he didn't buy a car every year. When you think about it, consider the parallels with the Unabomber. Although I personally think the Unabomber had less access to money than Forse did."

"But why couldn't Forse have a brand-new car?"

"Another educated guess. He was courting Bonnie—that costs."

"Highly speculative," Shui said.

"But, as it turns out, highly accurate." Vorpagel pointed at another spot on Klinger's profile. "Here, employment, Klinger puts down 'unskilled labor, clerical work. Typically a busboy, fry cook, janitor, laborer, clerk, or bag boy.' "

"Based on?"

"He is describing again the typical 'simple schizophrenic,' although now it has been changed to a disorganized schizophrenic, who—because of his feelings—doesn't want to have anything to do with people, avoids people, takes a job where he doesn't have contact with others, such as a busboy or a janitor or a laborer, or somebody who works in a semi-isolated low-paying job—I don't see that in a man capable of building this sort of explosive device, planning these sorts of things."

Shui said, pointing at the profile, "Klinger next states, 'mental health problems.' I don't see a problem of mental health here, because he has constructed something rather clever."

Vorpagel said, "When we see an individual who has had schizophrenic behavior, who murders or mutilates a female, there we will see more of an attack and assault on the body personally, where they personally make the attack, not from far away, such as this was done."

Vorpagel waved the profile, "Klinger says, 'Law enforcement history: Parking tickets, traffic offenses, residential burglary and voyeurism when young. Who knows why this is wrong?"

Marcus said, "I've studied this type in a few criminal textbooks I own. The voyeur is a window peeper who usually engages in sex crimes. And when he does get involved in violating or attacking a female, why, we see again mutilation of the breasts or the genitalia, sometimes masturbation. There is no indication here that this bomber has any background at all of being a voyeur or a window peeper."

"Again, right on target. Next, Klinger says the suspect is a 'loner, very few personal friends, all of them are male, and he's considered somewhat odd by his acquaintances.' This is virtually word for word from several of our profiles classified at the time as 'simple schizo.' "

Gary asked, "Any other criticisms of that profile that you haven't mentioned?"

"The last paragraph has a merger of several different types of personalities. Klinger is discussing, in the beginning, an individual who doesn't have anything to do with females. Then, he starts talking about an individual who becomes very dependent on the female, which is what we call, again, inadequate.

"It then goes on to show that he takes little pride in his personal appearance, which now drops all the way back to a disorganized 'schizo.'

"He says he tends to brag to his male friends of sexual conquests that never happened. Now he's dealing with the individual who is now called an antisocial personality."

Ava asked, "If he's antisocial, why brag to others?"

"He is egotistical and outgoing. Antisocial means that you do not conform to the mores and standards and laws of the community. An antisocial person can be gregarious. He needs other people to feed off their accolades.

"Klinger mentions that he can be expected to attend the funeral and to visit the grave site. He's not talking about the usual type of individual who kills on the spur of the moment and regrets it; and therefore, he feels bad and will go to the funeral, will go to the grave site, will send flowers and things of that nature."

Shui asked, "Don't premeditated murderers sometimes go to the funeral to deflect suspicion or to see if anyone suspects them?"

"Of course. But also, in some cases, to enjoy the pain and the tears being expressed by the family and loved ones."

Vorpagel studied the profile. "Klinger does have it right here: 'If arrested and charged with the crime, he may attempt to take his own life when he's locked up.'

This, usually, deals with the individual who has a

single, well-integrated mission in life and knows that he's going to have to die to accomplish it. He would also be called, in times of war, a patriot. We have certain people who feel that they have a mission in life. And in order to achieve that mission, they know they'll die. So now Klinger's bringing in that particular personality."

"Klinger says," Marcus said, "if he's unable to cope with the remorse and guilt, he may take his own life. And you said you agree?"

"We do have remorse and guilt here. But the individual who goes to the funeral is not going to be the one who is remorseful enough to kill himself."

"You stated," Gary said, "if arrested, he may take his own life. Then you said if he goes to the funeral, he will not be remorseful enough to take his own life. Isn't that a contradiction?"

"He's not going to take his own life if he's free. But sitting in a cell changes things. But, while still free, he has other defense mechanisms. Like using psychic erasure or restitution, which are subconscious acts of the mind that allow you to protect yourself."

Marcus asked, "Could you elaborate?"

"The superego or conscience dictates to you what is good or what is bad. The id tells you to do things for your own pleasure and not regard basic norms. When the superego is overcome by the id, the person can perform aberrations or antisocial behavior. When the superego 'recovers,' it cannot tolerate believing that it would have done a normally prohibitive act. In order to assuage this guilt feeling, subconscious acts are fed to the superego, showing acts of restitution or forgetting what really happened.

"It is a way of subconsciously lying to your conscience. And I don't see any of that in this man's behavior whatsoever.

"The FBI requires any individual from the outside who's going to be trained as a profiler to spend eleven months at Quantico with the Behavioral Science Unit. They have to have a minimum of five years on the street and a minimum of a degree or a minor in psychology before even being accepted. There's no way you're going to train somebody in a few days. As I told you earlier, I only include profiling in my lectures to give you a taste, and to show you the signs when it may be proper to call an expert in."

Vorpagel studied the faces of his students. "This story doesn't glorify my own ability at profiling. I'm more worried about the confused message it sends. The bomb that Randy Forse mailed killed one person. The bomb that my friend dropped in profiling this killer might send misleading ripples out for decades to come."

Marcus asked, "What credentials would you look for before using a profiler?"

"The same as most competent attorneys. The full course taken and completed at Quantico. At least a few years in the field getting hands-on experience, under more experienced guidance." Vorpagel paused, then continued, "Even then, the hiring attorney can get a surprise. I was hired in a murder case in Alaska. The attorney who hired me lost. His client received ninety-nine years."

Shui said in surprise, "This is an example of you as an expert witness?"

"The chips fell where they should have."

"What happened?"

"I was hired by the defense and wound up clinching it for the prosecution."

"How?"

"The defense sent me a copy of the interrogation of the suspect. The man had given the dead woman's unusual ring to his mother. The ring manufacturer stated only seven had been made. A gun registered to him matched the slug that had penetrated her skull. He had bragged to his friends about the deed. But now he claimed, and his attorney wanted confirmed, that a friend of his—the key to the prosecution's case—had done all these things.

"I insisted that my profile of the killer could cut either way. I would not tailor it to fit the defendant's case."

Shui asked, "And the attorney?"

"The defense attorney agreed."

"Then why did the case . . ."

"The circumstances leading to the woman's death illustrated a classic example of kinky sex gone bad. The young woman was a bank clerk. One afternoon, she took off early to do some errands at home. She was found with a light nylon cord—the type of rope used in parachutes—looped loosely around her wrists and binding her arms behind her. She was clothed, but it was obvious that some sort of fantasy had been played out before she was shot in the back of the head."

"What were the particulars?"

"She was a white woman. The suspect was a black man."

Marcus asked, "What kinds of racial overtones does that have in Alaska?"

"I have no idea. I was contacted by a private detective, Maureen O'Sullivan, and asked to do a profile. Various documents were delivered to my home. I did the profile. It fit the man who was testifying as a witness for the state. The defense was ecstatic and had me flown to Alaska.

"When I arrived, I asked to speak to the defense team. They were too busy to see me. Without preliminary conferences with the defense team, I was given permission to talk to the prosecutor for the discovery process—any witness's right. During my interview with the state's lawyer, I learned that I did not have all the facts when I made my original long-distance profile."

"And you did another profile," Gary said.

"I did another profile. This time, it matched the defendant. The next morning, I was called and, to the amazement and frustration of the defense, gave this new testimony. The defendant was found guilty."

Shui said, "Did you tell the defense you'd changed your mind?"

"Nope. Not my obligation. They didn't ask, I didn't volunteer."

Gary shrugged. "A lot of lawyers don't realize that when they hire an expert, they are also hiring objectivity."

"And the chips fall where they may. Tomorrow morning, we will have another field problem, then discuss another profiling case, a rather noteworthy one at the time, T. Cullen Davis versus Texas, big money, big attorney, 'Racehorse' Haines, and big drama."

"That happened a long time ago," Gary said.

"The crime itself did; and also the criminal proceedings. The civil end of it was over only a few years ago. Besides, I purposely stay away from current cases. What good would it do to discuss the O. J. Simpson case? Or the Oklahoma Federal Building bombing? Everybody in the world with access to a TV or radio knows those situations and the agonizing length of time before an outcome. Choosing mostly obscure, sometimes older cases allows me a fair certainty that my students haven't already formed an opinion. It also precludes possible civil suit or even a claim that a book or magazine article prejudiced a jury."

"What's the field problem?"
"Officer down."
"Shot?"
"Murdered."

HOLLYWOOD JUSTICE

The rolling terrain was sprinkled liberally with oak and manzanita. A narrow trail snaked along the face of the slope. It was dry, and only the drifting of sagebrush hinted at a breeze. Before the class arrived for the final field day of their training exercise, Vorpagel took time to scatter the evidence: a shell casing here, a fiber of clothing there, a cigarette butt, a matchbook, two empty bank bags, a bank passbook.

He stood on a knoll and checked the distances. Then he waved to another of his partners, Fred Bowman. Bowman was a retired police chief.

Bowman was dressed as a police officer. He was going to be the corpse. He asked, "Are you sure you couldn't get a student to do this?"

"I checked the school. Nobody was available. You can act as a control and a corpse at the same time."

Bowman took off his shirt. He shivered slightly in the chilly early morning air. Carefully, using mortician's clay, Vorpagel created four sucking chest wounds. The mounds were built; the stage blood was run into and out of the entry holes, creating realistic seepage. He placed three .38-caliber spent slugs into the fake wounds, then a .22 into the fourth.

Vorpagel stepped back. Bowman looked up expectantly and said, "That's it, right?"

"No, I've come up with a new touch."

Bowman groaned. "Why now? Why when I'm the corpse?"

Vorpagel held up a plastic bag. Inside was a red substance with hundreds of white thin lines about a quarter of an inch long. Black seeds were also floating in the bag.

It was a mixture of raspberries, with a handful of white rice tossed in. A piece of raw steak had been added as a catalyst. Vorpagel had made the concoction a week earlier—then let it cook in its own heat, sealed in the plastic bag.

Bowman asked, "What's this?"

"Realism," Vorpagel said and opened the bag. The FBI agent and the retired police chief, both consummate pros, both with over a thousand homicide investigations under their collective belts, gagged.

The sweet, pungent, putrid aroma of imitation death wafted from the plastic bag. Vorpagel grabbed the rotting steak gingerly between his forefinger and thumb and hurled it down the slope.

Bowman gasped. "You expect me to lie here pretending I'm murdered with that smell hovering over me?"

"Death stinks."

"I know, but I'm still alive. My olfactory senses are working fine. Your realism is going to go flying out the window once our students see the corpse puking his guts out."

"No you won't," Vorpagel said and held up two nose plugs. "Insert these, that'll help."

"What about my mouth? What about my taste buds? Right now, I'm gagging on the decay."

"I thought of that," Vorpagel said, and took a spray can out of his jacket. "Liquid Novocain. It'll deaden your mouth."

He sprayed a few mists of anesthesia into his friend's mouth—then a few into his own.

"Why raspberries and rice?" his partner gagged out.

"Raspberry seeds look like blood clotting and white rice looks like maggots."

Vorpagel went to work. He poured the horrific concoction of jam and rice and putrefaction around the artificial wounds he'd made on Bowman's chest. When he was finished he said, "I have a new twist."

"I thought I just smelled and tasted it."

"No. Something else that's new." Vorpagel opened his briefcase and took out another, larger, plastic bag.

"What now?" Bowman asked.

"The victim in our scenario was shot, but he was also gutted," Vorpagel said. He opened the large plastic bag and spooned turkey guts and cow intestines onto Bowman's stomach.

Bowman said, "I need more Novocain."

Vorpagel gave him another blast of aerosolized deadener. Working carefully, he drew red, puckered marks around the turkey guts and bovine intestines. When he was finished, the illusion was complete. Bowman looked as if he had been shot in the chest and gutted in the stomach.

Vorpagel said, "Lookin' good."

Bowman took a tape recorder out of his back pocket, scooped out a little earth, forming a miniature open grave, and placed the recorder into it.

Vorpagel asked, "What are you doing?"

"I'm going to have to lie on that damned thing for hours before some hot-shot student thinks to move the body. I'm getting as comfortable as I can."

Bowman lay back, spread-eagled, closed his eyes and asked, "Do I look like a corpse?"

Vorpagel watched humungous bluebottle flies congregate over the raspberry jam, turkey guts, and cow intestine. The flies contentedly flew weird and changing routes, all forming new and unusual parallelograms.

"Realistic enough," Vorpagel said, and went to meet his class.

The death investigation class of thirty men and woman arrived.

Marcus asked, "Why did you take our guns away?"

"To prevent accidents," Vorpagel answered, and handed out water pistols filled with a red liquid.

"We don't even get paint guns?"

"On our budget?"

The men and women, from every level of law enforcement and the criminal system, nodded their heads in understanding.

Vorpagel waved a hand at the rolling, gentle slope behind him. "One of your fellow officers, who patrols this area, failed to report in earlier. You've been sent out to find him."

Vorpagel held up the yellow police caution tape

that crossed the trail. He took out a Swiss Army knife and, dramatically, slashed the yellow ribbon. "The practical problem scene is yours. I must warn you, I will be observing—from an overall view—but I have four assistants positioned at various strategic locations with both video and tape recorders. What you do during this exercise will be recorded. Afterward, we will proceed to the local courthouse, which has been generously loaned to us. When we get there, a real judge—local, old, retired, curmudgeonly, who also volunteered his time—will be waiting. I will act as the prosecutor, my partner as the defense. What you do now, in fair warning, will be judged in a very harsh and scrutinizing way. By the defense. By the prosecution. By the judge."

The class shuffled nervously.

Vorpagel bowed and said, "Let's go to work."

Gary, from the Attorney General's Office, said, "Wait. I assume this will eventually involve a crime scene. Who's in charge? Who's the photographer? The crime scene artist? The lab? The pathologist? The coroner?"

"Why are you asking me?" Vorpagel said. "I told you this was an exercise. It's up to you—to think, to plan, to delegate, both authority and jobs. I'm just a humble teacher now, who anxiously awaits becoming a prosecuting attorney so I can nail anyone here who screws up."

The students held a conference. A command post was set up. The coroners were delegated jobs as coroners, lab team, and pathologists.

The play–crime scene took on an eerie look as the officers began their search.

Ava yelled, "I found the cop."

People congregated from all over the hillside. Both women and men gagged, turned, and became ill.

Marcus shouted, "This looks real. The flies, the maggots . . ."

Gary shouted, "Russ, this cop's really dead."

Vorpagel boomed, "He's part of the scenario."

"You brought a corpse out here?" Shui called indignantly. "A fresh, rotting corpse?"

"He's part of the scenario," Vorpagel repeated. He walked away. He was careful to stay on the narrow trail that snaked along the face of the slope. He knew approximately where the clues were, but not exactly, except that they weren't on the trail.

He walked to the top of the ridge line and stood by one of his assistants, who was carefully recording the events happening below on a camcorder.

Vorpagel asked quietly, "How are they doing?"

"Pretty good. Only a few have trampled on evidence."

"Around the body?"

"Yeah. They've been excellent protecting everything farther than ten yards from the body."

The officers searched the crime scene. They photographed the area. A crime-scene sketch was drawn. They made plaster casts. They found the matchbook. They found the shell casings. They found the cigarette. Then they moved the body and found the tape recorder under the make-believe corpse.

Ava rewound the tape and pushed the play button.

A weak, hoarse voice whispered, "Squad car's radio in a dead spot. Couldn't communicate. Used tape instead." The voice trailed off. Wheezing could be heard for ten seconds, then, "I saw a car parked out here in the woods. Dark bottomed station wagon with a white top. There seemed to be yelling coming from it and I went to investigate. A man was sexually assaulting a girl. I tried to stop them, but they stabbed me. I managed to crawl back here, but I lost my gun somewhere along the way." There was another pause. More wheezing, then, "Oh, sweet Jesus, they're coming back."

Loud shots popped over the tape, then the tape ran on. Sounds could be heard in the background, muttering, feet scraping against gravel. Then nothing.

On the ridge, Vorpagel watched through binoculars.

In the distance, a station wagon, white top, dark bottom, pulled out of the trees and headed toward the crime scene.

Dear God, Vorpagel thought, there wasn't supposed to be any station wagon. This was just a coincidence, right down to the description of the car. Who are those people?

From the top of the hill, he watched the law enforcement officers flag the car down. A man and a woman got out.

Vorpagel jogged down the hill. He didn't want the problem blown. He had to get these people to move on.

A woman got out of the vehicle. She looked at the incredibly real-looking corpse on the ground. She threw up.

He ran to their vehicle. "There's a police training exercise going on. The corpse isn't real. Don't worry about it, but please leave so we can continue."

The car sped off.

Vorpagel, out of habit, jotted down the license plate number. Twenty minutes later, he asked his class, "Did anyone twenty-eight/twenty-nine them?"

The class glanced at each other. No one had thought to run a standard makes and warrants on the car.

Marcus said, "No. You said they weren't part of the problem."

"This problem involves all aspects of crime-scene investigations. You are supposed to do exactly what you would do at a real crime scene."

A twenty-eight/twenty-nine trace on the license plate was run. The call came back. Both occupants of the car were wanted for armed robbery.

An all-points bulletin was issued. The couple was arrested two hours later. Two loaded revolvers were found under the seat.

Shaken, Vorpagel called the field problem off.

Fred Bowman said, "Loaded revolvers?"

"Yes."

"And all the officers here were packing water guns."

"If there'd only been a couple of cops flagging them down, I think they would have shot them."

"But no one was armed."

"They saw an army of law enforcement, so they decided to bluff it out. They didn't know we were unarmed. If they had, I think there would have been a lot of dead cops."

The class went back to the school. Vorpagel stood behind the dais. He told his students what had happened. After their initial startled reaction, they settled down. It was time to break the tension with a story taken from the pages of a Hollywood screenplay.

Vorpagel said, "The following case involves the use of profiling years after the crime."

Shui asked, "Shouldn't profiling be done right away?"

"It should have been done right away. But in the beginning, Bureau policy was that we would only profile a case with certain characteristics after all leads by the police had been covered."

"That's changed?"

"Yes. Back to the example. The people involved were celebrities. A sports hero was a victim. The ex-wife and her suspected boyfriend were gunned down. The trial became a media circus, with one of the country's top legal guns holding the jury in the palm of his hand.

"The following case illustrates that, without facts, and the proper education, no one should do a profile. Again, this course teaches when it is time to call in a profiler, not how to profile."

The trial of Cullen Davis had been advertised as featuring the richest defendant in a murder case in history. Certainly, it made his attorney a good deal richer. Richard "Racehorse" Haynes, whose nickname had stuck since high school days, already had a reputation for courtroom theatrics and successful criminal defenses against outrageous odds.

Davis was accused of attempting to murder his ex-wife, Priscilla. She claimed he shot her in the torso.

Davis was also accused of murdering Priscilla's twelve-year-old daughter, Andrea Wilborn, from her first marriage. The natural father's name was Jack Wilborn. Andrea had been murdered in the kitchen hallway and moved to the mansion's basement.

Priscilla's lover, former basketball star Stan Farr, had also been gunned down in the same massacre.

The fourth victim in the mansion mayhem was another friend, Bubba Gavrel. He had the misfortune of arriving just as the gunman was running out of the mansion in pursuit of the fleeing Priscilla. Gavrel was gunned down at point-blank range. Lucky to live at all, he was paralyzed, with a bullet in his spine.

Despite a parade of witnesses who identified Davis as the gunman in black at the mansion, the jurors voted first ten to two and then unanimously for acquittal. The key to the defense was hardly subtle, but effective: Demolish Priscilla's character.

Priscilla had been shot in the abdomen, had escaped and lived, had identified her assailant at the criminal trial—and yet he had gone free. She brought a civil suit against Davis for the loss of her child.

Jack Wilborn did the same.

Bubba filed a thirteen-million-dollar civil suit for personal injury with malice.

The family of Stan Farr also filed suit.

When David McCrory walked into the District Attorney's office in Dallas, in August of that year, 1978, with a story of a plot by Cullen Davis to "assassinate" fifteen people, including Judge Eidson, he was greeted with less than enthusiasm. McCrory had a long history as a handyman, of sorts, for Davis—a pool-playing buddy whose wife had produced a sensational document during the criminal trial to bolster Cullen's defense. In it, he had named numerous alleged drug groupies in Priscilla's retinue. Gratuitously, he provided his version of a conversation with Priscilla in the hospital after the shooting—in which she refused to say "what really happened." The "affidavit," as it was called—though he failed to sign it—was seen as a poorly disguised countermove by Davis.

But the charges were serious—a Federal judge was threatened. Events now began to fall in place rapidly. FBI agent Ron Jannings was called in to meet McCrory. The alleged plot seemed too fantastic to consider. After further consultation with other agents, however, Jannings wired McCrory with a recorder for a rendezvous with Davis. They were to meet to discuss guns, hired killers, and the amount of the payoff.

A van with shaded windows was parked in the restaurant lot when McCrory and Davis arrived separately. Inside the van were FBI sound technicians and cameramen. The meeting astounded the FBI agents; Davis not only approved a list of targets, starting with Judge Eidson, but haggled only over the fee for the hit man. McCrory bargained up to $25,000.

When the evidence was shown to Judge Eidson, he was stunned. The FBI now decided to make recordings of Davis paying off McCrory and McCrory returning the gun and accepting the next "hit."

An FBI helicopter hovered over the mansion on a bright Sunday morning when Davis left to get the payoff money from his office in downtown Dallas. When Davis arrived at the restaurant rendezvous, the same FBI van was waiting. This time, Davis circled it cautiously as the team of FBI technicians held their breath. He was not oblivious to the fact that an exchange of cash constituted the moment of truth in a transaction of this kind. McCrory drove up, exchanged pleasantries, and presented Davis with proof that the deed was done. The FBI had convinced the Judge that he had to act out a death scene. He had allowed bullet wounds to be painstakingly painted on his back. Polaroids of the "dead" Judge were in an envelope that McCrory offered as proof that the killing had happened. They were dusted with a traceable substance that could be detected when Davis was apprehended.

McCrory was handed a large, brown envelope containing $25,000, which Davis had taken from the trunk of his car. Through slats in the curtained van, FBI cameramen recorded the drop. The agents conferred briefly as Davis and McCrory parted. Within minutes, waiting police cars pulled Davis over and read him his rights. Early that morning Davis phoned his newest lover, Karen, to tell her he was back in jail again.

The second trial was moved to Houston in the usual concern for local, intense publicity—but the entire state was well aware of the Davis escapades over the past two years. Again "Racehorse" Haynes was summoned for the defense, and Jack Strickland, new on the District Attorney's team, was given the lead role in the prosecution.

In the protracted course of the "conspiracy to murder" trial, Haynes and Strickland sparred as much to define themselves as to defend their positions. Judge Gordon Gray presided over this play within a play with alternate fatherliness and boredom.

"Racehorse" and Strickland were in their early forties, and both were slight of stature. The Haynes trademark of elevator boots was a self-conscious admission of that fact. But Strickland was not aware of the vitriol of his adversary until the day that "Racehorse" skewered him during the cocktail hour. "Jack isn't that big," he said, "but he's competent. After seeing him with his coat off, I doubled my contribution to the muscular dystrophy society."

When all the testimony was in, "Racehorse" prepared Cullen for the worst. The jury would be returning a painful verdict in a day or two—no more. He spoke with Judge Gray openly in court about the time for sentencing. He had done all he could—in fact, his colleagues commended him for his inventiveness in asking the jurors to listen again and again to the FBI tapes— asking them to reinterpret what Davis meant by "Good" when McCrory said, "I got Judge Eidson dead for you."

The verdict came in. The jury had found T. Cullen Davis not guilty.

Much ink flowed about the role of "Racehorse" Haynes in beating an impregnable rap against Davis. The jury had been inventive, many claimed. They listened to the tapes—at Haynes's constant insistence— and began to hear other things. Haynes planted an alternative conspiracy theory: His client was the one being set up for murder, and the tapes hinted at it. McCrory was taping the conversations to protect himself.

The jury, in fact, talked to the press willingly about their reasons for acquittal. They had heard something on the tapes that no one else had called their attention to.

Clicks. Barely audible clicks that could not be traced to anything else in the car. These clicks were the sound of another tape player going on and off. The sounds of a conspiracy. Cullen Davis was just as believable as McCrory in projecting a plot. "Who was in charge of those tapes," one juror asked. "Cullen or the man out to get him?"

Bubba Gavrel settled his $13-million lawsuit for substantially less. It was clear that if Davis was to be convicted, this was the last chance.

When the civil suit finally came up on the calendar, in 1987, attorney Bob Gibbins, of Austin, told Priscilla Davis to fire him on the spot if she disagreed with his legal approach to the case. "Stay in the background," he insisted, "and dress modestly."

Priscilla bridled at the suggestion. She would be herself. Gibbins reminded her that Cullen Davis was no longer "himself." Shortly after his second trial victory, he had found Jesus. He was surely as "born again" as any: He and his new wife Karen had taken a leadership role in their local church. At last, Cullen said, he had found the meaning of life.

Faced with the prospect of losing one of the most respected trial lawyers in the country, Priscilla relented. The trial was on, though it would not turn out to be the "Super Bowl of my career," as "Racehorse" called his defense against the conspiracy trial. His firm, represented by Steve Sumner, again went to bat for Cullen Davis.

Gibbins, in effect, was taking on the prosecution's case in the first trial. On the positive side for him, eleven years after the event, he didn't have to show guilt beyond a reasonable doubt. As a civil case, the standard was only the preponderance of evidence. He had to show that Davis was the man in black, with the woman's wig, who shot four people, killing two, that August night in the centennial year.

Gibbins immediately set out to establish a motive for the first killing, that of the twelve-year-old Andrea Wilborn. The first trial had never come to grips with the question of why a man would single out his stepdaughter for murder. Gibbins had asked his research assistant, Francis Pan, to check out a motive, a drive to get back at Priscilla through her child, and then through her friends, and finally to get back at her.

Pan looked for similar cases in the major police departments of the country. Then, he looked to the criminology departments of universities specializing in this field. He checked with the FBI and its training people. Finally, he located two expert witnesses, who would analyze Cullen Davis and suggest a motive for his bizarre behavior.

The first was George Kirkham, an associate professor of criminology at Florida State University. He had already agreed to examine Davis's personality and state of mind, and suggest why he might have had a reason to kill a twelve-year-old girl in cold blood.

Gibbins could not do a rerun of the previous case, which had gone against the state eight to four. The facts were still persuasive, but he needed corroboration from a new source.

Pan entered Gibbins's office and said, "I think I've got the man you want."

Gibbins opened the file and asked Pan, "What qualifies Vorpagel to examine Davis's state of mind?"

"He has a degree in psychology. He is a lawyer sanctioned to practice before the Federal Supreme Court. Also, he worked for the Behavioral Science Unit of the FBI. In fact, he was part of the original team that created the science."

"And it does?"

"Profiles of murderers."

Gibbins's office in Austin contacted Vorpagel. The ex-FBI agent delineated what "profiling" could and could not do. He warned the plaintiff's attorneys that he could not predict the outcome in advance.

He asked Gibbins, "Are you willing to let the chips fall where they may?"

Gibbins agreed. He was sure of his case.

Vorpagel combed through transcripts and talked to people familiar with the two previous cases. The day before the trial, he came upon an inconspicuous form of four pages, answered in a clear script. It was entitled "Sentence Completion Exercise—M," and consisted of sixty-one short, partially completed sentences. The typewritten questionnaire had a space at the top for the name of the respondent and the date. These were "Thomas Cullen Davis" and "8/4/76."

Vorpagel took out a red pencil and began to make notes in the margin. The italicized words are Davis's handwritten compilations.

1. *I feel that my girlfriend seldom gives me any argument.*
   Vorpagel wrote after this: "Calculating."
2. *When the odds are against me, I usually don't gamble.*
   "Again—Calculating"
4. *If I were in charge, I would put in more qualified supervisors.*
   "Others are inadequate"

6. *The men over me are none.*
   "Superiority complex"
7. *I know it is silly, but I am afraid of nothing.*
   "Macho mentality"
8. *I feel that a real friend doesn't expect too much.*
   "Manipulative, doesn't give of himself"
10. *My idea of a perfect woman is too involved to put down here.*
    "There isn't one, in his opinion."

Some of the answers were clues to Davis's childhood and his dominating father. "If my father had not made me work so hard, I would probably regret it today." Vorpagel pointed this out to Gibbins and asked about the founder of Kendavis Industries.

"No question he was an autocrat," Gibbins answered. "His employees were driven by fear. He was a bantam rooster with a penchant for making bigger men squirm."

"I would guess that Cullen-the-kid felt dominated, and is now trying to rationalize it as a good thing."

"How much store can we put in speculation like this?"

"Very little in any one answer. A profile is like an Impressionist painting—hundreds of little strokes, none of them individually significant, create a meaningful picture en masse."

"Let me play the devil's advocate: What else would indicate this parental dominance?"

Vorpagel talked as he flipped through the questionnaire. "Notice the way Davis changed the question to a negative—it was hard for him to frame an answer without going into a negative. Ah, here—question 29, the sentence begins, 'If my mother had . . .' Here, he ignores the 'if' and says pretty much the same thing about her. In other words, his answer was so strong in his mind that he forced the sentence to work around it."

"So the sentence now reads?"

"My mother had a good way of getting me to see things her way."

"Again suggesting he was dominated."

"Which usually results in a domination of others. Repeatedly, he volunteers, remember, volunteers statements about his superiority over others. And when a woman is involved, look out!"

"I noticed that. He answered the question 'What I least like about women' by saying, 'is their complaining.' And 'I think most women are greedy.' He also says somewhere, about married life, that he likes living with a woman but not being married to her."

"The word 'love' never appears in these answers. Not even with respect to his children or his parents."

"Are you prepared to go on the stand with answers like these?" Gibbins let the question resonate, as if Vorpagel were already on the stand.

"The immediate aim is to show motivation?"

"That a man like Davis could shoot his own stepchild out of the torment of his personality."

"I am prepared to portray the personality of the man who answered these questions as one who could act compulsively, from cruelty and revenge . . ."

"Rather than from overt motivation?"

"Exactly."

"I warn you that the psychologist who took these

answers originally was raked over the coals pretty badly . . ."

"I read the transcript. It was two people talking in different languages. I think the defense lawyer and the psychologist ended their examination when they realized they weren't making sense to each other. And remember, this sentence-completion test was given to Davis only to see if he was too dangerous to be released on bail. Nobody really paid any attention to it during the original trial."

Two days later, in the courtroom, Cullen bolted upright from his usual slumped position when he listened to the lumbering, six-foot-two, former FBI agent describe Mr. T. Cullen Davis in a way he had never heard before.

Vorpagel's testimony was deliberate. "Selfish, egotistical, chauvinistic, emotionally unstable, insecure, domineering, paranoid, oblivious to his actions."

Vorpagel suddenly turned his attention to the events of the August 1976 massacre. "The man in black was no ordinary intruder," he said. "If he had wished to steal anything, he could have done it with ease and walked away. If he had wanted to rape, he had targets of opportunity upstairs. Instead, the intruder first shot and killed a child, then lay in wait for the others. His primary target was Priscilla herself. Only the strange comings and goings of others who lived in the mansion dictated those who died and those who survived."

Plaintiff's attorney Bob Gibbins led his surprise expert witness's testimony to its conclusion. "What is your expert opinion of the kind of person the intruder was?"

Vorpagel left no doubt as to his conclusion. Brandishing the questionnaire, he summarized, "The individual who filled out this form fits the profile of the killer to a 'T.' "

Sumner's cross-examination was unexpectedly timid. The psychological profile was accepted by default as he instead tried to pick away at what he perceived to be the conclusions not warranted by the evidence.

"You stated, Mr. Vorpagel, that Priscilla Wilborn Davis was the primary target of the intruder."

"Correct."

"But the man in black shot Stan Farr four times, and Priscilla only once. Does that add up?"

"Yes. Picture this scene: He has fired one shot into Andrea, four shots into Stan, and one into Priscilla. Now he has an empty gun. While he's reloading, Priscilla is running wildly away from the mansion across an open, dark field. Simultaneously, a car arrives in the courtyard, with the unfortunate Bubba Gavrel and his date. When the woman greets the gunman by name, he turns and shoots Bubba after reloading."

The defense attorney bit his lip at opening this line of questioning.

Vorpagel continued. "The gunman clearly came with ample ammunition. That showed me the man intended to kill more than one person. He knew he was going to use that weapon, and he knew he was going to use more than one gun load."

The motive was described as irrational. Vorpagel told the story of a kitten that Davis had killed. His adopted daughter brought home a bad report card.

Davis took her pet cat, threw it on the floor, and crushed its head with his foot.

Professor Kirkham followed Vorpagel on the stand and repeated Vorpagel's evaluation. His words were "expressive violence." And he defined that as irrationality, expressiveness, rage, and chaos—in short, no profit motive, no purpose.

But in the jury room, it became obvious it was eight against four from the very beginning. The four holding out for acquittal happened to be the least educated, the least responsive, on the panel. Two of them were scarcely literate; they adopted a "know-nothing" attitude about any instructions from the judge. In the end, two others joined them.

Davis had won again.

Marcus said, "How could he walk? With the evidence, the eyewitnesses."

Vorpagel answered, "Davis's demeanor during the course of the trial underwent a metamorphosis. Davis, the billionaire who bought everything, became the underdog who had found religion.

"Priscilla was now seen as the predator, the golden-haired society queen now coming back, after almost nine years of comfort and nightlife, again wanting to feed in the trough of Davis's wealth."

Shui asked, "Do you still think Davis did it? He was never criminally convicted."

Vorpagel shrugged. "Correct. However, interestingly enough, on the steps of the courthouse, minutes after reading the verdict, and with tears in his eyes, the jury foreman said, 'A guilty murderer is going unpunished.'"

"He walked," Marcus said in disgust.

"Not the first time for me that that's happened."

"What happened?"

"A party I thought was guilty walked."

"And that case was?"

"The Bell case. It didn't involve profiling, because it happened before there was a Behavioral Science Unit. It happened before I was an FBI agent. It happened when I was a cop in Milwaukee. But I'll tell you something. It taught me that history repeats itself, from Daniel Bell to Rodney King."

CHAPTER EIGHT

NO VIDEOTAPE

But first I have another little puzzle for you. All you have to go on are two photos and questions." Vorpagel opened his briefcase and held up two black-and-white photographs. He said, "These are somewhat grisly. They're shots taken on a railroad track. A track walker was run over."

The two photos were passed around among the students. The first picture showed the upper half of a man, wearing the striped shirt of a railroad employee. The second was a longer shot, showing the railroad tracks snaking off into the distance, a low retaining wall following the tracks on the left. Fifty yards from the upper half of the body was the lower half.

Marcus said, "The man looks like he's in his fifties."

"He was. He worked for the railroad for thirty-four years."

"What's the problem?" Shui asked. "He was run over by a train, an accidental death."

"That's not how the insurance company saw it. The

fact that he worked so long, as a track walker, made them . . ."

"What's a track walker?"

"He walked the tracks, head down, observing what railroad ties needed to be replaced or spikes driven in. The insurance company claimed he was despondent and wanted to commit suicide. The engineer stated that he had come out of a tunnel, saw the track walker—going the same direction as the train. The engineer knew he couldn't stop in time. He gave blast after blast on the whistle—to no avail."

"Was an autopsy done?" Ava asked.

"Yes."

"Was alcohol found?"

"No."

"What reasons did the insurance company give for claiming he was suicidal?"

"Only that there was no way this could be an accident, because he was so familiar with trains and their danger."

The class chewed on this information. Gary asked, "How was the man's hearing?"

Vorpagel smiled. "He was damn near stone deaf."

"Then the railroad company should have been sued for negligence."

"No, they provided him with two excellent, state-of the-art hearing aids."

Shui asked, "Did anyone check the batteries?"

"That's exactly what I suggested. He went to work without them because, by a wild coincidence, both batteries had gone dead at the same time."

"Coincidence?" Gary said. "Didn't anyone suspect possible murder?"

"Of course, but the only person who could have done it was the engineer. Remember? He saw the whole thing. No motive. And a train is a very unwieldy choice of weapons. This was followed by the insurance company's next salvo. They claimed that it didn't matter whether the hearing aids were working or not. A man with thirty-four years experience would know the feel on the tracks of an approaching train. He would have looked back and gotten out of the way."

"I remember when I was a kid," Ava said, "walking the railroad tracks. You can feel the vibrations, and you don't have to be standing on the rails themselves. The whole railroad bed shakes."

"So—suicide or accident? A whole lot is riding on the answer, the provable answer. And not just the money the insurance company was trying to save, but for the relatives. It makes a lot of difference to the bereaved whether the loved one intentionally took his life or died by accident."

"I know," Shui said, "I've been involved in cases like this. The family tends to blame itself in a suicide."

"Exactly."

The two photos were passed around and studied again. Nothing. The two halves of the body gave no clue. The railroad track was just a railroad track.

Marcus asked, "What's behind that retaining wall?"

Vorpagel grinned, "Another railroad track."

"Of course. You checked the schedules. There was another train going by at the same time, in the other direction. The track walker felt the vibrations, looked up, saw the train going in the opposite direction, then went back to walking the line."

"Exactly. And the insurance company paid off."

Vorpagel put the two photos back in his briefcase. "I give you these small puzzles as warm-ups for the class final, a case involving the question of murder, suicide, or accident.

"Now I have another case that influenced my career in law enforcement."

"Does this involve profiling?"

"In a way. This case I have used in teaching crime-scene investigation for years before connecting it to what happened to me in Korea. That connection led me to conclude certain things about the human mind. I found that understanding the motivation behind certain crimes that at first appear to be unmotivated helped in police work. It taught me that there are motivations we never thought of back in those days. Then, crimes seemed to be motivated by such simple things like lust, loot, lechery, and larceny."

Shui asked, "But it does involve murder?"

"It involved the question of murder or justifiable shooting. Everyone in this classroom, plus almost everyone on the planet, has heard of the Rodney King beating. Almost no one remembers the Daniel Bell case. This happened when I was a detective, years before I was accepted by the FBI. The final outcome was only resolved a few years ago. All testimony is a matter of public record. It happened in 1958."

"Isn't that ancient history?"

"Profiling didn't just spring up out of thin air. It took certain cases, experienced over decades, for myself and people like other police officers, and FBI agents like Ressler and Douglas, with years on the street, to formulate the basis of profiling."

Vorpagel paused. *Profiling*, he thought. Can you

really ever understand profiling unless you go through the entire FBI course?

Yes, you can understand what it does, just not how to do it.

He said, "What is profiling? It is the study and interpretation of the actions or nonactions in a crime scene. It is recreating what happened or didn't happen at a crime scene. The Bell case exemplifies this.

"I was the officer that interviewed the two police officers involved—at the scene. Their testimony is as vivid to me today as it was so many years ago."

Detective Russ Vorpagel sat behind the wheel of a 1956 Ford, the Milwaukee Police Department's unmarked squad car, across from the parking lot of a neighborhood bar. The street was glazed with black ice; it was a particularly bleak February.

He hadn't been this cold since Korea. In the years since that hell at Korea's Iron Triangle, Vorpagel had put his life together again. He had come back on the force at the First Precinct, working the headquarters building downtown. In a year, he was on the Vice Squad, using his primitive Spanish in the run-down near-northwest, across the Milwaukee River. Big, jovial John Polcyn, chief of police, had been a Marine and encouraged Navy and Marine vets like himself to move around in the department.

Vorpagel needed the push: His first son had been born while he was in Korea, and now there was a second son and a daughter. He had enrolled in law school at Marquette.

His partner that February night was an even more imposing figure. Howie Hughes was six-four, every inch muscle, with thin features and jet-black hair. Vorpagel and Hughes ended many a debate with the law just by walking on the scene.

Hughes pointed across the street and laughed. A heavy-set man stumbled out of the bar and was trying to get his keys in his car door. He put one hand on the car roof and slipped to the ground.

Stay down and sleep it off, Vorpagel thought. But the drunk got up, fumbled with the lock, and got behind the wheel. As soon as the car began backing up, Vorpagel clicked on the squad car's flashing spotlight. But then a voice crackled over his speaker.

The dispatcher was excited. "We got one down. Intersection of North Wright and North Sixth."

"One of ours?" Vorpagel asked at once.

"No, thank God. A suspect."

This was their beat—Crimes and Violence. As Vorpagel pulled away from the car in the parking lot, he called out the window to the drunk, "Your lucky day, but don't let us catch you driving."

When the unmarked squad car pulled up to the Sixth Street intersection, Vorpagel saw two officers standing over a prone body. He pulled out his notebook and recorded the time and place. He knew the officers by sight—Tom Grady and Louis Krause, both young. They worked traffic. The older of the two, Grady, also took photos of vehicle accidents and occasional shootings.

Vorpagel realized they were upset as soon as they started speaking. Their voices were high-pitched, both trying to talk at once. While Hughes left to canvass the neighborhood for witnesses, Vorpagel separated the two officers and began a standard inquiry.

"Louis and I were parked next to each other,"

Grady began. He stared into Vorpagel's steady eyes and caught his breath. A three-second nightmare flared before his mind, and he was at the center. He blurted out what he remembered.

Thomas Grady pointed to a few vacant houses. There were more these days. "The bums camp out in them and drink."

During the winter, when it was too cold to ride motorcycles, the two men were supposed to ride in "needle cars"—alone. Now, against regulations, they were in the same vehicle.

Grady saw a car drift by with its taillights out. He roared into the street with his siren on.

At North Seventh and West Wright, the man in the car saw him and pulled to a stop. A Negro jumped out. "You sons of bitches," the man said, "you won't get me for those holdups!"

Grady drew his pistol, with Krause behind him. The suspect ran. Grady yelled to his partner, "That guy matches the stick-up artist I saw on the daily bulletin."

Now running, Grady and Krause pursued the Negro to the next intersection, ordering him to stop. There, they commandeered a car and soon caught up with the suspect. When the man turned and tried to run back down the street, Grady ordered him to halt, then fired. The suspect went down.

"That is the truth as you know it?" Vorpagel asked Grady.

"Yes. He was a suspected felon, a fugitive."

"Anything you want to add?" Vorpagel watched

Grady's flushed face. He knew that killing a man does funny things to people. He also knew that this was the time, if there ever was, for a blurted confession.

"No."

Now Vorpagel had to get a statement from Louis Krause. He motioned Grady away and took out his notebook. The nightmare that Krause had experienced was different from Grady's, though it began the same. Krause spoke and remembered:

Grady waved him down, and Krause asked what was happening. "Nothing," Grady said. "That's just it—I need some more busts tonight. I'm going over to those boarded-up houses and nail some niggers."

"I got my quota."

At that moment, a car went by with a taillight out. "Look at that nigger," Grady yelled. "He's the bastard's been holding up liquor stores."

They gave chase, but very soon, the car slammed to a stop and a man bolted from the driver's side. It was "hot pursuit," so they asked a man just getting into his car to give chase. When the Negro tried to get away by running back to the intersection, Grady took off running after him.

Krause heard a shot. The suspect was lying face down in a pool of blood when Krause reached the scene.

An elderly Negro walked across the street, identified himself, said he saw "the whole thing." Grady ordered the man away with his gun drawn.

Krause leaned over the suspect and said, "He's dead!"

Grady answered immediately, "He's just a damn nigger kid anyhow."

Vorpagel looked up from his notebook. "Those were Grady's exact words?"

"Yeah. He always talked like that, but he didn't mean anything by it."

Vorpagel and Hughes took measurements. The distance from the dead man, and where Grady said he fired his weapon, was 23 feet and 9 inches.

Vorpagel directed two uniformed policemen to continue to knock on doors looking for witnesses. The officers reported back, giving Russ pages torn from their notebooks. There were no witnesses other than the old man. He had been chased away from the scene by uniformed officers.

Vorpagel bent by the body of the teenager. He saw a hole in the back of the head and no powder burns. It looked like a distance shot. There was no weapon in the man's hands.

Vorpagel went to Thomas Grady and asked for, and received, his gun and badge.

Vorpagel and Hughes arrived at the police safety building and began to write up their reports.

A newspaper reporter came in and asked why Russ had taken Grady's gun.

Vorpagel answered, "I always do in a police shooting."

"Even in self-defense?"

"What?"

"The suspect had a knife in his hand."

Vorpagel said, "What? I saw no knife."

• • •

The next morning Vorpagel entered District Attorney McCauley's office. He was joined in a few minutes by Krause and Grady. Also present were Inspector of Detectives Rudolph Glaser and Captain of Detectives Leo Woelfel.

"So what happened?" the District Attorney asked.

Krause said, "Grady shot and killed a fleeing felon, who had a knife."

"Why is there no mention of the knife in Vorpagel's report?"

"The fleeing felon must have fallen on it and his body hid it from view. Once the body was moved, the knife was found."

"From how far did you shoot?"

"About fifteen feet," Grady answered.

"Why did you shoot?"

"The felon slashed at me with a knife."

"From fifteen feet?"

"No," Grady said and paused. "It was more like six feet."

"Then why doesn't it say six feet in your report, Vorpagel?"

Vorpagel answered, "Because that's not the story I heard last night. The distance Grady pointed out to me was twenty-three feet, nine inches by my measurement. Also, Grady never spoke of being slashed at by a knife at the time of the shooting. And there was no knife in the kid's hand. If he fell on it and the knife was hidden when I examined the body, how did the knife get into the kid's hands after I left?"

Grady said in a mechanical voice, "As we approached the wanted man at 2650 North Sixth Street, the man made a threatening motion at me with the knife in his right hand when I ordered him to stop. At this time, I shot."

Vorpagel said. "Let's see what's confirmed by the autopsy."

The autopsy of Daniel Bell started at 11:32 A.M., and lasted an hour and a half. The Medical Examiner was Dr. L. J. Van Hecke. His deputy was Joseph LaMonte.

Van Hecke examined the wound and asked Vorpagel, "How far away did you say the shooter was?"

Vorpagel opened his notebook. "I measured from where Grady showed me. It was twenty-three feet, nine inches."

"Impossible. Look at these markings. The gun was only a foot away at best." Dr. Van Hecke pointed at the dead man's winter coat collar. The powder burns were underneath.

Vorpagel said, "That's why I didn't see them last night. The collar was down, hiding the powder burns. I really thought it was a distant shot."

On February 14, 1958, the coroner's inquest of Daniel Bell was held. During District Attorney McCauley's examination of Krause and Grady, Vorpagel watched in disbelief as the two police officers recounted the events of the fateful night without any mention of the distance of the shot.

The all-white jury quickly returned their verdict: justifiable homicide.

After the inquest, Dolphus "Dock" Bell, Daniel's father, wrote to his son Henry Bell in 1961. A few years later, it became a matter of public record, when it was published in Milwaukee.

> And he says to me, he says well, he said it's an unjust deal. He said, but son—he stuttered when he talked. He says son, he said, the truth will be told. He said you all childrens know exactly—the brothers and the one sister would know exactly how Dan got killed. And he said—that was around seven or eight days before Dock died. He said, because I done seen and I know. He said, whenever you do something wrong and dig a hole and bury it and cover it up, one day it's going to work out. And he said, my son has gone to rest. But he said his name would remain on to many, many thousands of people.

> Grady showed no remorse.

The guilt worked on Louis Krause month after month, year after year. The Milwaukee policeman was fired for drinking on duty a few years after he and Grady were investigated for the Bell shooting.

Krause drifted from job to job—even served time in jail for bouncing checks. The remorse built until, finally, he could no longer face what he had participated in. In 1978, he turned himself in and confessed to his participation in the cover-up. The investigator from the District Attorney's office tapped his phone and had him call Grady. They recorded the conversations.

> GRADY: And you know anything up to now repercussions and the problems for everybody way down the line and, ohh man. It would be inconceivable what could happen.

KRAUSE: I want to tell the truth.

GRADY: But you know how things go. Do you remember, ahh, everybody, ahh, ahh, down there, you know. I can't mention the names now, you know, everybody that backed us all the way down the line is, ahh, oh man, Christ, there'd be hundreds, hundreds of people that would be in the soup.

Even when faced with the incriminating tape, Grady refused to confess to the killing of Daniel Bell.

Except this time, Krause told the truth about what happened that night so many years before. The stenographer's fingers flew over the keyboard as she wrote down the testimony.

The commandeered car careened down the street and passed the running Daniel Bell.

Patrolman Thomas Grady jumped out of the car and shouted, "Halt."

Bell kept running.

Officer Grady caught Bell in front of the house numbered 2650 North Sixth.

Grady grabbed the man by the back, turned his service revolver counterclockwise ninety degrees, pointed the barrel upward at Bell's head, and fired.

Bell fell to the sidewalk.

Krause said, "You killed him."

"He's just a damn nigger kid anyhow," Grady said.

William Hochstaetter lived directly across the street from 2650 North Sixth Street. At 8:25 P.M. on February 2, 1958, he heard a shot. He walked across the street and saw two police officers. Then he saw the black man lying on the sidewalk. Blood was trickling out from a wound in his back.

Hochstaetter looked closely. There was no weapon in the slain man's hands.

One of the police officers shouted, "Get out of here."

The black man went back to his home and watched from the front-room window.

Vorpagel and Hughes arrived and investigated the scene. They performed the necessary duties at the crime scene and then left.

Grady pulled a knife out of his jacket pocket.

Krause said, "That knife ain't big enough, Tom."

Grady closed the jackknife, stuck it into one pocket and pulled another, larger knife out. He opened the dead man's right hand, stuck the handle of the knife into the palm, and closed the hand around it.

Vorpagel was in court the next morning. The tangled web had unraveled. The lies about twenty-three feet dwindling to fifteen feet, then six feet, then one foot came out; all became public knowledge.

The last few minutes of Vorpagel's cross-examination was the toughest part.

The defense attorney snidely asked, "And why, Mr. Vorpagel, after two decades, have you decided now to come forth?"

"I didn't come forward earlier because I had no proof. The District Attorney kept my original report."

"As far as we know, he still has your original report, if there ever really was one. So why now?"

"Because Krause's guilt has finally forced him to

talk. Now I can substantiate what really happened, as a witness."

"That's your only motivation?"

"No. I have been in law enforcement for thirty years. In all that time, I remembered Bell as probably the only case where I felt justice had not been served."

When Vorpagel returned to Quantico that year, in 1978, he received a call from an investigator with the FBI office in Washington, D.C. The business-like voice said he had information from the FBI office in Milwaukee that Vorpagel was instrumental in the cover-up at the scene of the Bell shooting. The trial was now focusing on Krause, and Krause had changed his testimony dramatically.

Vorpagel was told to go to D.C., to be charged with police corruption.

The FBI investigator said that Krause had claimed that Vorpagel had coerced him into changing his original testimony, and what really happened was that Vorpagel had killed Daniel Bell!

Vorpagel was enraged. He told the investigator, "I'm being charged with a Federal crime that didn't exist in 1958—murder wasn't a federal statute. I think the FBI should have allowed me the courtesy of giving an explanation. I'm a lawyer. Even if I admitted the whole thing, there's not a damn thing you could do about it now, in 1980. So I refuse to talk to you." He slammed the phone down.

Vorpagel calmed down and talked to Assistant District Director Jim McKenzie, who advised, "You should defend yourself."

Two weeks later, Vorpagel received another call

from FBI headquarters in Washington, D.C. The same investigator said, "You are now charged with lying on the stand as an FBI agent. We fully intend to prosecute you. See if you can laugh this off with some flip remark."

Vorpagel told him again what he felt as an attorney. He added a few expletives. He slammed the phone down again. He again talked to McKenzie.

The Assistant District Director advised him to take the charges seriously.

Vorpagel called Dr. Van Hecke, the coroner who had performed the autopsy. His records showed that Vorpagel was attending the Bell autopsy all the time Krause testified he tried to coerce him to change his testimony. The records were sent to the FBI in Washington, D.C.

The charges were dropped. But Vorpagel was still furious at the way he had been treated by his own agency.

Vorpagel told his class, "When you're told to be careful out there, it isn't always advice to protect yourself against the felon. Sometimes the enemy comes masked as friends."

Marcus asked, "Are you angry with the FBI?"

"Not the FBI, just a few representatives of the organization. And with people who use the FBI for sensationalism. I even have a touch of a problem with those that use the agency with good intent."

"An example."

"*The Silence of the Lambs* was a very popular movie, made with the cooperation of the FBI. But in real life, do you think a case of that magnitude would have been given to a rookie? That's not the Behavioral Science Unit at all."

"What was the outcome of the Grady trial?" Gary asked.

"The Grady trial ended a few months later: $1.7 million was awarded to the Bells and a seven-year sentence to Grady."

He studied his students' faces. "There's one glaringly huge logical error in Grady's testimony, even after all the lies, on what happened those last few seconds of Daniel Bell's life. Recreate the scene and think."

The class pondered the problem. Some heads were bent, one man stared at the ceiling, some wore frowns.

Ava said, "Pretend you're Bell. How can you brandish a knife, and so threaten the patrolman that he shoots you, if you're facing the other way?"

"You're right. Bell was shot in the back. Daniel Bell was murdered. You can tell that without a videotape."

Marcus asked, "How did the Bell case impact on your ideas regarding behavioral science?"

"The sociopath, the antisocial personality, and the psychopath all are the same. They are, unfortunately, related to the word *psychotic*. But the psychotic deals with serious mental problems, and the sociopath deals with personality problems. In my opinion, Krause was an inadequate personality—a follower. Grady was a classic antisocial personality, or a sociopath.

"This case caused me to wonder how a person could take an oath to uphold the peace and protect the innocent, and then commit murder. How could this happen? Why did this happen?

"This led me to begin thinking about the how and the why of the different kinds of criminal minds."

"The how? The why?"

Gary asked, "Where did the Bell case lead you?"

"To other interviews and interrogations. What people feel when in conflict. What they can justify. People do not all share the same values. I began to realize that there are many more motivations than loot, lust, lechery, and larceny. This led to more in-depth analysis on future cases."

Vorpagel opened his briefcase. "Some unusual cases to finish up with before we have our final test problem. Cases from A to S, autoerotic to secretors."

FROM AUTOEROTIC TO SECRETORS

Vorpagel rested his hands on the dais. "Recognizing that no one is perfect, my next presentation is designed to assist police officers, coroners, and even medical examiners in their determination of the *manner* of death. Too often, I have seen misidentification of household pets, identified as the bodies of infants, in fires. Blatant mistakes happen with gunshots, sharp force wounds, bodies recovered from water, hanging/asphyxia deaths, and even vehicle deaths."

"I see that all the time," Shui said.

Gary rebutted with, "Or claim you have to a jury."

The public defender glared at the prosecuting attorney.

"Now, now," Vorpagel chided, "let's not kick sand at each other, at least anywhere besides the courtroom. *Equivocal*, two equal voices. This happens frequently in autoerotic death: *auto*, meaning self, and *erotic*, meaning arousal. Autoerotic means sexual feelings or sexual gratification that are self-induced without having sexual relations with another human."

"I've seen this kind of death," Marcus said.

"Really?" Vorpagel said. "How long you been walking a beat?"

"Less than a year."

"Some cops go a full thirty and never see an auto-erotic death. What happened?"

"We found a teenage boy hanging from a rafter in the garage. I was the initial cop who responded to the call. I wrote out suicide, but the precinct captain arrived and told me to slow down. We searched the boy's room and found certain paraphernalia and magazines that changed the report to accidental death."

"Smart precinct captain. This illustrates exactly what I'm trying to convey. No matter how bad something looks in one direction, take your time; think whether there's another possibility. There are two categories in autoerotic activity: nondangerous and dangerous. Some nondangerous examples are masturbation, fantasy, voyeurism, pornography, and sex toys or props. Even a necrophiliac can catch germs. Dangerous autoerotic behavior involves the need for pain, use of hypoxia, extreme stimulation, and being unaware of the danger."

Marcus asked, "That's what I still can't figure out. How is hanging yourself a sexual stimulant?"

"To someone born without this sexual craving it isn't. And to one who has, it is not the intent to hang oneself. Only the suffocating sensation, the lack of oxygen, is desired, not death. Usual ways that this is achieved besides a rope or a plastic bag, are laughing gas, carbon monoxide, ether, sniffing glue, or oral plugs. Anoxia leads to fantasy.

"What was the first thing your precinct captain did when he arrived at the scene?"

"He checked the rafter for other marks. And he found some."

"Right on. First thing, he checked for signs of life, then checked for marks on suspension points, which can be almost anything: branches, beams, doors, bars, handles. Was the teenager wearing strange attire?"

"Just a mask."

"And you jumped at suicide? Didn't the possibility of a homicide type execution come to mind?"

"No."

"At first glance, your hanging could have been any one of three: murder, suicide, accident. The psychological autopsy can be used to determine if a victim is truly a victim of foul play or died of suicide, or accidentally in some bizarre sexual pastime."

"An example?"

"Of course; one is short, the other long. In 1991, I was giving a death investigation class in Florida when the local police asked me to look at a crime scene. It was one of the bloodiest scenes I've ever encountered. The victim was seated in a chair in shorts, socks, and boots. All were blood soaked. Two fingers and an ear were cut off and missing. His scrotum was in his mouth. His severed penis lay on the floor."

"What's the problem?" Gary asked. "With two fingers and an ear missing, and a scrotum and penis cut off, it sure looks like foul play."

"That's what the local authorities thought. I did a profile. I talked to friends and neighbors, searched his room, and came to the conclusion that this was death by accident."

"Why?"

"In extreme cases of sadomasochistic behavior, self-mutilation and self-torture are not uncommon."

"The missing ear? The missing fingers?"

"I attended the autopsy the next day. Along with a large quantity of drugs . . ."

The room became suddenly silent.

Vorpagel blurted, "In the poor man's stomach were found the missing body parts."

Marcus said, "Good Lord, he ate them himself? What else led you to believe this was an accident?"

"Putting the victim's shorts back on was puzzling behavior. Killers don't do this. Not when the victim is a male. This was not restitution. From his friend, I learned that the victim was into autoerotic behavior."

"What drives a person to this kind of activity?"

"Many things. Many things could be a type of transference, for example, imagining he was doing it to someone else, or a punishment to self, or 'to get even' by making a significant other feel guilt . . . They can be ashamed or embarrassed about sexual preferences. It can be experimentation. They could be mentally ill. In the last case, I found evidence of solo sexual activity, of sexual fantasy aids, and some evidence of prior autoerotic practices. What I didn't find was any apparent suicidal intent. For example, no good-bye letter. No suicide note. Not even depression noticed by anyone close to him."

"What else should we know about this?"

"To handle relatives with extreme kindness. They blame themselves. 'I should have known,' they say. 'I should have seen the signs and done something to help.' But the practitioners of this kind of sexual activity try to hide the signs."

Vorpagel opened his briefcase and removed a file. "Follow along while I tell you about a case that does not involve the possibility of a suicide. Only two choices this time: accident or murder."

Even though the recently divorced Molly was eighteen years older than her son, a senior in high school, she was considered very hot stuff by his friends. They'd joke among themselves that the day Molly got divorced was the day that the boys in the class of '92 would find out what making it with a real woman was like.

Molly was insatiable.

And Molly was creative.

The seventeen- and eighteen-year-old high school students that she seduced thought that a fast romp in the back of the car was the ultimate sexual thrill.

Until Molly got them into her bedroom.

She liked props: magazines, oils, videos, exotic creams, exotic positions.

None of these young men had ever heard of the *Kama Sutra*.

Molly, using the illustrations in her book and the visual aid of a mirror, helped them learn.

Her son didn't know. His friends would take turns keeping him out of the house.

"Let's play baseball for a few hours."

And Molly's bedroom and house would be free.

"Let's see a movie. Better yet, a double feature."

Molly's house would be free for an entire afternoon.

She was reasonably discreet. She told neighbors

that she was tutoring some of her son's friends. In a way, she was telling the truth.

Then Molly was found dead.

Vorpagel was giving a class on *Differential Diagnosis in Death* in Missouri, when the deputy sheriff walked into his classroom unannounced.

Vorpagel did a sidebar with him by the door.

The deputy said, "Got a bad one. I took your class a few years ago and I heard you were in town. Mind taking a look before the body bag's brought in?"

Vorpagel apologized to his students for canceling the class and went with the deputy.

The cottage was modest: white stucco, white fence, browned-out lawn, yellow police caution tape everywhere.

Fire trucks were parked by the curb. Sooty-faced firemen rolled up hoses, put away axes, and dogged down the hydrant.

"Was the victim burned to death?" Russ asked.

"Nope. The firemen got here in time to extinguish the flames before she was burned. Her name was Molly." The deputy led the way into the house.

The front room was still smoky. The deputy opened a few windows and the kitchen door. He pointed at a door down a hall.

Vorpagel stood in the doorway. At the foot of the bed was Molly's body. She was on her back. Her dress was up over her waist. She wore no panties.

The deputy stood just behind Vorpagel and said, "Pretty bizarre."

Vorpagel nodded. A chest of drawers was directly

in front of a side door, about a half a foot away from this rear exit. On the floor, leaning against the bureau, was a mirror. The mirror was tilted so that the woman's private parts were visible from her point of view. A Tootsie Roll bank, shaped just like a Tootsie Roll but capable of holding dozens of the candies, was lying on the floor directly between her legs. It looked like a dildo.

Next to the body was a magazine. It was open and displaying a photo of a nude male in a state of arousal.

The deputy said, "At first, I thought it was autoerotic death, but I remember you telling me that was usually brought on by some type of strangulation. Where's the means? No rope. No plastic bag. No nothing."

Vorpagel glanced around. The bedroom still had smoke hovering near the ceiling. "Maybe she accidentally inhaled too much smoke when the fire started. That would be death by suffocation."

"Wouldn't she have run when the fire started?"

"Not necessarily. She could have had something to drink. Performed masturbation. Then fell asleep." Vorpagel bent forward. "This looks like the fire was started with a cigarette. She could have lit up, then dozed off."

"That's kind of what I thought. Sorry to have . . ."

"I'm not through. Or someone could have manually strangled her and then arranged everything to look like an accidental death. Let's wait for the autopsy. Also, I want to do a psychological autopsy."

Vorpagel talked to the neighbors and learned about the frequent teenage visits. He talked to Molly's son's friends. He found out that there were five regulars who visited Molly.

He interviewed each one.

Four of the teenagers had been playing touch football with Molly's son.

Vorpagel talked to the fifth boy, Frank.

They stood just outside the school yard. A few boys were playing basketball on the other side of the fence.

Frank called out, "Nice shot."

Vorpagel asked, "How well did you know Molly?"

"She's my friend's mom."

"I know. Did you go to her house the day she died?"

Frank clutched the wire fence with both hands. He said softly, "Yes."

"For tutoring?"

"No."

"For what then?"

"I had sex with her. But then I left. Honest. She was all right when I left."

Vorpagel went to the lab. He learned that there was seminal fluid found in Molly. The bedroom had been dusted. Frank's fingerprints were found on the doorknob. But they were not found on the mirror, the magazine, or the Tootsie Roll bank.

Vorpagel studied his students. "So, what would you have done?"

Ava said, "This seems like a pretty straightforward case of autoerotic death."

Gary said, "But if that was the case, why would Russ be giving us this problem? I vote for murder."

Vorpagel sighed. "You can't keep using me or my reactions, or my original participation, to come to conclusions."

"I'm a prosecutor, that's how I think."

"I'm a lawyer too, but . . ."

"Really," Shui said. "What type law have you practiced?"

"I always liked that phrase," Vorpagel said. "Lawyers practice all their lives. Plumbers don't practice once they're journeymen. Neither do electricians, bartenders, or steelworkers. Just professionals have a practice. Doctors, lawyers . . ."

Shui interrupted. "Talk about misdirection. All I asked was what type of law have you practiced."

Vorpagel sighed. "If you must know, I'm sanctioned to appear before the U.S. Supreme Court. Also, back then, Hoover wouldn't accept an application to the FBI unless you were a lawyer or a certified public accountant."

Vorpagel held up the file. "What would you have concluded on this case?"

Marcus said, "Maybe Frank wore gloves when he moved the mirror, magazine, and Tootsie Roll bank."

"Nope. No signs of it in the lab report. The only fingerprints on any of that stuff were Molly's."

Ava asked, "What else did the autopsy reveal?"

"There was no evidence of a broken hyoid, that's located in the throat. No bruises around her throat, except a slight one under the jaw. Her son said she did that by accident the day before."

Ava asked, "What did the autopsy discover in her lungs?"

"Very good," Vorpagel said. "That's the right question. No smoke was discovered in her lungs. Frank was picked up. He was interrogated. He broke down and confessed. While having sex with Molly, he got carried away. He placed one hand on her throat and gently squeezed. She started to thrash. He thought she was enjoying it, until she quit moving. He panicked. He lit a cigarette and started a fire to hide what he had done. Then he fled."

"Wait a minute," Gary said. "And I suppose the magazine, the mirror, and the Tootsie Roll bank just magically arranged themselves to make it look like an autoerotic death."

"Something like that," Vorpagel said with a smile. "Think. How could three objects do just that?"

The class became very silent.

Vorpagel hummed softly.

Ava raised her hand. "Where did you say the chest of drawers was located?"

"About a half a foot from the rear exit to the bedroom."

"How did the firemen enter the bedroom?"

"Bingo! Excellent. They entered by the rear exit. I interviewed them. They said something felt like it was obstructing the door, they had to shove it to get in."

"Are you telling me," Gary said, "that those three objects just happened to drop exactly in the right place?"

"There are stranger things, Horatio, under the heavens, than man can ever tell. That's exactly what happened. Molly's son told us that she usually kept the magazine tucked into the side of the mirror. And that she loved Tootsie Rolls and always kept the bank on the chest of drawers, which, he further informed us, was always shoved against the rear door to make more room in the bedroom."

"What happened to Frank?"

Vorpagel shrugged. "I finished my course and went home to California. Never did find out what sentence he received. He was an adult, eighteen, and Missouri's a pretty tough state. But I don't really know. I use this example, as I do most, to show you over and over again not to jump to conclusions. Use Sherlock Holmes's logic. When every possibility is eliminated, whatever remains, no matter how improbable, is the answer. Most of the time, the obvious will be the answer, but sometimes it won't. And that sometimes is what I'm preparing you for. A lot's at stake. No one wants to lose a loved one, but it's a lot easier to handle if one knows it was an accident rather than a suicide. Believe it or not, even a murder can be easier to handle than a suicide. The victim's relatives have a place to aim their rage and grief in a murder. In a suicide, many times, that rage and grief get aimed at themselves."

Vorpagel glanced at his watch. "One more example before we take a break." He opened a file and read, "A man found his girlfriend dead in her apartment. He claimed she committed suicide by shooting herself. I will now read his interrogation. No names will be used. However, the detective conducting the interview was of the old school that liked to use sarcasm to rattle the suspect. This is how he told it to me."

"How long did you know her?"
"About a year."
"And you had just broken up with her?"
"Yes, the day before."

"Why did you go to her apartment the next day?"

"I talked to her on the phone. She sounded very down."

"What's *down* supposed to mean? Down on the floor?"

"No. Down. You know."

"No, I don't. Down is the opposite of up. Heaven is up. Hell is down. Do you mean she sounded like she was in hell?"

"No, more like she felt like hell."

"She felt like hell?"

"Yes."

"As in depressed?"

"Yes."

"That worried you?"

"Of course."

"Worried how?"

"Worried."

"About what?"

"That she might do something."

"Like blow her brains out?"

"No, I didn't think she'd kill herself."

"But you were worried. She was down. Depressed. Potentially suicidal?"

"Yes."

"You stated that you arrived at her apartment door, knocked, then heard the sound of a gun firing."

"Yes."

"What did you do that morning, after learning that she was down, before arriving at her apartment?"

"After talking to her on the phone, I started for her place."

"Because you thought she was down, depressed, maybe suicidal?"

"Yes."

"You were in a hurry?"

"Yes. But I got a flat tire."

"That delayed you?"

"Yes. I put on the spare tire. Then, I decided I didn't like driving around without a spare so I went to a filling station a friend of mine owns."

"Then what?"

"I decided as long as I was there that I would get a grease and oil change."

"More time chewed up?"

"Yes."

"I thought you said you were concerned about your ex-girlfriend?"

"I was."

"You stated she sounded down."

"Yes."

"Depressed."

"Yes."

"Maybe suicidal."

"Yes."

"Have you ever heard the expression 'Time is of the essence'?"

"I think so."

"You think so. What do you think it means?"

"I'm not sure."

"Not sure. How about an example of 'Time is of the essence'? How about a guy who dumps his girlfriend? Then, he talks to her on the phone. She sounds down. Depressed. Suicidal. He thinks he should talk to her in person. And very soon. The clock's ticking. Time is of the essence because getting there in quick time might enable the prevention of an untimely death. You follow?"

"Yes."

"But you decided to have your car's oil and grease changed?"

"Yes."

"I guess the 'Time is of the essence' concept was more important on your engine's maintenance than it was in talking to a down, depressed, suicidal ex-girlfriend?"

"It's just that I was already at the gas station."

"You stated your friend owned the gas station?"

"Yes."

"Was he suicidal?"

"No."

"All this filling station friend had at risk was whether you'd have your oil and grease job that morning, or maybe the next?"

"I guess."

"But the woman you'd been sleeping with for the past year, whom you said sounded down, maybe suicidal, might not see another tomorrow. Who needed your decision regarding 'Time is of the essence' more? The gas jockey or your ex-girlfriend?"

"You're confusing me."

"What happened after the grease and oil change?"

"I couldn't find a parking spot near the apartment building."

"Could you usually find a parking spot near the building?"

"Yes. Almost always."

"You eventually found a parking place?"

"Yes, about six blocks away."

"Then what?"

"I walked to the apartment building."

"You walked. Didn't run?"

"No."

"You thought your ex-girlfriend was down. Maybe suicidal. And you'd just wasted—what? An hour? An hour and a half? A new tire. An oil change. New grease job. And you didn't run?"

"I'm not in good enough shape to run one block, let alone six."

"Did you run one block?"

"No."

"So you sauntered to the apartment building. Now what?"

"The lobby was crowded with people. I've never seen so many. They were waiting in line to get onto the elevator."

"This ever happen before?"

"No."

"Never had to wait for long for an elevator during the whole year you dated this girl?"

"No."

Detective's note: I stare directly at the suspect and begin tapping my pen against an ashtray. The suspect studies his hands. At least twenty seconds pass before he asks a question.

"Is that it?"

"What is that it?"

"You're finished with the questions, right?"

"Far from it."

"Then why aren't you asking questions?"

"You ever heard of thinking?"

Detective's note: I went back to tapping the pen against the ashtray. The suspect is staring at his hands. Another twenty seconds tick by before I ask a question.

"So, you say a big crowd decided to visit the building just at that particular moment?"

"Yes, a big crowd. Had to be over a hundred people in the lobby."

"A hundred people? How tall was this apartment building?"

"Four stories. My girl lived on the top floor."

"How many apartments per floor?"

"About ten."

"We have forty apartments in the building. And a hundred of their friends all decide to come calling at the exact same moment. Is that what you're telling me?"

"Yes. I couldn't figure it out."

"That I believe. What did you do next?"

"I was getting worried about how long it was taking to get to her apartment."

"You were frantic by now?"

"Yes, that's right. I was frantic."

"So, in this newfound frenzy, what did you do?"

"I took the stairs."

"Run up, did you?"

"All four flights."

"Can't jog six blocks, or even one block, but you can dash up four flights?"

"I told you, I was getting worried."

"Frantically worried."

"Yes. Frantically worried."

"In a frantic, frenzied worry?"

"Yes."

"You must have been out of breath when you arrived at the fourth floor?"

"I was."

"Did this apartment complex count the ground floor as one, or did it count the ground floor as the lobby?"

"The lobby."

"You must have really, really been out of breath when you arrived at the floor numbered 'four,' which is really five stories above the street?"

"Yes, very out of breath."

"Stood there at the top floor, hands holding your sides, gasping for breath. That's what happened?"

"Exactly."

"What happened next?"

"I went down the hallway."

"Kind of staggered down the hallway. Right? Being out of breath and all."

"Yes."

"Had to support your exhausted body by steadying yourself, by placing a hand on the wall?"

"How did you know?"

"We found your fingerprints on the hallway wall."

"Oh."

"Then what did you do after walking down the hallway sucking in oxygen?"

"I knocked on her door."

"No answer?"

"No."

"Of course not. I forgot. She's slumped at her dining-room table, with the gun on the floor and a bullet in her head. No way could she have answered the door. Right?"

"That's right."

"So you stood there knocking and waiting for a corpse to let you in?"

"I didn't know she was dead."

"Of course not. You'd just spent all morning in a frantic, frenzied worry having your tire fixed, your car greased, your oil changed, looking for a parking spot, sauntering six blocks, waiting in the lobby, dashing up the stairs, stumbling down the hallway, and knocking on your dead ex-girlfriend's door."

"She wasn't dead yet."

"How do you know?"

"Because, when she didn't answer, I put my key in the lock."

"Your key?"

"Yes, my key."

"To her apartment?"

"She gave me one after we'd been going together for a few months."

"Didn't ask for it back when you broke up?"

"No."

"Did she have a key to your apartment?"

"No."

"Why not?"

"I just never gave her one."

"She gave you one. Didn't it occur to you that maybe some sort of reciprocation might be in order?"

"No."

"No what? No, it didn't occur to you? Or no, you didn't feel the need to reciprocate?"

"It didn't occur to me."

"It must have occurred to your dead ex-girlfriend when she made such a gesture of trust."

"Trust?"

"Giving you her key meant she was telling you that you had an exclusive relationship. Pop in any time. No one else will ever be here."

"Oh."

"That didn't occur to you?"

"No."

"Were you screwing around with someone else?"

"No."

"Didn't occur to you?"

"No."

"It appears many things didn't occur to you."

"I guess."

"You weren't screwing around with someone you didn't want your dead ex-girlfriend popping in on?"

"No."

"Just how did you and the deceased break up? I mean, before she supposedly put a bullet in her brain?"

"I took her to lunch the day before . . . before . . ."

"The day before she supposedly put a gun to her temple, pulled the trigger, and splattered her brains all over her dining-room table."

"I don't like to think about it."

Detective's note: I start tapping the pen against the ashtray. The suspect is looking around the room. He has never made eye contact since the interrogation began. It's about twenty seconds before the suspect breaks the silence.

"Thinking?"

"Aren't you?"

"Yes."

"You just said you didn't like to think."

"About it."

"It?"

"You know? It."

"You think of a woman you bedded down with for a year as an it?"

"No."

"Then what is it you don't like to think about?"

"What she did."

"Oh, you mean the blowing her brains out it?"

"Something like that."

"If it's not something that's exactly like a blowing her brains out it, what exactly something like it do you mean?"

"You're twisting my words."

"Did you or did you not say 'I don't like to think about it'?"

"Yes."

"Did you or did you not then say 'Something like that'?"

"Yes."

"Exactly those words?"

"Yes."

"Then how can you claim that I'm twisting your words?"

"You're confusing me."

"Did you or did you not take her to lunch?"

"Yes."

"You took her to lunch and then dumped all over her?"

"I told her it wasn't working out."

"What wasn't working out?"

"Our relationship."

"Why wasn't it working out?"

"We never seemed to talk anymore."

"No talking. What else?"

"We'd grown apart."

"Grown apart. What else?"

"Nothing."

"How about sex? Was she still delivering?"

"She cared about me."

"We have this loving, caring girlfriend who trusts you enough to give you her apartment latch key, but you felt she didn't talk enough and you had grown apart?"

"Yes."

"What does 'grown apart' mean?"

"We felt uncomfortable around each other."

"We? We felt uncomfortable? Is that the editorial *we*, or the *we* meaning you and your girlfriend?"

"I felt uncomfortable around her."

"Ah, *you* felt uncomfortable around her. At lunch, how did you tell her you didn't want to feel uncomfortable around her anymore?"

"I let her down gently."

"You let her down gently? So gently that now you claim that she brooded over this gentle letdown and then blew her brains all over her dining-room table."

"I thought I let her down gently."

"I talked to some of your drinking buddies. They say you have quite a hot and volatile temper."

"Only when I get riled."

"Only when riled. Were you riled that morning when you went to your ex-girlfriend's apartment in a frantic, frenzied, sauntering hurry?"

"No. Why would I be riled?"

"I don't know. What kinds of things rile you up?"

"You know, sometimes the guys start needling and it gets to you."

"Gets to me? Why would it get to me?"

"I meant me."

"What else riles you up?"

"That's about it."

"Just the needle riles you up? How about a girl-friend who's cheating on you?"

"She wasn't cheating on me."

"That's not what you told those drinking buddies who rile you up."

"They said I thought she was cheating?"

"Sleeping with another guy. Balling her brains out. Humping someone other than you. You know. Cheating."

"I was just kidding around."

"Kidding around, about a mythical guy balling your girlfriend?"

"You know, guy stuff."

"Do any of your drinking buddies who rile you up talk about their girlfriends betraying them?"

"No."

"So this guy stuff only includes one guy, you?"

"I guess."

"What if somebody else told you your girlfriend wasn't as loving and caring as you thought? What if they told you she was giving most of that loving and caring to someone else?"

"I wouldn't believe it."

"But if you did believe it, would it rile you up?"

"It would hurt me."

"Sure. Even though you'd grown apart. Let's say you heard she was banging somebody. Would that rile you up enough to go over to her house, stick your key in the lock, confront her, really, really get riled up, pull a gun, and blow her brains out?"

"Of course not. The gun went off when I stuck the key in the lock."

"You stick her key into the latch, and then—POP goes the gun. That what happened?"

"Yes."

"Then you enter the apartment?"

"Yes."

"And see?"

"See her sitting at the dining-room table."

"Sitting?"

"Slumped over, her head on the table."

"Any blood oozing about on the table?"

"No."

"Notice any brain matter scattered around the table?"

"No."

"Where was the gun?"

"On the floor."

"What did you do with the gun?"

"I picked it up."

"I know, your fingerprints were on it. Why did you pick it up?"

"I didn't want her shooting herself again."

"She's got a bullet in her head, her blood and brain particles scattered and oozing all over her dining-room table, and you didn't want her shooting herself again?"

"I didn't realize she was dead."

"You didn't, did you? You're under arrest."

• • •

Vorpagel looked up from his notes. "Conclusions?"

Gary said, "What an interrogation. That detective's a bulldog."

"I said old school, but not the old school of bring out the brass knuckles until the suspect confesses. It was a legal interrogation."

Shui added, "But ruthless."

"Why ruthless?" Vorpagel asked. "The detective thought he had the girlfriend's killer on his hands. A ruthless girlfriend killer. He had already spoken with the suspect's fellow employees. He had learned that this guy had a very hot temper. He also learned that the boyfriend thought the girlfriend was cheating on him. So why not an in-depth questioning, aimed at breaking resistance down and getting a confession?"

Shui shrugged. "Was his attorney present?"

"The suspect was informed of his rights. He declined representation."

"Big mistake. And so many people make it."

Marcus asked, "What's the point of telling us this?"

"Exactly. What's the point? The very fact that you asked that question is the point. Every person in this room, including defense attorney Shui, thinks the boyfriend's story is a crock."

"It wasn't?"

"No, it wasn't. The detective thought he had a murderer, but he was a very professional police officer. He checked. Guess what? The filling station verified the flat tire and the oil and grease change. There was a wedding on the roof of the apartment building that day, which explains the lack of parking places for blocks and the hundred people in the lobby."

Marcus asked, "How do you explain the finger-prints on the gun?"

"Don't have to. The fingerprints were his."

"Then all the stuff about why it took him so long to get to her place means nothing. Who cares when he arrived? All I care about is the fingerprints on the gun."

"The story about why it took him so long to get there is what made him look so suspect. Like he was ly-ing about everything. But he wasn't. And because the photographer who photo'd the scene was as thorough as the detective, proof was found."

Vorpagel held up a photo. "This is a photograph of the woman's hand. As you can see, there is an indenta-tion quite noticeable on her trigger finger. She shot her-self, and in the act left proof that her ex-boyfriend didn't do it. When shooting oneself, that indentation is usually found, due to the loss of tension in the skin, and remains for almost an hour before disappearing."

Marcus asked, "I thought cardiac spasm caused the hand to clutch the gun. And so hard that the fingers have to be pried from the weapon."

"Sometimes. Sometimes the hand clutches the in-strument of death in an iron grip; sometimes it doesn't. Nothing is absolute or continuous from one violent death to another. There are similarities. A woman jumped off a building holding her baby. Dead on im-pact. Her body cushioned the baby. Her arms had to be pried off the baby."

"But why was an indentation left on the trigger fin-ger, but the hand didn't freeze on the weapon?"

"It happens. Different people's chemistries react differently to a bullet plowing through their brain."

Marcus pressed on. "Couldn't the boyfriend have placed the gun in her hand, put it to her temple, and then squeezed the trigger, using his finger on top of hers?"

"No, not in this case."

"Why not?"

"Because the boyfriend was a secretor. About sixty percent of the world is."

He looked at the puzzled looks on his students' faces. "A secretor is a group-specific substance in the bloodstream that makes it possible to determine the blood group from body fluids like urine, semen, tears, saliva. A secretor also has a chemical reaction when his or her skin comes in contact with metal. The detective immediately had the boyfriend's hands placed in a black felt box and dosed in ultraviolet light. That's a metal trace box with hydroxyquiniline that only works on secretors. If done soon enough, like in less than twenty-four hours, it will show where skin has come into contact with metal. The boyfriend's palms were clear; the only metal traces found were on his fingers, from picking up the gun. The girlfriend's hand was also done. Metal traces were found on her palm and trigger finger."

There were puzzled looks around the room.

Vorpagel held up another photograph. "The FBI has done tests involving this science. We had three volunteers hold three metal objects: a badge, a gun, and a coin. They were told to squeeze these objects in the palms of their hands. The next day, there were trace metals detected. Not only were metal traces discovered on all three hands, but also the very identifiable shapes of a coin, a gun, and a badge appeared."

Vorpagel shoved the file back into his briefcase. "I tell the story of the ridiculous alibi made by the boyfriend to make a point. By now, you should all know what this point is."

The students chorused, "Don't jump to conclusions."

Vorpagel said, "Correct. Tomorrow I will give you your final problem. It is long. It is complicated. And, as usual, it involves the question: Was this death suicide, accident, or murder?"

CHAPTER TEN

ALL As

It was a case Vorpagel always saved for last, the type of story that absorbed every investigator. An airplane crash. An intriguing puzzle. And the human element in the background. It was the final exam in a class in which everyone got A's, but the only A that counted was in the hearts of the students.

Vorpagel said, "One last problem, much longer, much more complex. This case involves the question of whether a death was a suicide, a murder, or an accident."

Pensacola is notched into the westernmost part of Florida. It is the entrance to the "Miracle Strip," the hundred-mile continuous beach that runs all the way to Panama City. It has an airport with a history.

The flight controller at the tower studied the overcast sky. Heavy, bloated clouds hung seven hundred feet over the runways. A Beechcraft King Air 200, N30PC, broke through the angry sky. The plane was given clearance to land.

The controller watched it gently bounce down and thumbed his microphone. "Okay, three zero Papa Charlie, ground point niner clear of the runway at the next left."

"Papa Charlie."

The controller smiled at the sound of the voice. The captain of the King Air was Joe Holmes, who'd worked for Southern Company Services for years, since Saint Patrick's Day 1971. Holmes was an excellent supervisor and pilot. He had logged 12,200 hours in turboprops, 150 in jets, 1,120 under instrument conditions, and 2,020 at night.

The flight controller said, "Thirty Papa Charlie to the ramp IFR to PDK."

"King Air thirty Papa Charlie to the ramp instruments to PDK."

"Anyone working ground?"

The controller knew this second voice as well. The first officer was John Major. He'd worked for the company since April 9, 1989. He'd logged 12,050 civil pilot time, 250 in the last six months. The controller answered, "Affirmative one two one point nine."

"I tried—twice."

"All right, taxi to the ramp if you want to check it again. I'd appreciate it."

"Okay."

Captain Holmes said, "Ole Jake just drove up."

The controller looked through binoculars. He watched Jacob F. Horton, Senior Vice-President of Gulf Power Company, get out of a car.

Why, the controller wondered, did Horton schedule the plane himself? That was usually done by his secretary.

Jake Horton gave two pieces of luggage to the hangar attendant, a hanging bag and a suitcase. The attendant was also carrying a small bag—the pilot's lunch. Horton took a small red bag and another black bag, which looked like a bowling ball bag, out of the trunk.

The controller thought, a bowling bag?

The flight controller heard over the tower speakers the sound of switches clicking. Then, a ratcheting sound. He thought, Holmes is switching radio frequencies.

The controller pushed the button on his mike. "You read ground Papa Charlie?"

"I'm not getting anything."

"Okay, we just rotated the position here. Let me check something." He looked at the controls on the radio panel.

Captain Holmes said, "Thirty Papa Charlie back to twenty-one-nine."

"You're loud and clear."

"We're on the ramp now, we're IFR to Peachtree-Dekalb."

"Three zero Papa Charlie is cleared to Peachtree as filed. Maintain three thousand, expect flight level two one zero one zero ten minutes after departure. Departure frequency will be one niner one niner point zero squawk one zero three two."

The flight controller watched Jake Horton walk up the short metal stairs and enter the plane.

Jake's voice came over the radio. "Hi, guy."

The captain said, "How you doin'?"

"Messy over there."

"It's cold and wet, but it's not a real bad thunderstorm."

The flight controller pushed the button on his radio. "I'll tell you what they got—a full route clearance here. I didn't see that. They got you going to Crestview, Montgomery, Lagrange mike three arrival."

"Okey, doke. Crestview, Montgomery, Lagrange mike three and that's not too far out of the way."

"Thank you," the controller said, and then listened to an exchange coming from the cockpit.

Jake Horton said, "It's almost like winter out there."

The captain said, "Sure is."

The flight controller watched John Major leave the airplane and jog to the hangar.

Jake Horton's voice came over the radio speakers, "Where'd John go?"

"To the men's room."

The tower's radio filled with the harsh, shrieking sound of static, then picked up Horton's voice in midsentence. "Don't get excited about these clothes. I just, I don't think I'll have to stay."

"What's that?" Captain Holmes asked.

"I brought these clothes, just in case."

"In case you have to spend the night?"

"Yeah."

The cockpit voice recorder went dead. The flight controller knew that Holmes had shut it off to restart the left engine. This was a normal procedure for the Fairchild recorder.

The radio in the tower sputtered back to life. Delta flight 654's captain said, "Six five four cleared Crestview, Montgomery, Lagrange six three thousand feet, seven zero ten minutes later, one nineteen on departure and one zero two six the squawk."

The flight controller said, "That's correct." He watched First Officer Major reboard the King Air. He and Horton exchanged hellos.

The first officer then said, "Montgomery?"

Captain Holmes said, "Yeah."

"You filed Montgomery?"

"Nah, I filed Lagrange."

The controller thumbed the button on his mike. "Three zero Papa Charlie taxi runway three four—wind three six zero at one two."

"Papa Charlie."

In the tower, the flight controller listened to the sounds of switches being thrown in the plane. Then Holmes asked, "Say your altimeter again."

"Pensacola altimeter three zero one eight."

Another harsh shriek blared from the tower's radio speakers. The flight controller thought, sounds like they have got a CVR problem. He listened to the two pilots drone through the flight check.

"Trim," Flight Officer Major said. "Flaps. Flight control. Autofeather."

"Autofeather is armed," Captain Holmes said.

"Flight and engine instruments."

"They're okay."

"Ice protection."

"Leave 'em off for a while. The doctor took an X ray of my head and he said I'm one of the three per-centers—population that has no frontal lobes."

"So, is that bad?"

"Nah," the captain answered, "he said that's good. I don't know—whenever I have a sinus headache, it's always right there . . . right in the frontal lobe . . . in the cavities right up above your eyes . . . above your eyebrows."

"You got cavities all over your head . . . sinuses all over . . . nose, eyes, ears. An X ray?"

"Yeah."

"My next-door neighbor, when I saw him, I said the doctor told me that I had a sinus infection. He said, did he take an X ray? I said, no. He said, how in hell does he know . . . I said, hey, I don't know—he's the doctor."

"This is the doctor you want me to see?"

"Yeah. Well, like I said, he ain't an eye-nose man . . . but whatever he gave me helped . . . I think. . . . Maybe it didn't. . . . Maybe I just got well on my own."

The flight controller cleared the King Air for take-off. He watched the Beechcraft roll down the taxiway and stop at the end of runway three four. He said, "After departure, turn right heading zero one zero."

"Papa Charlie cleared for takeoff zero one zero."

The flight controller watched the plane glide down the runway. The captain said, "Mitchell gave me a shot last Monday and it had all kinds of powerful stuff in it, gave me some antihistaminic decongestant and all this stuff, and it didn't do a damn thing."

The first officer said, "The decongestant I had didn't help me at all. Ignition . . . autofeather . . . lights. Ninety knots."

The flight controller pushed the button on his microphone. "King Air three zero Papa Charlie, contact departure. Good day."

"Right on. King Air Papa Charlie with ya out of one for three."

The flight controller watched the airplane gain altitude and disappear into the gray, thickening clouds.

John Major's voice came over the radio. "I got a carrier on but no modulation."

The controller heard the sound of the altitude alert alarm buzz softly. What? he thought. They have to be at least fifteen hundred feet off the ground.

Captain Holmes' voice came over the tower's radio speakers, "Tower, thirty Papa Charlie."

"Thirty Papa Charlie Pensacola."

Again, the sound of ratcheting crackled over the speakers. An indistinguishable blur of static followed. Then, barely audible, "Unable," static, "Nineteen," static, "Nothing."

They're having trouble with their radio, the flight controller thought, or maybe it's just the connection with departure. He said, "Two three zero Papa Charlie reattempt one niner point zero and if no contact, return this frequency and I'll tell 'em."

Again, the sound of ratcheting filled the tower.

The captain's voice came over the radio. It was tense, both words said with force. "Holy . . . shit!"

The first officer, the excitement evident in his voice, said, "What the hell was that?"

Jake Horton said, "Fire."

The flight controller listened to the sound of ratcheting. Then, he heard it again. Then, a third time.

The captain said, "God, Vance."

The controller thought, who's Vance?

First Officer Major said, "We got a fire in the back."

The landing-gear warning horn began its mournful song. The roar of the engines suddenly turned to a purr. The flight controller thought, he's pulled back on the power.

The captain's voice echoed out of the tower's radio. "Drop the pressure!"

The first officer answered faintly, "Huh?"

"Drop the pressure. Tower, gotta 'mergency . . . thirty Papa Charlie got a 'mergency."

The flight controller listened to departure call the Beechcraft. "King Air three zero Papa Charlie Pensacola departure, how do you hear?"

The flight controller listened to a sound, like rushing air, whoosh over the tower's radio speaker.

The captain said, "We're on fire!"

The flight controller listened helplessly to indecipherable sounds pouring over the speakers. Then, he heard propeller noise blended with static.

Suddenly there was nothing—not even background static.

The flight controller's hand was shaking as he made the sign of the cross.

Vorpagel asked, "So, murder, accident, suicide?"

Gary answered, "We don't have enough information."

"You're absolutely right. The insurance company claimed that Jake committed suicide, thereby nulling the insurance policy."

"What did they base that on?"

Vorpagel took a number of slides from his briefcase. "These contain an airplane accident report from the National Transportation Safety Board (NTSB)." He fiddled with the slides, turned off the lights, and flashed an image on the screen. The following appeared:

The passenger, Jake Horton, was a Senior Vice-President with the Gulf Power Company, Pensacola, Florida. It was reported that he had been employed with Gulf Power since 1956. Mr. Horton was reported to be a person who gets things done. It was also reported that the company was his life and that he would not allow anyone or anything to stand in his way.

Mrs. Horton said he had spent an unremarkable weekend prior to going to the office on Monday, April 10, 1989. On the day of the accident, Mrs. Horton said that Mr. Horton had arrived home about 12:00 noon and had departed between 12:30 and 12:40. He reportedly told her that he was going to Atlanta to see Edward; he was tired of all the finger pointing.

Marcus asked, "Who's Edward and what does 'finger pointing' mean?"

"Edward was Jake's old boss. Ed Addison ran Gulf Power for years. At the time of the accident, he was president of the Southern Company. Gulf Power was a subsidiary of Southern, as was the aviation company, Southern Services. The finger pointing takes a longer explanation."

"Bad management?" Ava, the woman from the Department of Corrections, asked.

"Among other things. That is, if you call graft, misuse of manpower, illegal political donations, and illegal misuse of funds bad management."

"So," Shui said, "the management got caught. Then, they started pointing the finger. I assume most of the fingers ended up aimed at Jake Horton."

"Gulf Power's audit committee voted the previous Friday to fire Horton."

"He was to be the fall guy."

"Yes," Vorpagel said, "but no one told him that day. Jake heard about it from a lawyer friend of his, Fred Levin, on Monday morning. Horton had a memo from the President of Gulf Power, Douglas McCrary, to meet him and Doctor Reed Bell, chairman of the audit committee, that afternoon. Horton knew why—he was getting the ax."

Ava asked, "How did Addison feel about all this?"

"He was quoted as saying, 'I'm sick about it.' Horton knew that his only chance to hang on to power was to get to Addison. Jake called . . ." Vorpagel paused, scanned a sheet of paper, then continued, "at quarter to ten, Monday morning, Southern Company Services and scheduled a flight to Atlanta. That's where Addison lived."

"So he was flying to Atlanta when the plane crashed."

"A few things happened before he got to the airport. His wife said that before leaving their home, Jake went to a private bathroom off the garage. He washed his hands, but he left his wedding band and university ring, from Auburn, on a ledge. Then he . . ."

Gary said, "The two most important rings in a professional man's life. Is this why they suspected suicide?"

Vorpagel answered, "Among other things. This man was known as Mr. Gulf Power throughout the Florida panhandle. He'd worked for the corporation for over three decades. His life was crumbling before him."

"You said," Marcus rasped, "it was a case of either suicide, accident, or murder. How can any of this lead to suspected murder? And why? Cover-up? Fear of Horton blowing the whistle?"

"All of the above, plus a few other things—like two anonymous phone calls and a few dead canaries."

"What?"

"I'll get to that later. Jake packed a few things while he was in that bathroom, sans wedding and university ring. He'd had a colostomy. He packed the necessary equipment for cleaning the defecation that would periodically fill the bag. He also placed an old T-shirt and a Mason jar, full of alcohol, into a bowling bag."

"Alcohol?" Shui said. "Do you mean distilled spirits for drinking? Or rubbing alcohol?"

"The alcohol wasn't for drinking."

"So the investigators think he started a fire, using the alcohol and T-shirt."

"Let me show you the last page of the National Transportation Safety Board report." Vorpagel changed the slide.

Mr. Douglas McCrary, President of Gulf Power Company, reported that the Monday meeting with Mr. Horton was to tell him that he would be separated from the company. Mr. McCrary also reported that an effort was made to have Mr. Levin talk to Mr. Horton and try to get him to take a reasonable approach to the separation. Mr. McCrary stated that during the meeting when he told Mr. Horton of his impending separation from Gulf Power, Mr. Horton reportedly took it very calmly and asked what his options were. After being given the options, Mr. Horton reportedly told Mr. McCrary that he would give him his answer later in the afternoon and left the office.

Ava said, "To head for Atlanta and Addison. He was not going to go gently into that sweet night—Horton was going to rage, rage, rage."

Vorpagel nodded and pointed at the screen.

While at the crash site, a conversation was overheard that Mr. Horton had a thing about shining his shoes and always carried shoe polish and a jar of alcohol with him.

Shui said, "This explains why he carried the flammable on board."

"It does?"

"Who made the statement about Horton being a fanatic about shining his shoes?"

"Exactly. We've never found out."

"Was it true?"

"Yes, Horton used alcohol to spit polish his shoes. But this alone does not eliminate the possibility of suicide. Jake Horton was an intelligent man. If he was bent on self-destruction, he was clever enough to use material he knew would not give away his plot. To kill himself and still have the life insurance go to his wife."

Vorpagel changed slides. Another portion of the report appeared on the screen:

All during the on-site investigation, there was continual talk about the Southern Company being investigated by a Grand Jury for fraud, misappropriation of funds, illegal political contributions, and so on.

During the briefing at the PNS ATC facility it was reported that within a few hours of the accident, the

FAA control tower had received an anonymous telephone call that said something like: You can stop investigating Gulf Power now. We took care of that this afternoon. The Escambia County Sheriff's office received a similar call at about the same time frame.

Marcus said, "There's no mention of dead canaries."

"Ah, yes. Now we come to the dead canaries."

Gary asked, "Where does this information come from?"

Vorpagel reached into his briefcase and removed a wad of papers. "While this was going on, newspapers from Atlanta to Miami covered the story." He held up the papers. "A magazine called *Florida Trends* covered the story." He peered at the papers. "In a two-part article, 'Abuse of Power I,' and 'Abuse of Power II,' written by Elizabeth Wilson."

Vorpagel tossed the papers on his desk. "Later the PSC covered the story, then the IRS covered the story."

"What about the canaries?"

Vorpagel said, "The canaries began to appear on people's doorsteps. Levin, Horton's friend, received three. One outside each of his two homes, the third at his Pensacola law office."

Gary said, "What in the devil was that all about?"

"I'll get to that. But there was something else. Frank Patti was Horton's next-door neighbor for seventeen years. He saw Jake as he was leaving his home for the airport. He asked Patti to arrange a meeting of their local Bayou Chico restoration committee."

"Would he arrange a meeting if he was going to commit suicide?"

"A clever man would." Vorpagel pointed at the screen.

Information received April 1990 from the NTSB indicates that Mr. Horton paid off the remaining principal of $7,740.99 on his house mortgage on April 10, 1989. That just "happens" to be the day of the crash. Mortgage records indicate that from 1980 through the end of 1987, he had only made the required monthly payment of $193.32 and had never made any payments in addition to that required monthly payment.

Shui said, "I find this significant."

Vorpagel asked, "In which direction?"

"That this was a suicide. He was cleaning up his affairs. It's a common reaction when we know, or think, we are going to die."

"So a big point lands as a vote for suicide."

"Except," Shui said, "I have two big votes cast under murder: the canaries and the phone calls."

Gary said, "And why was he killed?"

"You don't have enough information yet," Vorpagel said. "Let's talk motives, for all three possibilities: suicide, accident, murder."

Marcus said, "There's no motive in an accident."

"How about intentional negligence?"

"Sabotage? Something completely unrelated to Horton's death?"

Vorpagel shrugged. "Possible. Before you can start eliminating possibilities you have to consider them all."

"The motive for suicide is easy," Shui said. "Horton was facing public disgrace. He was losing the job he loved, the life he loved, the power and prestige he held."

"What about the motives for murder?"

"I'd have to hear more about what type of misbehavior was going on at Gulf Power."

"They were misbehaving all right. There was big money floating about. Southern Company's gross in 1988 was $7.2 billion, with a net of almost a billion."

"That's a big pot to play with."

"They played with it. Gulf Power employees remodeled Addison's home."

"Pro bono."

"Yes, for free, materials and labor. According to published accounts, the company's heads liked entertaining. They blew $89,000 on one weekend. During the entire eighties, they funneled illegal contributions to politicians. The Gulf Power Company was charged with 123 counts of improper transactions with its own vendors. They used phony receipts to the vendors to raise cash for the politicians. The company faced fines totaling over fifty million."

"But why should Horton have to hold the bag? Big corporations sweep fines under the balance sheet like advertising costs."

"Horton was big time. He was connected. The kind of guy who gets mail with fancy autographs. Like personal Christmas cards from Reagan, Bush, Quayle."

"No Democrats?" Gary asked.

"Gary Hart and Michael Dukakis sent thank-you notes also. The donations were a guarantee that no matter who won, a friendly face would be in office."

"Companies don't just suddenly start defrauding everything in sight."

"Neither did Gulf Power. The President before Addison was Ellis. He started using company employees for a few odd jobs: reseeding his lawn, building a fountain, putting in a sprinkler system. Years later, near the end, some of the company hot-shots were using one of their vendors, West Florida Landscaping, to maintain their yards. In Wilson's article, she wrote that employees claimed that Addison provided women and booze for politicians. Some of the power company's best customers were appliance stores. Free refrigerators, freezers, stoves, on and on."

Ava said, "Big perks."

"Exactly. You have to remember, this was a utility company. The rate payers were picking up the bill for all this. Fishing-trip weekends ran ten to twenty thousand."

Vorpagel looked around the room. The others were rapt. They were listening to a lot of facts. Facts are supposed to lead to the truth, a logical conclusion.

The mentor had an advantage. He knew the punch line. He could dole out information as he pleased.

He said, "Here's something for you to think about."

He thumbed through a stack of papers; some appeared to be newspaper clippings and legal briefs, the usual stuff he carried with him whenever he made a presentation like this.

"Gulf Power was never very bashful about how it spent money or how they could get their customers to foot the bill. We're talking millions of dollars. Some of it may have been legally spent, but a lot of it wasn't."

"But they're a public utility," Gary said, "a regulated agency. Where's the oversight? What about the

Public Service Commission? Maybe the PSC's a player?"

"Not likely," countered Vorpagel. "Gulf's graft was too well disguised. They were thumbing their nose at the public and getting away with it."

Gary said, "If that was true, then the IRS would never be able to prove anything."

"I don't think that the PSC was guilty of anything intentional besides sloppy procedures and protecting Gulf's interests in political issues, and looking out for executives became Horton's forte."

Ava said, "Horton was the procurer. That's what made it easy for everybody to point at him, to make him take the fall."

"For everybody else." Vorpagel referred to some legal papers. "I do not use Gulf employees' names during my presentation. This is about Jake Horton, not what was going on at Gulf Power. But what the company was doing raised the specter of the possibility of murder by someone."

Gary said, "Murder, the mob, and canaries."

Vorpagel nodded. "Two members of the Gulf Power team were also in the soup."

"Horton took the fall for them, too?" asked Marcus.

"Let's look at their roles before we jump to that conclusion. One was supervisor of general services. The warehouse, building maintenance, transportation. That sort of thing. He was in a position to procure, and then cover the procurement. He was a fox in the hen house."

"What about the other?"

"He ran the warehouse. Between the two of them, covering up executive expenses was pretty easy."

Shui asked, "Like how?"

"They could get anything they wanted. And they often did. Then, they used the spoils to enrich some companies they ran on the side. But they couldn't do it alone."

"Inside deals?" asked Marcus.

"Sure," nodded Vorpagel. "They used Gulf employees, outside vendors, accountants. Whoever could help in the scheme. They didn't mind sharing the wealth. They were making a lot of people happy."

Gary shook his head. "I've seen this sort of phenomenon before. One hand goes into the cookie jar and the next thing you know, everybody's hand is in the cookie jar."

"And the cookie jar becomes empty."

Vorpagel continued. "Quite a few Gulf Power employees, especially those that worked for these two, knew what was going on. Things got casual; the underlings began to attach their nicknames to some of the stuff. When they did something for an executive or a fellow worker, it was called an 007 job. The repair shop became known as the hobby shop. Pretty soon, they were using company trucks with Gulf's name covered up. Even private citizens noticed what was going on."

Marcus said, "They became more and more blatant."

"When Doug McCrary took over as President, he hired an outside security agency to investigate. He demanded and got both men's resignation."

"But that didn't stop the activity."

"What happened, the terminated supervisor began

to seethe about getting the boot. Everyone else besides him and his buddy were still playing the same old tune, at least in his mind. He sued every top executive.

"Believe it or not," Vorpagel said, "he claimed he had no choice but to go along with things. He said that Gulf executives made it clear that he was to help provide assistance to the politicos, the Gulf VIPs, whoever needed something."

"Maybe," Ava said, "they shouldn't have let him go."

"That's exactly what an FBI agent said." Vorpagel glanced at some legal papers. He wanted to be sure he had the right date. And the right plea.

He said, "Let's move ahead to the federal court in Atlanta. October 31, 1989. Quite a date for Gulf Power."

"Time to pay the piper?" asked Ava.

"But with a safety net for some."

"Confess and cover your butt?" offered Marcus.

"And how," replied Vorpagel. "The company pled guilty to two charges of conspiracy. Felony charges. They admitted to a tax fraud deal that involved some illegal campaign contributions. And they confessed to rigging some vendor invoices."

"Kind of a public absolution," Shui said.

"Exactly."

Marcus asked, "So what was their penance?"

"A cool half-billion dollars. For violating the Public Utility Company Act. Of course, they said it was Jake Horton's fault, and the federal court bought it. No doubt about it, Jake was wearing the black hat, and Gulf wanted the whole world to know."

Marcus said, "Blame the dead guy."

"Who else? Now you're getting close to why my firm became involved in all this."

Ava asked, "The court ruling must have been good news for the Gulf execs?"

"For some, sure. But it was bad news for Horton's widow and friends."

"Jake was the fall guy," Ava said.

"Absolutely," agreed Vorpagel. "There was an 'us and them' mentality at Gulf headquarters. And Gulf's big boys thought they were bulletproof."

Gary said, "Everyone involved wanted deniability."

"This is a case," Vorpagel said, "that obviously involves greed, but did that greed lead to suicide, or murder, or was the whole thing just a coincidence, an accident?"

Ava said, "I have checks under murder and suicide, none under accident."

"Perhaps you should read more of what the National Transportation Safety Board discovered."

At 12:49:38, the Cockpit Voice Recorder (CVR) tape indicated that the crew observed the passenger drive up while they were still taxiing toward the hangar. . . . Upon boarding, the passenger sat in the left rear seat and placed the luggage he was carrying in front of his feet. . . . The hangar attendant made the comment that he did not notice any irregularities with the aircraft such as smoke, leaks, or odd sounds while the aircraft was on the ramp or while it taxied out.

The hangar attendant and another Southern employee noted that the passenger did not have a suit coat or briefcase with him, as he normally did. Also, Mr. Horton did not use the phone in the facility, nor was he using the car phone when he pulled up, which he normally did.

Gary asked, "Did the NTSB find this significant? I mean, the guy was facing termination, and headed toward the one man—for a face-to-face—that he thought could save him. Why place an emphasis on not using the phone?"

"State of mind."

"Of course, but indicative of what? Intent on saving his job, or committing suicide?"

"That's part of the puzzle."

"I don't think we have enough specific knowledge either. I'm a lawyer, but I have to get the raw data. I expect that this puzzle will, sooner or later, end up with interrogatories and depositions."

Vorpagel flashed on a slide from the NTSB report:

Radar indicated the aircraft reached a maximum altitude of 2,400 feet in a left turn. The aircraft then made what appeared to be a normal descent to 1,900 feet, then a rapid descent to 500 feet, then climbed to 800 feet, then descended to 300 feet, at which time radar contact was lost.

Several witnesses observed the aircraft descending out of overcast and reported a continuous trail of dark smoke coming from the aircraft as it descended to the surface.

"I'm not a pilot," Marcus said. "Is there anything significant about the descent that I should know?"

"The pilot was obviously fighting the descent, in a rather erratic manner."

"Caused by?"

Vorpagel shrugged and pushed a button on the projector.

There was extreme thermal damage to the inspection cover under the left rear seat. The inspection cover was partially melted and was sagging below the floor area.

The location of the broken tree limbs showed that the aircraft was in a near wings level attitude when it traveled between the trees. . . . The aircraft continued on a heading of 185 degrees and contacted a cluster of trees along the north side of an apartment complex. The aircraft then collided with the north side of a four-plex apartment building, continued through the four-plex, and entered the second four-plex where it came to rest in an upright position. . . . Impact forces and postcrash fire destroyed two four-plexes and most of the aircraft wreckage.

Ava asked, "How many died on the ground?"

"Miraculously, none. All eight units were being renovated. The roofs of the entire complex were stripped off. I have a photograph. I also have photos of the remains of the fuselage, a pencil sketch of the seating layout in the plane, and a sketch made by the Escambia Sheriff's Department of the crash/crime scene."

"Crash/crime scene?"

"When you read some of the depositions, you'll find that some witnesses refer to the site as a crash, others a crime scene." Vorpagel passed two photos and two sketches to the class.

Marcus pointed at the picture of the plane's wreckage. "It looks like the plane landed in straight and level flight, even after skimming off the top of eight apartment buildings."

"Which means?"

"I'm not sure. Another confusing point. First, the pilot appears to be affected by the carbon monoxide, the erratic descent; then, he suddenly starts to fly the plane again."

"Which leads you to conclude?"

"Nothing. Yet."

Shui pointed at the pencil sketch of the plane. "What's the remains of a Mason jar doing there. I thought it was in the bowling bag?"

"It was when he entered the plane."

"So I'm supposed to believe he's polishing his shoes while he's in an airplane that's just taken off?"

Vorpagel shrugged again and hit the projector's button.

Remains of a briefcase that contained expense reports and personal papers of one of the pilots were located in the aisle alongside the left seat. In front of the left center seat were the remains of a suitcase that contained a hair dryer and shoe brush. Under the left center seat, there was a vinyl bag that resembled the shape but slightly larger than that of a bowling ball bag. The bag sustained some fire damage but was generally in fair condition. The zipper closure was open.

It was reported that a book of safety matches was

adhered to the outside of the bag. The contents included among other things, a ring and cap for a "Mason" jar, a white T-shirt that disintegrated when any force was applied to the fabric, more safety matches, other clothing, and two containers of shoe polish.

Shui asked, "Was Jake a smoker?"

"Nope," Vorpagel answered and flashed another slide.

The cockpit fire extinguisher located under the co-pilot's seat was still secured in the mounting bracket with the safety pin installed. Two quick-donning oxygen masks for the crew were located in the cockpit area. One of the masks had the dust cover installed. The other mask did not have the cover installed and was plugged into the outlet fitting.

Marcus asked, "How long was it from the time the Captain said 'shit' to impact?"

Vorpagel glanced at a folder in front of him and said, "The pilot said 'Holy shit' at 12:59:15—the last engine propeller noise was at 13:00:01."

Marcus did a rapid calculation. "Forty-six seconds. Why didn't they try to use the fire extinguisher? Why weren't the gas masks donned?"

"Why indeed?"

"Was a maintenance schedule given to you?"

Vorpagel opened a file. "This is another report from the National Transportation Safety Board. The NTSB called it a Factual Report Aviation, as opposed to the first report I gave you, which is called a Narrative

Report. The maintenance report is on 2e." He placed a
slide in the projector.

> There was a system of oxygen system leaks in 1988.
> . . . A leak at the valve for the first aid outlet above the
> "Potty was found and the valve replaced." . . . No fur-
> ther write ups of the oxygen system pressure were
> found until February 12, 1989. The write-up stated
> "O_2 is low." No record of a corrective action was
> found.

Ava said, "This might indicate that there was no
oxygen available, but it still doesn't answer why they
never donned their masks in the first place, or used the
fire extinguisher."

"Play a game that I have over and over," Vorpagel
said. "Imagine what happened that fits the facts available, if this was murder."

Vorpagel watched them concentrate. Marcus
raised his hand. "I can think of what might have happened, if this was murder."

Jacob F. Horton, Senior Vice President in Gulf
Power Company, got out of the car. He gave two pieces
of luggage to the hangar attendant. They were a hanging bag and a suitcase. The hangar attendant was also
carrying a small bag—the pilot's lunch. Horton was carrying a small red bag and another black bag that looked
like a bowling ball bag.

The left engine of the King Air was shut down to
facilitate boarding the passenger. Jake Horton walked
up the short stairs, entered the plane, and said to the pilot, "Hi, guy."

The captain said, "How you doin'?"

"Messy over there."

"It's cold and wet, but it's not a real bad thunderstorm."

The flight controller and the captain exchanged information about takeoff.

Jake Horton said, "It's almost like winter out there."

The captain said, "Sure is."

John Major left the airplane and jogged to the hangar.

Marcus finished with, "How does anyone know what was really in the supposed lunch bag the hangar attendant was carrying? He could have been paid to place a bomb. The plane was only in the air for forty-six seconds after fire was noticed. If the killers used altitude bombs that go off after a certain height is reached, it would fit the scenario."

"How does that work?"

"If they used one of those and set it low, two thousand feet, the bomb would be safe from detection. The killers knew no one would open a lunch pail until the plane reached flying altitude. This scenario would explain the phone calls and the dead canaries."

"So, there is a possibility that this was murder?"

"Except one problem," Vorpagel said. "If this was murder, if they used a bomb, then it either misfired and only partially detonated, or the killers were hopelessly inadequate. If I were going to blow up a plane, I'd use a bomb big enough to do the job in the air. Remember the Unabomber's first few, feeble efforts at bombs. His altimeter was fine, but his explosive was the wrong type. In this case, despite all the confusion surrounding everything else, the pilot still managed to hit the trees in straight and level flight. If he'd been lucky enough to come down over a field or a parking lot, he might have landed safely."

"And the people who usually send dead canaries are not known as being hopelessly inadequate," Marcus said. "However, semibureaucrats who work for entities like public utility commissions have been known to botch jobs, especially if the job is out of their area of expertise."

"So, this could be a badly planned murder."

"Keep the thought. But what if this were suicide?"

Gary said, "I still can't get over Horton leaving his two most important rings behind."

"If Jake Horton were a suicide, isn't that just the thing he would do?"

"Why?"

"He might leave the rings behind if he knew he was going to cause a plane to crash. His wife was going to get back a charred corpse. Couldn't Horton have wanted her to have his wedding ring intact?"

Shui said, "I can imagine a possible scenario, if this was a suicide. Except it didn't start at the airport, it started in Horton's home."

The attractive Asian woman closed her eyes and began speaking what her mind was visualizing.

He opened the colostomy bag and dumped the contents down the toilet. Then, as he had so many times since having the operation, he went through motions that—in some parts of the world—give rise to terms like the "clean hand" and the "foul hand."

First, he removed his University of Auburn ring. Then, his wedding band. He cleaned the colostomy bag, running tap water into it, and flushing the last remnants of defecation down the sink.

Using a bar of soap, he vigorously scrubbed his hands. He paused. He looked up into the mirror attached to the wall above the small sink. He studied his own eyes—really looked inside.

It's over, he thought, I'm ruined. Disgraced, front-page news, the wife and kids on a media parade—look at them—family of the man accused of raping Gulf.

Would Addison help?

Could Addison help?

Even if Addison wanted to, would his intervention make a difference?

In the distance, he heard the bark of a dog, a plaintive howl, filled with loneliness.

I am that dog, he thought. Alone—after accomplishing so much—alone. Except for my wife, my family. And, if it truly comes out, stained for the rest of their lives with my mark.

The insurance was in force. Paid in full.

All I need is means.

He went into the garage. A five gallon can of gas was resting against the rear wall.

No good. Too easy for the investigators. There is only one way for automobile fuel to end up on an airplane—it's lugged on.

What was available that would not be suspect?

He opened his look-alike bowling bag that

carried the paraphernalia he took on trips. The items he needed to maintain his colostomy bag. A few personal items for cleanliness. A few items for maintaining his clothes.

He picked up the shoe polish and held it in his hand. Then, he set it down on the sink. He removed the soiled T-shirt he used to buff his shoes and set it next to the shoe polish. Then he removed the half-filled Mason jar—the glass canister containing alcohol for spit-shining his shoes.

He put everything back in his bag.

He checked to make sure that he had matches.

Then, he looked at the two rings still resting on the ledge above the sink.

How dangerous was it to leave them?

This would be investigated.

He smiled. He was right—this would be investigated, by intelligent men. The rings would shout: suicide!

But only at first.

Just as the early payoff of his mortgage would shout suicide—but only at first.

Then, the investigators, the psychiatrists, the police would start to dig. What would they find? An organized man—a fighter—a member of the intelligentsia.

Would one of the elite— one of their own—be so stupid?

Of course not.

They would analyze. They would reconstruct. They would decide that someone with his education would not do this. Someone with his education, if he really were contemplating suicide, would realize that leaving the rings would be a fatal flaw. *Ergo*, he would never do it. *Ergo*, if he did, it was simply an oversight, caused by the upcoming emotional meeting with Addison, a meeting only he was sure was doomed.

He finished drying his hands.

He filled the Mason jar with rubbing alcohol. Then he left for the airport.

· · ·

Shui said, "Eliminating suicide, at least intellectually, is not as easy as murder."

"I agree," Vorpagel said. "If Horton was really contemplating suicide, then—and remember he was intelligent—he would have prepared. In that case, he never would have left his rings behind. However, if he was distraught, planning his defense, preparing his pitch to Addison, then he was distracted. We've all been there. We have a fight with the wife, or our kids, we plan what we are going to say, reworking the presentation, rewording the delivery. We do this while doing other things, driving, eating, showering, shaving. We think about other things while performing the routine."

Gary said, "I saw him readying his colostomy bag— for him, a routine. He was washing his hands, but he wasn't really in the bathroom off the garage. He was mentally in Addison's office in Atlanta. He was preparing for the pitch of his professional life. There's a possibility, when he left that bathroom. He was not distraught, he was not depressed. He was coolly analytical and in control of his anger, like a knight of old before a joust, or a professional athlete before a game. Horton was working himself up for what was to come."

Vorpagel commented, "He seemed calm when he talked to his neighbor Patti and to the airplane's pilots."

"Outward calm," Ava said, "doesn't always equate with inward peace."

"Exactly," Vorpagel agreed. "But Horton did do other things. He planned to attend a meeting with Patti the following week. In Mrs. Horton's testimony, she stated that he had told her that if he came home that night, there was a TV show he wanted to see. How would you imagine this case if it were an accident?"

"I wouldn't try," Marcus said. "That should be left in the hands of the investigators. I know how varied and complex things can be—and look—in an accident. I still keep coming back, in my mind, to Horton's demeanor before he got on that plane."

"Have you ever been with a man before he goes into battle?"

"Yes," Marcus said, "I've been there."

"Then you know he will mention the most inane things: nice weather, I think I'm getting a cold, chow was the pits. Anything but what he is really thinking: Am I going to die? Am I going to be maimed? Horton planned a meeting for the next week with Patti. His wife said he told her that if he came home that night, there was a TV program he wanted to watch. He mentioned the weather to the captain; then, there was the odd conversation explaining why he brought clothes for an overnight stay. Mundane, everyday chitchat. His mind was elsewhere."

"Wouldn't his mind be elsewhere if he knew he was going to die soon? Like a soldier before combat? The soldier is wondering: Am I going to die? Not I am going to die in few minutes. Different: one a possibility, the other an absolute."

Vorpagel said, "I was called in to investigate this

particular case on March 8, 1991, by Bill Wagner, the attorney representing Jake Horton's widow. Wagner's a hardworking, honest lawyer—with his client's interests at heart. If you ever need a lawyer, I hope you get one the caliber of Bill Wagner."

"Quite a testimonial," Shui said.

"No, just the truth. Once I got back East, I reviewed the autopsy reports. I also saw the aircraft. I reviewed the pathology found at the autopsy and concluded that the failure to use the oxygen mask resulted in the pilots' inhaling the smoke, which contained carbon monoxide, which had some physiological effect on them, which may have contributed to this crash."

Ava asked, "Do you know how fast a person is affected by carbon monoxide?"

"Just two or three breaths is enough. Your blood circulates through your body in your major vessels about three times in one minute. Normally, we only breathe about twelve breaths a minute, but you take a couple of deep breaths under stress or excitement and there is going to be rapid absorption of carbon monoxide."

"How do you reverse the . . ."

"Inhalation of oxygen."

"Was the time that the fire lasted long enough for the pilots to lose consciousness?"

"No."

"Would it affect their ability to operate the plane?"

"I can only speculate. It would depend on how healthy they were. Whether they were in good shape or not."

Gary asked, "How about the failure of the pilots to use the oxygen masks?"

"Correct. That would impair them."

"How so?" Marcus asked.

"By using the argument of exclusion, they crashed."

"That doesn't necessarily lead to a conclusion. They could have been flying in the highest standards and . . ."

Ava said, "From the aerial photographs I've seen, it appeared that the pilot was attempting to land. He almost made it. I think he was aiming for a large parking lot and didn't quite make it. I think he didn't make it because he was impaired. Remember the wildly erratic descent? Plummeting then soaring?"

"Yes," Vorpagel agreed. "What else?"

"The carboxyhemoglobin count . . ."

"Yes, the difference between the count in the three occupants of the aircraft."

"That would be explained by the fact that neither pilot donned his oxygen mask."

"That would appear to be the case. Except . . ."

"Except?"

"One oxygen mask was off the hook. That appears to be an attempt on the part of the pilot to at least try and don the mask."

"The copilot?"

"Mask still on the hook."

Shui scanned the NTSB report. She pointed at a line and asked, "What made the whooshing sound?"

"What do you think?"

"When you examined the wreckage, were the windows open or closed?"

"One was smashed open."

"The captain's."

"Yes."

"Then, I think I've figured out part of the problem. Whatever happened, accident, murder, or suicide, a fire starts. The carbon monoxide affects everyone on board—witness the erratic descent. Then, the captain smashes his side window and inhales fresh oxygen. It clears his head; he regains control of the aircraft. He almost lands it safely, but catches the tops of trees and the apartment complex."

Vorpagel said, "I agree. That re-creates what I think happened on the airplane that last forty-six seconds."

Gary asked, "To save time, tell me where the fire actually broke out."

"There were two hot spots. One of them underneath and in front of the copilot and the instrument panel. The other, the open vent just to the rear of Mr. Horton's seat."

"Two hot spots? To the same degree?"

"No, the one near Horton was a much more intense . . ."

"Didn't the plane catch fire upon impact?"

"Absolutely. But there are ways of determining what started first, and to what degree."

"How?" Ava asked.

"Various tests, done by experts. I didn't perform the tests myself, just analyzed the results."

"And they were?"

"The first hot spot was near Horton's seat."

"Then that would indicate he started the fire."

"It would?"

Shui said, "If Horton didn't start the fire, what else

could have? Do fuel lines run underneath the floor of the main body of the plane?"

"Yes."

"Did anyone test for a leak?" Marcus asked.

"One was found."

"So the fuel ignited by accident and . . ."

"What could have sparked the ignition?"

Ava said, "The second hot spot was behind the instrument panel?"

"Yes."

"In the NTSB report, it mentioned the pilot was having trouble with his radio."

"Yes."

"Then a possible explanation is that fuel leaked into the bottom of the airplane, fumes built up, and a short in the radio sparked the fire."

Gary said, "Horton paid off the remaining balance of his mortgage the morning he died. You have his mortgage record from 1980 to 1987. What happened in 1988 and 1989?"

"In 1988, Jake paid off $4,806.68 in principal, in addition to his monthly payment."

"I thought you said he only made straight payments for years."

"He did. But then, he changed patterns. On March 13, 1989, he made a payment of $5,193.32."

"So the early payoff was part of a plan, a long-range plan, and it was only coincidental that the final payment was on the day he died."

"That's the way I saw it."

"So," Gary said, "it wasn't suicide. That leaves murder or accident."

"My gut hunch," Marcus said, "is I don't think it was murder, but I can't get the dead canaries out of my mind. Or anonymous phone calls."

"Think," Vorpagel said, "think, imagine, create scenarios in your minds."

Gary said, "A possibility. The local underworld saw this accident as a possibility to cash in very cheaply on something they didn't have a thing to do with. Make a few calls, kill a few birds, and scare everyone to death. It left the door open, before the case was determined to be caused by accident, to create a bunch of very frightened executives. What a great potential for extortion."

"You're right," Vorpagel said. "That was the buzz back then. Bill Wagner said that, while this was originally going on, he conducted a straw poll. Asking waiters, taxi drivers what they thought. He asked one cabby, 'You ever heard of the Jake Horton case?' The cabby replied, 'You mean the guy the mob offed?' "

The class grinned.

Gary said, "So maybe they did just kill a few canaries, for publicity."

Vorpagel nodded. "If organized crime really had killed Horton, for a fee, would they have so blatantly, and publicly, advertised it by leaving canaries around?"

"No way."

"What about this," Ava said. "A Gulf Power executive saw Horton's death as an opportunity to scare everyone involved in the company's fraudulent activities into silence."

"Possible," Vorpagel said.

Marcus asked, "What materials did Horton carry in his bowling bag to take care of his colostomy?"

"Part of the normal paraphernalia was match-books."

"Why matchbooks?"

"To diffuse the odor from the bag when he cleaned it. You know, sulfur. The insurance company placed great importance on the matchbooks and that certain trace chemicals found in nitrocellulose were present at the scene. They didn't follow through on what chemicals Horton was carrying in his colostomy kit. The same ingredients, except in minute quantities."

Vorpagel picked up a piece of chalk, went to the blackboard, and said, "I am now going to walk you through a postautopsy on suicidal tendencies."

Gary asked, "What is your method for doing them?"

"Attempting to find out as much of the individual's background, past, and recent past, especially the prior ninety days, and any history of suicide in the family. Whether or not he's made good-bye phone calls, which we call hello phone calls. By that, I mean calling people that he hasn't talked to in ten or fifteen or twenty years saying, 'Hi, Uncle Charlie, this is your brother's kid. Yeah, I know I haven't talked to you.' That sort of thing. They're good-bye calls."

"What for?" Marcus asked. "Why call someone you've lost contact with over the years."

"Precisely. A change in pattern. He knows he's going to die. He wants to talk one last time to people who mattered to him over the course of his *entire* life. Not just lately."

"What else is a sign?"

"Whether or not he has made specific recent gifts

to others, such as, 'Here, I'm no longer a cop. I won't need this off-duty gun anymore.' "

"Is this a list you've developed," Shui asked, "or is it a list that you've derived from other sources?"

"It's a list that has been derived from four psychiatrists' writings that we have compounded and put together, and that we use when we teach crisis intervention in barricaded gunmen, suicide. By cop types of hostage negotiations. Now what do we know about Jake Horton?"

Gary said, "Jake Horton had short-range planning. The meeting next week with Patti; the TV show to watch with his wife. People planning suicide, even if they're trying to cover it up, and don't know what things like short-range planning mean to a psychiatrist, don't even think to do them."

"All right. What else?"

Shui said, "There was not an incendiary device used to ignite or set fire to the plane."

"Based on?"

"There were several other 'hot spots' in the wreckage other than the one near the deceased's chair."

"You're right. Reports of 'traces' of hydrochloric and sulfuric acids in the area are attributable to other materials in the plane, and the use of certain chemicals used to put out the fire. They are not *indicia* of a hypergolic substance used for an incendiary device."

Ava said, "It is my opinion that some other source was the precipitating factor. Probably a puddling of fuel in the low spots of the airplane's inspection holes that partially were left open and the fumes of which were ignited by a hot gear or electrical shorts emitting sparks that ignited the fumes. The NTSB report shows that there were prior problems with maintenance in this plane, and no corrective procedures were reported."

"Again, good. In order to make a determination in this type of case, we must use the process of elimination and exclusion. There are many possible sources of fire. Here, it has been established that the sources of such fire were *not* explosives, incendiary devices, lightning, smoldering trash, chemical spontaneous combustion, resulting in a spread from some other nearby source. Therefore, we must speculate as to other possibilities. Think."

Marcus said, "Improper maintenance. The NTSB report suggests a puddling of gas, this would indicate a definite lack of maintenance. Combined with comments in part one as to other repairs not made, we have a confirmation of such speculation, or at the least, some corroboration of same."

Excited, Gary said, "Yes. There is also the question of a 'missing' inspection panel from the floorboard under and adjacent to Horton's seat. This panel was located during an examination of the wreckage. Photos were taken to show its condition."

Ava, now agitated, stood. "Of course, the picture! The fire extinguisher rack in it was empty. Also, that it was burned in a manner to preclude Horton having removed it and starting a fire in the hole."

Vorpagel said, "When all logical reasons disappear, the only remaining possibility is some sort of negligent maintenance. Once the fire was discovered, the pilots should have immediately donned their oxygen masks. To not do so resulted in their inhaling of toxic and noxious fumes. Depending on the heat of these fumes, they could seal the windpipe by their inhalation, causing almost immediate incapacitation. There is also speculation that the window was opened. This is not the proper way to contain a blaze. Fire academies teach that windows and possible drafts should be prevented so as to deprive the fire source of oxygen. The opening of the window in this case very easily would have caused an acceleration of the blaze. This scenario then proceeds along to show a confusion in the mind of the pilot. Asphyxia, semiconsciousness, and confusion would have led him to misjudge his landing speed and misinterpret what he saw—the roof of buildings as a possible landing area in a large parking lot. This slight area alone could be the contributing factor in the crash."

"What was the conclusion of the case?" Gary asked.

"The airplane company settled out of court. They paid Mrs. Horton a million dollars." Vorpagel stuffed his briefcase with papers and photos. The students stood. He said, "I want to thank you for your attention and participation. You have all earned top marks."

Marcus buttonholed Vorpagel by the door. "You said if I got an A, you'd tell me about the Rastafarians."

Vorpagel said, "A top grade in my class is a B."

Marcus's face fell. The young man turned and walked out into the parking lot. His shoulders were hunched, his hands stuffed into his pockets.

Vorpagel sighed in resignation. He called to the rookie and led him to a nearby park bench. The young man leaned forward in expectation.

Vorpagel said, "You have to understand that I learned much of this after the fact. Ressler conducted the investigation. He interviewed the ultra-Rastafarians. He interviewed almost everyone involved.

Over the years, talking to Ressler and other agents, I pieced together what happened."

He stared at the ground.

Marcus prompted, "What did happen?"

"What happened in Saint Croix was an anatomy of an assassination."

ANATOMY OF
AN ASSASSINATION

A few miles outside Saint Croix, by a meadow with a stream twisting through it, was a shack. Inside, Jean Claude O'Reilly wove long strands of hair into a braid and tied it off. He studied his image in a small, cracked mirror. The braids cascaded down, encircling his rich ebony face with a crown of dreadlocks.

Each braid had a tiny colored ribbon on the end.

Jean Claude's face was clean shaven, but it looked grizzly. He had large, soulful almond-shaped eyes, a broad nose, and a lantern chin.

The malnutrition of his youth still showed. At five-six and a hundred thirty pounds, he looked hungry and wiry, for all his muscles.

He left the one-room hovel of corrugated steel and stolen lumber. A goat was tethered to a tree outside.

The West Indian bent by the animal and picked up fresh dung. He worked the manure, kneading it in his hands like a sculpture of warm clay. Then, he carefully massaged the goat defecation into each of his dreadlocks.

The ritual completed, he went to the stream and washed his hands. Then he dug into the moist clay of the bank and worked it in his hands, just as he had the goat dung.

Jean Claude sculpted the clay into an oblong shape the size of a small potato. He made other shapes, some long—like earthen cigarettes, others round—the size of small apples. He used twigs to connect the clay pieces together. When he was done, he had a small, rather ugly, clay doll.

Using straw, he matted-in imitation hair. He tied his rainbow-colored kerchief around the doll, creating the illusion of a woman's dress. Two black pebbles made the eyes.

In the distance, the clear azure water of the Caribbean crested with white caps from a stiff breeze.

Jean Claude removed a tattered paper from the rear pocket of his jeans. Is was the front page of the *Saint Croix Avis*. The bastard nation to the north is at it again. Uncle Sam's sending a team of FBI agents to my island.

Seventy-nine law enforcement personnel, representatives from many of the Caribbean countries, were gathering to learn how to curtail terrorism. The head of the FBI team was Russell Vorpagel.

Jean Claude tucked the article back into his pocket. At the rear of the shack, a dozen chickens clucked, pecked, and strutted. Moving with lightning quickness, he feinted one way and then scooped a scrawny rooster into his arms.

He headed down a narrow path that meandered through thick underbrush. Three miles away, he entered a clearing with a small hutch in the center. He waited, ten meters away, motionless, his left arm clamped on the rooster.

The sun rose in the distant sky, its glare hitting him full in the face. Beads of perspiration trickled down his strong features. Still, he stood, unmoving, except for closing his eyelids into slits, to protect his pupils from the sun's harsh rays.

A woman, bent forward in a half-circle—not because of age (she was mid-thirties), rather from a birth deformity—left the hutch. She squatted, hitching her scarlet dress up to her knees. She had luxurious black hair, and, despite the hideous twist in her body, a well-formed figure.

Jean Claude removed the doll from his shirt and placed it on the cracked earth in front of the *mambo*—the Caribbean female version of an African witch doctor.

The woman said, in a low, husky voice, "Do you believe in Agwe?"

"I do believe in the Shell of the Sea."

"Are you a descendant of Rada?"

"My heritage follows a true path to Rada, to Dahomey, to Africa."

"What do you want?"

"I need to capture an enemy."

"Death?"

"Not at first. My brother is in prison. I wish to negotiate his release, promising an exchange, then kill my enemy. The rooster is my sacrifice."

The *mambo* went inside the straw house. She reappeared, carrying a tiny earthen bowl and a pouch. She poured crystals from the pouch into the bowl and, using a smooth rock, crushed them into a fine powder.

Jean Claude gathered dead wood and made a fire. The *mambo* placed the bowl on the fire and thin wisps of smoke rose. They both bent forward and inhaled deeply.

Miraculously, the woman straightened, her posture regal. She began to dance, a sensual, sinuous movement, circling the fire and Jean Claude. The tempo of her movements increased until they became frenetic. She grabbed the rooster from him, twirled it high above her head, then snapped its neck. She clawed the dead fowl's throat, tearing into the artery. She held the bird aloft and let the blood flow into her mouth.

She dropped the bird, then folded her body back into its normal, grotesque position. She dipped a finger into the neck of the rooster and made two bloody signs of the cross on her cheeks.

Jean Claude felt the spirits emerging from the surrounding trees and brush. The *loa* were coming. These were the evil *diab loa* of the red sect, not the benevolent *loa* of the white sect.

The woman said, "A *mapous* has appeared."

"The largest of all the *loa*," Jean Claude said reverently.

The *mambo* cupped her hands into a chalice. The *mapous* telescoped its shape into a ball. The priestess gently brought her hands to the clay doll and opened them.

"The *mapous* has now entered the doll," the woman said. "The doll will now help you. But you must bring me two possessions of your enemy. After I have chanted the incantations around them, only then will you be ready."

"What do you want in return?"

"Two teens, to take part in the Rite of the Snake."

"I have passed the Snake Rite."

"I know. Otherwise, I would not talk to you."

Jean Claude picked up the clay doll and thanked her.

She said, "What you are going to do is dangerous. You will need an amulet. Bring me the tooth of an alligator."

"I will. Does it have to be a fresh kill, or . . ."

She smiled, her lush lips moist. "No, I'm trying to protect you, not get you killed."

The plane swung in an arc over Saint Thomas and began a steep descent. Russ Vorpagel could see Saint John's Island off to his left. The sky was cloudless, the view incredible. He could make out two of the British Virgin Islands, Tortola, and the Virgin Gorda in the far distance.

Vorpagel's wife, Nancy, asked, "How long do you have to work every day?"

"I'm giving five four-hour lectures, one each morning. They don't start until Monday, and we have two days on the other end that are free, plus every afternoon."

"Almost like a vacation."

"Almost." Russ patted her hand gently and stared out the airplane's window. He had asked the Special Agent in Charge (SAC) if he could take his wife on this assignment and had been told that there was no problem. His partner, Bob Ressler, had told him that he had heard rumors that the Rastafarians were active. They considered the FBI's help to local police an intrusion on their unacknowledged claim of sovereignty.

When they had done their last-minute preparations in Quantico, Vorpagel had said, "I don't know much about the Rastafarians, except the most publicized stuff: Bob Marley's Reggae music, dope's a holy weed."

"It's a little deeper than that," Ressler said. "First, they believe Haile Selassie is the living god. That he is Ras Tafari."

"Where's he living?"

"In Ethiopia."

"God picked a hell of a place to live."

"That's another one of their tenets. Jamaica is hell, Ethiopia is paradise."

"Have any of these guys been to Ethiopia?"

"Russ, this is serious. They believe that the black person is superior to the white person. They believe that the Invincible Emperor of Ethiopia's going to bring every expatriated African back to the homeland."

"Does this Haile guy have that kind of money?"

"He's dead. And the Jamaican Rastis believe he did not die of cancer. They believe the whole story of his demise was fabricated by the enemies of the true reincarnation of ancient Israel."

"These guys are Jewish?"

"No, they believe that the history of the world has been altered to arrange things for the white man's benefit."

"These guys don't sound like a potent threat."

"They believe that, soon, the blacks will rule the world. And they are ready to act on that principle."

"In other words, they are dangerous."

"Exactly. Remember, Selassie defied Mussolini before World War II and lived into our era."

"With Nancy and Helen coming along, let's take our weapons. You never know."

They had both packed service revolvers, .357s, plus extra rounds in a belt pouch.

If, Russ thought, I'm worried enough about security to bring a gun, should I have brought my wife?

He glanced at her. Her face was pressed inches from the airplane's window. She was excited.

He thought, if the SAC said it was okay to bring the wives, then it must be.

Jean Claude lived seven miles from Christiansted, the second largest town on the island. The harbor town lay nestled at the base of low surrounding hills. An island, the Cay, was centered in the bay. Sailing boats and yachts dotted the south side of the Cay.

Jean Claude walked into the town. For the first six miles of his trip, the only people he saw were black. As he headed down the path into town, he could see a cruise ship disgorging its payload of fat, old, white people.

The Rastafarian felt disgust rise from his belly and crawl into his mouth.

Fight the hatred, he thought, channel it, use it, don't let it control you. He had work to do. He checked the newspaper article again, got the name of the condominium complex where the FBI agents were staying, and went to the service entrance at the rear.

He waited patiently, nodding to maids hurrying into the building. He knew whom he wanted to talk to, one in particular. Alicia had spurned his advances once at a local festival. She worked in the laundry from noon to nine.

The condominium complex was housing only the law enforcement students for the classes and the FBI instructors.

Jean Claude removed the newspaper article and re-read it again. Russel Vorpagel was the agent in charge of this mission.

I want the man at the top, Jean Claude thought. Vorpagel.

Across the alley, at the rear of a warehouse, some-one had written: THE GROWL OF A HUNGRY STOMACH THE RICH KNOWS NOT.

That, Jean Claude knew, was as true as the sun rising in the east.

Underneath another slogan was painted in bright red: ONE GOD, ONE AIM, ONE DESTINY.

My destiny, he thought, is to kill Vorpagel and purge my island of the infidel from Babylon.

He saw Alicia coming down the alley. Her dress swayed in a sensuous movement, miming the swing of her hips. She saw him and frowned.

He asked, "What rooms are the FBI agents going to be in?"

"Whatchóo talkin' 'bout? Getta outa here before I call . . ." She stopped and stared at the doll Jean Claude had just removed from his shirt. Then, she laughed. "You take me for a fool? Believin' in that mumbo . . ."

"I took this to Rita. She called up the spirit, not me."

"Getta outta here."

"Rita," Jean Claude repeated.

Doubt entered Alicia's eyes. She said, "I won't tell you, but ask Maria at the bank. She cashed his check. They have to put the room number on the back."

Jean Claude went to the bank, sent inside a small boy, who asked Maria to come out. He told the bank teller what he wanted. Then, he showed her the doll.

Maria's mouth turned down. "Rita made this?"

"The crooked woman in the hills."

"You lying to me."

"Touch the doll."

Maria's thin, dark hand stretched out tentatively. One finger grazed the doll's face, barely touching one of the black pebbled eyes. Her hand shot back as if zapped with electricity. She crossed herself, kissed her thumb, and whispered, "A *mapous*."

"I saw him. He was huge, dark, with jagged teeth. He looked angry—and hungry."

Maria blessed herself again.

"Tell me Vorpagel's room number."

Maria nodded. She entered the bank, looked at the back of the check, came back, and told Jean Claude the room number.

He said, "And I also need a photograph of Agent Vorpagel."

Her hands clenched at her sides. "How'm I suppose to do that?"

"Tell him you're happy that he's here, teaching your people his ways."

"I'm not happy he's here."

"Lie. Tell him you're happy that he's sharing his knowledge. Tell him you want a souvenir of his coming."

Her head bobbed again in reluctant agreement.

"Get movin', woman."

Vorpagel and Nancy sat in the condo's cocktail lounge with Bob Ressler, his wife Helen, and Agent Daniel Borden from Puerto Rico. They were drinking banana daiquiris and getting in a vacation mood. It was election time in the states.

Ressler had bought a book on the Rastafarians. He said, "Listen to this. The Rasties believe that the whites' god is really the devil and the font from which all evil flows into the world."

"From," Vorpagel said, "a Caribbean's point of view, they have a valid foundation for that position. How did Haile feel about being anointed god?"

"He was never told. He was actually a Christian."

Vorpagel started to laugh.

Ressler waved a hand, stopping him. "The Rastafarians, or at least some of them, are very militant. Our presence must infuriate them. It's an insult."

Borden said, "I thought this was a plum assignment."

"It is," Ressler said. "I just want everyone to be careful."

Jean Claude waited on the sandy beach that fronted the condominium. The room number Maria had given him was on the second floor, the second room from the end. The sliding glass door was dark.

Jean Claude climbed a tree and stood on the lanai patio. If Vorpagel entered his room, Jean Claude could always escape down the fire ladder and across the beach. There were two chairs, a small table, and a huge plant on the lanai.

Jean Claude tested the sliding glass door. It

opened. In the bedroom, he searched the drawers. Just clothes. He searched the end tables. Just FBI manuals.

He felt under the mattress and recoiled in surprise: A Colt .357 lay there. He rummaged under the mattress again and removed an FBI badge and credentials.

He looked at the credentials; they were made out to a Daniel Borden.

Jean Claude thought, Borden? Maria gave me the wrong room number. He held the .357 against his chest, then smiled. He would kill Vorpagel with his fellow officer's gun. He picked up the badge. A potential symbol.

A young woman approached the bar and hesitated.

Vorpagel studied her for a moment, then said, "I saw you in the bank. Can I help you?"

She said shyly, "I read in the paper why you are here. Can I take your picture? As a memento?"

Vorpagel shrugged and stood.

Even though expecting it, he was caught in the bulb's flash by surprise, momentarily blinded. When the stars that swam in front of his eyes dissipated, the young woman was gone.

Nancy said, "That woman looked awfully nervous."

Jean Claude walked down a side street. He thought, now I need two teenage recruits, to pay Rita and to get her to perform her magic on the badge and the gun. But first, I need what she wanted for my amulet.

He entered a dingy shop. He explained to the dark, ancient shopkeeper what he wanted.

The old man said, "Are you buying everything for the amulet—the gad—or just the alligator tooth?"

"Rita didn't say."

"Better buy everything she'll need. Rita's not one to fool with."

The shopkeeper hobbled about his store. He placed an alligator's tooth on the counter. He got a can of gunpowder, a vial of water taken from a tannery, and a small jar of ashes. He said, "The ashes are the most expensive."

"Why?"

"They were taken from the church—they're Shrove Tuesday ashes. You can only get them once a year."

"Is this all I need?"

"No. But this is all I have. You must also get the bile of a bullock and a goat."

Jean Claude left the shop. He decided he needed two killers more than Rita needed two new recruits. He knew Ciro, fourteen, and Ricardo, fifteen, had already been initiated into the Snake Rite, but they had done it on the west end of the island, near Frederikstadt.

The crooked woman never left her clearing—except to go to the sacred altar two miles from her home.

Jean Claude felt uncomfortable. Lying to a *mambo* was very dangerous, but not unheard of. Ciro and Ricardo would be no problem. The Rite of the Snake was intense, but so were the narcotics. The lure of the drugs would snuff any argument from the two teens.

And they'd both been bloodied.

Ciro had kidnapped and killed a baby a month ago. The kid was one of seven hundred and fifty people who died before Jamaica's October election. The Jamaica Labor Party won in a landslide.

Ricardo's kill was only a goat. Not exactly a human kill, but still a kill.

Blood would not bother either of them.

But should he lie to Rita? The *mambo* was very powerful, very knowledgeable, but she was not a seer.

My own power will ascend, Jean Claude thought, if I fool her.

He stood on the south road and tried to hitch a ride to the west end of the island.

The small tourist buses, filled with flaccid, fat, blanched faces, did not stop to give a native a lift. The Nortes averted their eyes when they passed, pretending not to see the dark native son of Saint Croix.

They want, he thought, our sun, our beaches, our bauxite, our labor, our women, our land. They give nothing except complaints, manure, and garbage. They give insults, take heritage—give disdain, take morality. They swap money for souls, money for freedom, money for everything.

Or so they think.

Money meant nothing—liberty, everything.

My brother, Jean Claude thought, not of the flesh, but of the spirit, rots in the Governor's jail.

My brother, not of the womb, but of the movement, lies chained to a wall.

And I will offer to swap Vorpagel for him—and once my brother is free, I will kill the agent. I will place the badge of one of his fellow officers on his forehead. I will mark his chest, in his own blood, with the sign of the Rastafarians.

An old man, in an equally old donkey-drawn cart, stopped by the side of the road. The man was blacker than Jean Claude.

The Rastafarian asked, "Are you one of the brothers?"

The old man eyed the dreadlocks cascading down Jean Claude's face.

Jean Claude said, "Don't you know all black men are brothers?"

"Do you want a ride? Or do you want to walk?"

Jean Claude remained quiet on the trip to the west end of the island.

Vorpagel and his wife went to Sunday services, attending the Methodist Church in Christiansted. Then, they toured the town. They learned the Virgin Islands were named by Christopher Columbus, after Saint Ursula and her maidens. They visited Buck Island Reef National Monument, with its colorful coral and tropical fish. They toured the ruins of Princess Plantation, a sugar cane farm.

Nancy said, "You have to teach tomorrow. Do you want to get home early or see Frederikstadt?"

"I know how much you like Victorian architecture. Let's go look at the houses."

Jean Claude saw Vorpagel and Nancy. The couple watched a cargo ship load bauxite. Painted on the wooden dock, in bright green, were the words: COWARDS CANNOT WIN.

I am not a coward, Jean Claude thought, and looked at the couple.

The Rastafarian didn't believe it at first. He kept checking the photo Maria had given him. There was no mistake—his quarry was there, a hundred feet from him, watching the workmen.

Vorpagel's big, Jean Claude thought, way over six feet, and at least two hundred and forty pounds. But a bullet from his partner's gun will turn that giant hulk into a rotting corpse.

The Rastafarian put the photo in his pocket.

Russ Vorpagel and his wife walked in his direction. The agent wore a short-sleeved shirt. Jean Claude noticed the green dragon tattoo crawling down the agent's left arm.

An FBI agent with a tattoo? Maybe that stupid bitch Maria had photographed the wrong person at the condominium, not Vorpagel.

No, Maria wouldn't make a mistake. Not on something this important. This huge man was Vorpagel. But to make sure, Jean Claude decided to recheck with Maria, to show her the photo and ask, "Is this Vorpagel?"

He followed the couple on their walking tour by the Victorian homes, with their showpiece galleries, on the streets of Frederikstadt.

Slogans were sprayed on the pavement in black and red. Jean Claude read: INFORMERS BEWARE.

Did he have to worry about Ciro and Ricardo? Would they betray him, after he told them what he wanted?

No, he decided, the threat of the doll would be enough, as long as he replaced the scarf dress with a white handkerchief, folding the linen to resemble pants.

The pistol he had stolen from the condo felt heavy in his coat pocket. He thought, I could blast Vorpagel where he stands. Just walk up and put a round between his eyes—except that would not help my brother chained in the Governor's jail.

I must wait.

Until I talk to Ciro and Ricardo. Until Rita evokes the spirits and blesses the gun and the badge. Until the huge agent is taken prisoner. Until my brother has been freed in the hope of an exchange.

Then, I will kill Vorpagel.

The next morning Agents Vorpagel, Ressler, and Borden drove their rented car from Christiansted to Frederikstadt. They reached the south road. The local authorities had warned them not to take the north road that meandered through the hardwood forest. The ultraextremist Rastafarians controlled that forest, using it for military training.

Borden confessed sheepishly, "Someone broke into my room last night. I didn't get back to the hotel until late. My gun's gone . . . and so is my badge."

"You're going to have to fill out a report," Ressler said. "The SAC's not going to like it."

"What good does it do to let us have a gun in a foreign country, and then tell us we can't take it out of our room?"

"At least," Vorpagel said, "it gives you some protection when you're in your room." He parked the vehicle in front of the training school.

Vorpagel entered the classroom assigned to him. He checked the roster. There were seventy-nine law enforcement personnel in his class. They represented every country from the Caribbean Islands, including Jamaica and the British Virgin Islands, to Brazil.

He stood at the dais and said, "We will begin with the unaltered and disorganized crime scene. The overall imprint of this crime scene is that the act was committed suddenly and with no set plan of action for deterring detection. The crime scene shows great disarray and disorganization. The weapon is often present at the scene. No attempt has been made to conceal the body."

A lithe, wiry man stood. "My name is Manuel Garcia, from Colombia. We have many such murders as you've just described. Yet they are committed by organized crime, the Cartels."

"I'm not speaking about the professional, rather the sociopath. This type typically is preoccupied with recurring, obsessional, and primitive thoughts, and is in a distressed frame of mind. The offender may explode with aggression and kill the victim in the frenzy of the attack . . . or the offender behaves by carrying out instructions—auditory hallucinations."

A woman stood. "I am Mary Salscea, from Jamaica. I also have investigated many deaths like you described. We normally find that the hallucinations were drug induced, and accompanied by the black magic of religious ritual."

"Again," Russ said, "I am not speaking of the sociopath. Ritualistic killings usually fall into the area of the altered crime scene. Obsessive-compulsive traits surface in the behavior. The ritualistic killer brings a weapon with him. The disorganized kills spontaneously and with weapons of opportunity."

The woman said, "I've seen some terrible things at those scenes."

You're not alone, Russ thought. "If the killing involves torture, where death comes in a slow, deliberate manner, then you have a demonstration of power—the attempt to dominate another person's life."

• • •

Jean Claude found Ciro and Ricardo at the beach. Both teens were sitting, backs against boulders, and smoking marijuana. They nodded languidly at him and offered him a puff.

Inhaling deeply, Jean Claude felt the first wave of gentleness sweep through his mind. He enjoyed the *ganja*, the holy weed. It let him forget about toppling the infidels from Babylon. It let him forget the terrible rumors that Haile Selassie had died.

Impossible! How could the Messiah die? No, the great prophet waited in Ethiopia for the return of his beautiful black people. The man who was the true Jesus foretold in the unaltered version of the Old Testament—the testament that had not been twisted by the Europeans—could not die.

And even if he did, he would rise again.

The narcotic spread its message from his brain to his body. He rested his head against the boulder. The sun was high—a bright circle of beauty—sending its warming rays to bathe his face.

Ciro snapped on a portable radio. The words of a Bob Marley song poured forth. It was a Nyabingi chant.

I'll wipe my weary eyes,
I'll wipe my weary eyes,
Dry up you' tears to meet Ras Tafari,
Dry up you' tears and come.

Jean Claude closed his eyes. Dry up my tears and come. I will, I will successfully complete my mission.

He inhaled again, sucking the smoke deep into his lungs.

The thoughts began to wander from images of sexual encounters, both real and imagined, to darker thoughts of how he should kill Vorpagel.

Quick? Slow? Clean? Torture?

He decided to send a message with the Norte Americano's death. He would not set the badge he had stolen on Vorpagel's forehead. He would heat it over hot coals and brand its image onto the man's cheeks.

Vorpagel glanced at his notes, then said, "Specific areas of the body may be targeted for extreme brutality. Overkill or excessive assault to the face often is an attempt to depersonalize the victim. Destruction of the face may indicate the victim resembles or represents a person who has caused the offender psychological trauma. We have successfully closed numerous cases on that fact alone. In one, a man murdered seven women. They all resembled each other—short, brunette hair, small gold earrings, oval faces, all between twenty and twenty-five. Each had her face beaten beyond recognition. Then, the murders stopped suddenly. The Behavioral Science Unit of the FBI found that a woman in her forties had been murdered. She had an oval face, fancied small gold earrings, and had short, brunette hair. We proved that her murderer was also the killer of the seven young women. He was killing his mother over and over. When he finally got around to actually killing his mother, he was released from his turmoil. A few months later, he turned himself in, plea-bargained before he confessed, and got life in prison without possibility of parole."

Police Officer Manuel said, "This Behavioral Science sounds like mumbo jumbo. I work with clues, hard facts."

"So far, in the first year, the FBI has profiled sixty-five cases throughout the United States. Fifteen evaluations were reported, resulting in arrests for twenty-seven homicides, fifty-five rapes, and four arsons."

"That adds up to eighty-six, not fifteen."

"The fifteen evaluations resulted in fifteen arrests. The fifteen criminals were responsible for the eighty-six felonies. We in the Bureau expect the number resulting in successful arrests at least to double next year."

Police Officer Mary asked, "Can you be more specific about disorganized crime scenes?"

"The offender uses a blitz style of attack for encountering the victim. He either approaches the victim from behind, suddenly overpowering her or him, or kills suddenly, as with a gun. The attack is a violent surprise, occurring out of the blue, and in a location where the victim is going about her or his usual business. The victim is caught completely off guard. The offender may wear a mask or gloves, or cover the victim's face as he attacks. There is little verbal interaction except for orders or threats."

"Do they usually know their victims?"

"In the disorganized crime, the victims are selected at random. Age and sex do not necessarily matter. If the murderer is selecting a victim by randomly knocking on doors, the first person to open a door becomes a victim. The offender feels very insecure with people. He kills instantly to have control; he cannot risk that the victim gets the upper hand. He often is sexually and socially inadequate. Most often, he has never married, lives alone or with a parental figure, and his residence is in close proximity to the crime scene. The offender is fearful of people and may have developed a well-defined delusional system."

"What about the altered crime-scene offender?"

"The initial observation at a concealed crime scene is the sense of organization aimed at deterring detection. The offender takes precautions against discovery of himself or the victim. The body and the other evidence are hidden from view or disposed of far from the death scene. Few, if any, weapons or fingerprints are found. The crime appears to be deliberate, calculated, and preplanned."

Vorpagel saw that he was finally reaching his audience. "Investigators find little evidence to work with in developing a profile of the suspect. Often, the offender has stalked, abducted, abused, and murdered the victim, first encountering the victim at one location and transporting him or her to another location."

Manuel said, "I've investigated many homicides in my life. And many were completely different than what you've described."

"Please keep in mind that this class is about psychotic killers. Better than two-thirds of the murders committed, at least in the United States, are done by very ordinary people—the housewife who snaps after her husband asks her, for the zillionth time, 'Get me a beer, honey,' and plunges the carving knife into his throat."

The audience laughed knowingly. Domestic problems were the same the world over.

Vorpagel continued, "Even the premeditated, cold, calculated murder—of a partner, a spouse, a friend— done with every intention of getting away with it, often solves itself. Those killers, the sociopaths, suffer from death trauma just as peace officers in a righteous shoot do. Some handle it, suppress the guilt, and are never caught. Others' consciences gnaw away at them—they're the ones who walk into police stations all over the world and blurt out confessions."

Vorpagel paused. Using a handkerchief, he wiped perspiration from his brow. It was hot, humid. No air conditioning, and not even a pitcher of water available.

He thought, talking for hour after hour is not easy, even with something to soothe the larynx. He looked out at his audience. Though attentive, they weren't connecting with him. Latin America had mass murderers, but they fell into different categories from the sociopaths who seemed to roam every state in the United States. The Latin murdered for passion, money, revenge, insult, or just plain machismo. Whacking up someone's sexual parts and keeping them as trophies didn't occur south of the border—not very often.

Even the terrible ritualistic killings that Vorpagel had read about involving black magic and the dark side of voodoo were really just religious convictions gone evil.

He thought, I should try to give them something they can use, something Latin. He said, "I don't know the statistics in your various countries, but in mine, there were 19,555 murders last year. Sixty-three percent were firearms, mostly handguns. In contact wounds, there will be a muzzle impression, due to blow-back of the skin, caused by the gases coming from the barrel. In contact wounds over bone, such as in the head, a star-shaped wound of entrance is often produced by subcutaneous expansion of the gases between the skin and bone."

Vorpagel smiled.

His seventy-nine students weren't sitting politely with a vacant look in their collective eyes anymore—they were scribbling in their notebooks. Latin America was very familiar with murders involving contact wounds.

Jean Claude napped for an hour. When he awoke, he talked to Ciro and Ricardo. As he expected, neither teen had any problem with his plans, either with being reinitiated into the Rite of the Snake, or kidnapping the FBI agent.

They would meet that night at the altar of the crooked woman. They would experience the dream state of the mind of the Green Snake; they would drink blood. They would dance and copulate.

Then, they would go to the hotel, capture the agent, and free their imprisoned brother. Then, they would brand Vorpagel with his own badge, place the muzzle of an FBI revolver against his temple, and blow his brains out.

That night, Jean Claude walked to the crooked woman's altar. With him were Ciro and Ricardo. A few minutes earlier, they had gutted a goat and a bullock, and drained both animals' bile into a clay bowl.

When they arrived at the altar, there were fifty people waiting. The clearing was surrounded by bougainvillea, flame trees, hibiscus, and canaria. The crooked woman stood on top of an immense boulder, carved flat at the top. Draped over the edge were three sheets of linen, each the color of the holy movement: black, red, and green. The *mambo* stood next to a large, wrought-iron cage. Inside the cage was an enormous green snake. Centered on the cage was the symbol of the *Damballah-wedo*, a crest formed out of two snakes entwined around a drum.

Rastafarians milled about, smoking the holy weed, chanting, singing.

Jean Claude heard a female voice, perfectly tuned, crystal clear, sing in French, "There is no night in Zion, there is no night there. Ras Tafari is the light, we need no candlelight. Hallelujah, there is no night there."

People swayed in time to the music. A man, dreadlocks at least two feet long, handed a pipe to Jean Claude. He sucked in the smoke, letting it do its work.

The pipe owner said, "The taking of rum has eaten out our head."

Jean Claude knew the poem. He answered, "They who continue to take it will end up dead."

"Remember, one is created, the other manufactured."

"On the evils of white men we have always lectured."

The woman, who had been singing, heard them. She sang, in a perfect soprano, "So cast not your verdict before making a test, true conscience in you will show you the best, for rum we know will pronounce your doom, all hail to great ganja, the solvent of doom."

A cheer went up, and together they shared more of the holy weed.

Jean Claude knew how easy it was for these things to get out of hand. If the delirium experienced by the crooked woman was intense, she could be out for hours, even a day, after the ritual.

He needed his amulet tonight. He motioned to her. He removed the vial containing the two animals' bile, the alligator tooth, the gunpowder, and the other items, and set them on the ground.

Rita crouched. Her long, disfigured spine pressed up against her scarlet dress. Using a bowl, she poured the blood, sprinkled the gunpowder and Shrove Tuesday ashes and water from a tannery, then soaked the alligator tooth.

She said, "I have also had a *maman-loa* prepare a charm lamp for you." She held out a crab shell. The shell was filled with oil. Two bones floated on the oil, forming a cross.

Rita, using a bone-handled knife, poked a small hole through the alligator's tooth. She threaded a thong into this, then placed the handcrafted necklace around Jean Claude's neck.

She said, "I will keep the oil burning while you seek your prey."

WEB OF VIOLENCE

Vorpagel and his wife had dinner with the Resslers. They ordered fried conch and turtle soup. They drank a few exotic concoctions made with rum distilled on the island.

Then, they went to the beach and walked barefoot in the sand. The night was balmy, the sky clear, the stars almost touchable. The surf was less than a foot high, the waves gentle as they fell on the beach.

Vorpagel rolled up his pants legs. Nancy tucked her skirt around her waist. They walked in the surf, holding hands. After thirty years of marriage, they were having a spontaneous second honeymoon.

Jean Claude slumped to the ground. He lay on his back and stared at the heavens. The stars did a waltz with the quarter moon. Red comets shot toward the earth, only to slow, stop, then shoot outward again.

His heart slowed to less than forty beats a minute.

His body felt like it was flooded with Novocain. He tried to blink his eyes and found them frozen into immobility.

Deep in his mind, one portion still grasped a sense of reality. Rita had made a concoction of drugs, from herbs and mushrooms. Whatever she'd used, it was the most powerful he'd ever experienced.

He turned his head to the side. All about him were macabre shapes of people dancing, making love, staggering.

He saw Rita on top of her boulder-turned-altar. She held the green snake aloft and spoke in tongues, a strange combination of French, Creole, Portuguese, and Spanish. The frenzy of her contortions was such that her body blurred. Her writhing matched the rhythm of her oracle.

Rita held the snake high above her, then, swinging it like a bull whip, snapped it out and broke the thin neck.

Those still able to move danced or crawled to the foot of the altar. Each ate the raw flesh of the green snake.

Jean Claude tried to move—he knew how powerful that meat would make him. His body refused the messages from his mind and remained immobile.

He sensed everything. The moonlight's rays shimmering above, near, touchable. He felt his dreadlocks, the symbol of the lion's mane, brushing his cheeks.

Again the *danse vaudou* began. The reveling figures' shadows, cast down from the faint light of the quarter moon, appeared to dance as separate entities from their owners.

Ciro and Ricardo stood in front of the altar. Their bodies trembled—not from fear—from ecstasy. Each quivered in time to Rita's chanting voice.

Suddenly, the *mambo* withdrew a wooden spoon from her scarlet dress and tapped each teen on the forehead. They both fainted, collapsing to the ground. The others also keeled over.

The Rite of the Snake was over.

Vorpagel talked briefly with Ressler about a rumor of a planned kidnapping. It was serious, but the wives shouldn't be put on alarm.

"These guys are fanatics," Ressler said. "It would be foolish not to take a defensive posture."

"The condo's doors have chains. But it gets too hot at night to leave the sliding glass door to the balcony closed."

Vorpagel looked around the hallway of the hotel. He went to a laundry closet at the far end, rummaged about, and found a mop. He unscrewed the handle.

He went to his hotel room. The suite contained a front sitting area, two bedrooms, and a bath. The large front room had sliding glass doors that gave access to a balcony and a vast view of the sea.

He placed the mop's handle onto the sliding glass door's track. The door now could only be slid open six inches before being stopped by the wedge.

Vorpagel left his room and knocked lightly at Ressler's. Bob opened the door.

"Did you tell Borden about the threat?"

"No, can't find him. He's not in his room."

"I used a mop handle to block my sliding glass door."

"Good idea," Ressler said and padded down the hall to the laundry room. He returned, carrying a broom, and said, "I hope this place doesn't have a house detective—wouldn't look good having us agents busted for stealing."

Vorpagel grinned and returned to his room.

He removed his clothes and went into the second, cooler bedroom. His wife was on her side, curled up, face relaxed, hair slightly mussed. A wave of affection spread through him. He kissed her goodnight and went back to the other bedroom. Ressler had forewarned him. If anything went down, he didn't want Nancy in the same room.

Just before dozing off, he reached under his pillow. His hand felt the comforting steel of his .357 revolver.

Daniel Borden was ten blocks away, sitting in a bar, arguing with the owner. He didn't want to leave, he didn't want to sleep, he didn't want to dream, he wanted another drink.

The owner was a small but very determined man. He wanted the intoxicated *gringo* out. He wanted to go home to his wife and three daughters.

But Borden was adamant. He threw a twenty on the bar and said, "For one more rum, dark, neat, and poured heavy."

His thirst, for alcohol, for relief from his feelings of despair—about his loneliness, his losing his gun and his badge—saved his life.

At least, for a while.

• • •

It had taken Jean Claude two hours to come completely out of his stupor and to get Ciro and Ricardo out of theirs. The three Rastafarians walked down the sandy beach to the hotel where the FBI agents were staying.

Jean Claude had checked with Maria. She had assured him that she had given him the right room number, that the other agent, Borden, must have just left his gun in Vorpagel's room.

The three Rastafarians stood on the beach, the ocean at their backs.

Jean Claude was trying to remember from which one of the second-floor rooms he had stolen Agent Borden's gun and badge.

His head felt fuzzy, full of cotton. He tried to recreate his actions. He held the alligator tooth amulet and prayed that he would.

He did. Vorpagel's room was second from the end.

He led his two accomplices across the white beach. They climbed a tree. Each of the hotel's rooms had a balcony. The balcony contained a small table, two chairs, and a thick bush. The plant was taller than Jean Claude.

The three men drew their weapons. Ciro and Ricardo held .22's; Jean Claude, the stolen .357. He stood behind the huge bush and motioned to his two accomplices.

Ciro knelt by the sliding glass door, Ricardo stood. Ciro tugged at the handle and the door slid open. The two teens entered. Jean Claude followed. There was no one there.

Jean Claude thought, where could Vorpagel be?

And this late at night? He was traveling with his wife. I saw them at the dock. Nothing was open this late.

He sat on the bed and thought, should I wait? What if they're having a party with the other agents? What if they all come back together? What if they decide to come to this room for a last drink?

I'd be facing them all, and every one of them, besides Borden, would be armed.

This is no good. This is too dangerous.

He glanced at the end table. A wallet was next to the lamp. Using the bedspread, he covered himself, the lamp, and the wallet. He flicked on the lamp and opened the wallet. The driver's license, the credit cards, were all made out to Daniel Borden.

God damn Maria, Jean Claude thought, damn her to hell. She *did* give me the wrong room number.

The three men crept out of the hotel room, scrambled down the fire escape to the sandy beach, and headed for Alicia's house.

Jean Claude thought, Alicia knows the right room number. Maybe she's not afraid of a *mapous*, but she'll tell me the right room number or I'll blow her head off. Alicia did know the right room number. Maria had inverted the numbers: Vorpagel's room was 12, not 21.

Vorpagel awoke. He glanced at his watch: six-ten. He yawned. He heard a sound coming from the front room. Still groggy with sleep, he slipped out of bed and went into the front room.

He froze. Two black men, or, most likely from the appearance of their faces, two black teens, were trying to force open the sliding glass door. The mop handle was doing its job, stopping the door when it was only six inches open.

Both men saw Vorpagel. One of them was standing. He drew a gun and aimed it at the FBI agent's head. The other was on his knees. He drew a revolver and aimed it at Vorpagel's privates.

Vorpagel thought, I'm naked as a jaybird; my gun's back in my bedroom, under the pillow. My wife's asleep in the second bedroom.

One of the men said, "Open the door, we want you, mon!"

Hostage situation, Vorpagel thought, then added: Not quite, they haven't got me.

"Open the door. We want you, mon!"

Vorpagel thought, after all my lectures, for the life of me, I can't think of hostage negotiation procedures.

He started to grin, his humor bubbling up. Of course, he thought, I've never done it with two guns aimed at me, I've never done it in my birthday suit.

Another random thought hit him: Kings X, start over, let me put my pants on.

Both men cocked their weapons.

Vorpagel thought, I'm not a negotiator. I'm a potential hostage. What does the hostage want most? Safety.

The man standing said, "Open the door or we'll blow your head off."

Inadvertently, Vorpagel looked at the man kneeling. His aim hadn't changed.

The agent took a half step forward.

Both men shouted, "Don't move."

Vorpagel took a full step back. He'd gained six

inches, half a foot closer to his bedroom door, half a foot nearer his weapon.

He said, "I can't open the sliding door if I can't move."

"Open the door," the kneeler said. "We want you, mon."

"We won't hurt you," the stander said.

Vorpagel thought, I know, you just want me, mon. He took a tentative partial step forward and made a sudden movement with his left arm.

"Don't move!"

Vorpagel took a big step backward, feigning fright. He'd picked up another eighteen inches of territory. He could just see the edge of his bedroom door in his peripheral vision. He said, "This is dangerous. Those guns are cocked. An accident could happen."

"Open the door."

"I will, I will," Vorpagel said and thought, like hell, I will. "Put the guns down, please."

The standing man grunted, a low guttural snarl. "The mon think we fools."

"I didn't mean put the guns down. I meant aim the guns down, away from me. Then I'll open the door."

The two teens hesitated.

"I'm a professional peace officer. I know how easy it is for an accident to happen." Get another concession, he thought, and added, "Just point the guns at the ground and uncock them. I'm naked." He turned slowly, giving them a full 360-degree view of his body, and at the same time giving himself a full view of exactly how far he really was from the bedroom door.

He thought, I have to do a tuck and roll. Once I'm

in the bedroom, I have to grab my gun and go into a crouch position. No, I have to get Nancy onto the floor on the other side of the bed. Wrong, can't do that— she's asleep in the second bedroom. What is she doing? Is she listening to what's happening?

Good God, if she wakes up, sleepy, as I was, and walks in here, she could get killed.

Maybe I should go with them.

No, once I open that sliding door, they'll have me—and my wife.

Vorpagel said, in as soft and unthreatening a voice as he could, "I don't want to get accidentally shot. I'm not making an unreasonable request."

He saw the hesitation in the two teens' eyes. Almost there, he thought, almost there. Once I do the tuck and roll and get my gun from the clothes bag in the closet, I should let off a round into the floor. That will wake up Ressler and Borden—and better the odds.

Vorpagel held his hands up. He said, "I'm a professional negotiator. I know that if you were going to kill me, I'd be dead now. I know you want me as a hostage. That's fine with me. I don't want to die. But I also don't want to get killed accidentally. Just uncock your weapons and point them at the floor."

Come on, he prayed, dear God, please listen.

The kneeling man uncocked his gun and pointed it down.

Vorpagel had to suppress an insane urge to laugh. He thought, at least I've untargeted the most important body part. Still, he decided, this is a good time to blade my body. He slowly maneuvered to his left, giving the two gunmen only his profile as a target, instead of a full frontal position.

The standing islander was still pointing his .22 at his brain.

No problem, Vorpagel thought, my head's tough, it took a direct hit of shrapnel during Korea and I'm still alive.

The standing man uncocked his weapon, then, almost defiantly, aimed it down.

Vorpagel whirled and flung his body into a tuck and roll. He did a somersault. He felt as if he were moving in slow motion. He could see the room spinning, first the floor, then a backward look at the two startled teens, then . . .

Then a muzzle flash from behind the huge bush sitting in the corner of his balcony.

A third man, Vorpagel thought, and felt a searing pain explode in his brain.

A head shot, he thought, good, dear, sweet Jesus, not a head shot, please not a head shot. But his head felt like a ball hit by the full swing of a baseball bat.

His forward momentum propelled him through the open doorway into his bedroom.

He thought, molten lava's being poured into my skull.

Yet, he realized in awe, I'm still functioning.

He crawled across the floor. Across the hall, he noticed Nancy was still asleep. She must be wearing her ear plugs, he thought, and grabbed his weapon.

A head shot, he thought, I've got four—maybe five—minutes before I die. The brain fluid is draining down my back. I can feel the liquid. I've got a few moments to kill those men—before they kill Nancy.

He crawled across the hall and into the second bedroom. He awakened Nancy. He told her to run for help. She opened the condominium door and turned to the left.

Vorpagel thought, she's headed for the stairs. She's going to run up a flight and wake up Ressler. Groggy, he stumbled down the hallway and pounded on Borden's door.

The FBI agent came out at once and followed Vorpagel back to his condo.

Vorpagel said, "Check the lanai."

Borden said, "I don't see anyone."

Nancy returned with Bob Ressler and his wife, Helen.

Vorpagel lay on the floor, on his back in Borden's room.

Vorpagel tried to rise, felt a wave of nausea, and slumped back to the floor.

Surrounding him were Nancy, Ressler, Helen, and Borden. Vorpagel said, with a weak grin, "Would somebody please get me a pair of pants?"

Jean Claude felt like shooting Ciro and Ricardo. The dumb bastards had let the agent talk them into pointing their weapons down.

He had stood, hidden behind the huge bush on the balcony, and tried to hiss at them not to do what the FBI man wanted them to do.

He had pointed the .357 through a break in the branches and lined up on the agent's head. When he had tried to throw himself into the bedroom, Jean Claude had fired.

Did I hit him? I had to shoot through the glass of

the door. He moved so quick, tumbling and rolling and disappearing, that I'm not sure.

The three men had jumped off the balcony and landed in the soft sand. They had run down the beach a mile to the cottage of a friend.

They sat on the porch. Ciro and Ricardo smoked dope.

Jean Claude fumed.

Vorpagel lay on the floor of Borden's hotel room with a blanket wrapped around his body.

Ressler said, "The ambulance is on the way."

"It's a head shot," Vorpagel said. "Why waste anyone's time?" He noticed the shock in Nancy's eyes. He grasped her hand and held it close. He couldn't think of the words to say, the last words he'd ever say, to this woman he had loved and lived with all his adult life.

Ressler knelt beside him and peered at his face. "It looks like the slug lodged in your cheek bone, just under the right eye. I can see the slug lodged under the skin."

"Is there cranial fluid seeping?" Vorpagel asked in a garbled voice. Speaking was difficult because both the upper and lower jaw had been shattered by the ricocheting slug.

"No, not that I can see."

"Then it must be oozing out the entry hole. My back is sopping."

Ressler lifted the blanket and said, "I see a lot of blood, your back's covered with it. Hey, the entry hole is in your shoulder."

"How did the slug end up under my eye?"

"It must have traveled . . ."

"What can I do?" Borden interrupted.

Vorpagel said, "They got away. Go outside and see if you can find anything."

He left.

"There was a third man," Vorpagel continued, "hiding behind that bush. It never dawned on me. I kept looking at those two guns aimed at me. I never thought about a third man."

"Why should you have?"

"Bob, my head's killing me."

"There's no cranial fluid on your back. I'm beginning to think you're the luckiest guy alive."

"I'm laying here with a bullet sticking out of my face and you think I'm lucky?"

"I said you were alive."

Vorpagel thought, I should have someone treat me for shock. No! Not shock. Can't raise the feet for a head shot. Shock causes a temporary collapse of the nervous system and circulatory system. But, please, no blood to the brain.

He couldn't see out of one eye. He waved at Ressler and pointed to his right eye.

Ressler said, "You've got blood seeping out of your eye from internal hemorrhaging."

"You ought to rope off the crime scene," Vorpagel said and looked around the room. "You need to take pictures."

"Vorpagel," Ressler said, "are you going to conduct your own crime scene investigation?"

Vorpagel smiled faintly. He felt like closing his eyes. Just let go, a voice whispered in the shadowy recesses of his brain. Suddenly, an old friend's face appeared in his mind's eye. A police officer, Ken

Hagopian, had been shot in the face with a shotgun earlier that year. He had survived, even though most of his face had taken the full brunt of the blast. Russ saw the 8 x 10 colored photo behind his desk saying, "I made it."

Vorpagel kept repeating in his mind, over and over, if Ken could make it, with his face shot off, then so can I. I want to live.

The ambulance arrived. Vorpagel was put on a gurney and loaded into the van. The vehicle sped toward a nearby clinic. A med-vac helicopter lifted off an aircraft carrier near Guantanamo Bay.

Ressler joined Borden on the beach. The agent pointed: There were three sets of footprints, starting at the base of the balcony, where there were deep impressions, then leading west down the beach.

Borden said, "I don't have a gun."

"I have mine," Ressler said, "and I have Russ's." He gave the .357 to Borden. The two men followed the clear trail of prints down the beach.

Borden asked, "Will he make it?"

"It's a head shot. Dan—I'm amazed he's conscious at all, let alone alive."

A mile down the beach, the three sets of tracks turned inland. They aimed toward a small cottage. The two agents hid behind a clump of low shrubs. They could see two men sitting on the porch.

"Now what?" Borden asked.

"We don't have jurisdiction."

"So?"

"I don't want to blow the case with an illegal arrest. I'll wait here. Go get the locals."

Borden left. Ressler kept the cottage under surveillance, but his mind was elsewhere, praying for his friend to live.

Jean Claude went out on the porch. Ciro held out a roach.

"No dope. Get your heads on straight. We don't know if the agent is dead. We don't know what's happening. Did you see anyone else come into the room before you jumped off the balcony?"

"Not me," Ciro said.

"No, mon," Ricardo added.

Jean Claude fingered the alligator tooth hanging around his neck. Wasn't it supposed to bring luck? No, he thought, it was supposed to protect me. I was unlucky. I didn't kidnap the agent. But I might have killed him.

And I didn't get hurt.

Maybe Rita's amulet's working after all.

Vorpagel opened his eyes. He saw the clinically white ceiling. A blur moved off to his left.

I'm still alive, he thought in amazement.

A technician appeared, hovering over him. The man was wearing a white smock and a troubled look. He said, "I have to move your head to take an X ray."

Move my head? Vorpagel thought. What for? The bullet's sticking out of my cheek. Good Lord, if my head is jostled, it could dislodge the slug, releasing brain fluid. I would die in four or five minutes.

The technician grabbed him firmly, placing his hands on his jaw.

No! Vorpagel thought, dear God, please, no! He could not articulate his plea.

His head was twisted to the left. He moved his eyes around, fully expecting to see the spent bullet plop down to the table, followed by a geyser of cranial fluid.

The technician aimed the X-ray machine at him and took a picture. He said, "Got to turn you over and get the other side."

Why? Why? Why?

The technician rolled him over, grabbed his face again, and twisted it until it was angled properly at the X-ray machine. Another picture was taken.

A doctor entered and asked in a high, shrill voice, "What are you doing?"

"Taking X rays."

"We know where the bullet is, for God's sake. You could be killing this man. I'm having him med-vacked to the Roosevelt Road Hospital in Puerto Rico. Don't move him again, not his body, and especially not his head."

Thank you, God, Vorpagel thought, thank you very much.

The cottage was surrounded by Saint Croix police. There were snipers on the roofs of adjoining buildings. Men with shotguns were hiding behind the two pickup trucks in the driveway. Across the street, two men were pumping tear gas shells into grenade launchers.

Ressler said to the local man in charge, "If at all possible, can you take them alive?"

"Why?"

"We want to interrogate them."

"Why?"

"To see what their motives were."

"I know those men. They're bad. I am a Rastafarian myself. But these men, these ultraextremists, they take my beliefs and meld them with the black magic of voodoo. Jean Claude likes to kill. If you interrogate him, all you will find out is he likes to kill."

"I might find out why he wanted to kill my friend."

"Because he's white. Because he's a policeman. Because he's American. Because he's here. I'm not risking my men for scum, or for you."

The front door of the cottage opened and three men came out. They were unaware that they were in the gun sights of dozens of weapons. They argued as they walked to one of the pickups. The two policemen hiding behind the truck stood and aimed their shotguns at them.

All three raised their hands and surrendered.

"That was easy," Ressler said. "Can I have first crack at them?"

Vorpagel was in a military helicopter. He was lying on a gurney. The roar of the whirling blades penetrated his mind, thumping and thumping their repetitive message.

He thought, what happened? I was hit. I was hit with artillery fire. I was running across a field, a shell burst, I got caught in the back and buttocks.

No, that's not right. That was three days ago. I was running across a field and got caught by incoming. The shrapnel hit me in the head.

That's it! I'm being airlifted back to the aid station. How bad am I hit?

Did the flying pieces of metal penetrate the brain?

Am I dying?

His mind wandered back to those bloody battles.

The thump of the rotating blades lulled him into semiconsciousness.

I'm hit, he thought, hit good.

Ressler sat in the interrogation room. Chained to a chair across the table from him was a man in his early twenties, black, hair done in dreadlocks, with some sort of tooth hanging around his neck.

"Why did you do it?" he asked.

"Do what?"

"Shoot my friend?"

"I hit him? My shot hit him? Is he dead? Is the bastard dead?"

Ressler, controlling his explosive temper, left the room. He would come back.

Vorpagel stirred. The sound of the helicopter blades stopped.

Someone poked a finger into his left shoulder.

He opened his eyes. A doctor was bending over him. Vorpagel was naked. A medic was shaving his chest.

The doctor said, "I've seen the X rays of your jaw. The upper is shattered. I can't put you under with an anesthetic. If I do, you'll die. The throat needs to be kept open because the internal bleeding is pressing against your windpipe. But I have to desensitize the pain, so I'm giving you a hearty concoction made out of heroin and cocaine. I'll stick it on a swab and coat the right side of your nose. I don't know where the bullet went as it traveled through you. If it had gone in a straight line, you'd be dead now."

Vorpagel watched through bleary eyes as the medic started shooting shaving lotion onto his public hair. He thought, wait a minute, wait a minute, what's happening? Did I get shot twice and not notice? What's happening!

The doctor bent down and looked into his open left eye. "Are you all right? You look scared to death."

"Why are they shaving my chest?"

"We may need a rib to replace a jawbone."

Vorpagel tried to point at the medic, who was now happily honing a razor blade on a leather strop.

"Why are they shaving down there?" he mumbled. The doctor looked down, then grinned. "Don't worry. I'm just taking the precaution that I might have to replace the carotid artery with the saphenous vein, which is located in the groin."

The doctor went to work. Vorpagel could see a clock hanging on the wall of the operating room. The hours ticked by. He did not mind. The medic kept a steady supply of cocaine and heroin coming. He was aware enough to understand the passing of time. He was now in the present. He was about to retire. . . .

Five and a half hours later the doctor said, "I have to stop. Your blood pressure is dropping."

The young rookie police officer who had attended Vorpagel's Criminal Investigation class stood silent for a moment, then said, "Shot in the head. And you lived."

"Obviously. So did Reagan's secretary."

"Amazing."

"And educational. Like in that hospital in Korea,

watching my fellow Marines, watching as they tried to mentally cope with what they had experienced, that was when I first became interested in the workings of the human brain. I coupled that with observations on the Bell case.

"Why do people act like they do? Why do they sometimes commit acts that defy a reasonable explanation? After I returned home, I began studying psychology."

Marcus asked, "How long were you hospitalized?"

"Only a week. The bullet had traveled up the muscle of my left shoulder blade, to the top of the scapula, the bone that allows you to raise your arm. Then, it ricocheted up along the muscles, missing the spinal column, and hitting the skull, the occipital bone, to be exact. That's the large, thick bone at the base of the skull."

He paused, smiled a rather tired smile, and added, "I was very lucky. When the third assailant fired, the bullet hit the sliding glass door, deflecting its spiral flight. The slug hit me on its flat side, rather than nose in, slowing it considerably. The doctors found glass fragments, from the sliding door, in my skull. The hollow-point bullet also picked up a three-quarter-inch piece of bone—they found it stuck in the bullet. After hitting the occipital, the slug traveled between the skull and skin, the maxilla and the mandible under the cheek—shattering both, and also tearing up the salivary glands, and lodging up in the right sinus."

"What happened to the bullet?"

"That's a cop's question," Vorpagel said and grinned.

"I really wanted that bullet. The doctor slit open my face and pulled it out, but it got lost someplace. I didn't need reconstructive surgery on my jaw. Three days later they took another X ray, and it had almost totally grown back together."

"What happened to the Rasti?"

"Jean Claude was being transferred as a prisoner to another island; he was shackled, hands behind his back, with heavy chain. He fell overboard. He went to the bottom of the Caribbean like an anchor. The body was never found, except by the sharks."

"Pushed overboard?"

"Who knows? This was one mean man. He was under suspicion of beheading two people and staking their heads out on a golf course. He was also under suspicion of raping the U.S. attorney's wife, and later, shooting an airline pilot. That makes for enemies. The Bureau did pick up a rumor that Jean Claude had angered some local *mambo*—a witch. One word from a *mambo* could have arranged the 'accident.' But, as I said, who knows? Just another part of a web of violence that involved many people."

"Many people?"

Vorpagel started walking with Marcus toward their cars. He thought about the secondary victims.

Borden withdrew psychologically, blaming himself for losing his gun, the gun that shot Vorpagel. He got divorced a year after, then committed suicide eighteen months later.

Marcus repeated his question. "Tragedy to many people?"

"It's personal."

Vorpagel remembered more. Nancy withdrew and went through incredible mental stress and years of treatment, before she could handle what happened. He was in a hospital for a week—she took three years before recovering, after months in the hospital.

A bad time in their marriage. But they had survived the pain, the distance, and had remained together.

Marcus asked, "It was no tragedy that Jean Claude got his in the end."

"I must admit, when I first heard Jean Claude was sleeping inside Davy Jones's Locker, I felt a fierce joy. But, I'm a Methodist, a Christian. A believer. So I've felt, from time to time, twinges of conscience for that kind of reaction."

Vorpagel grinned. "Of course, from time to time, to tell the truth, I still imagine Jean Claude's last moments and feel elated. But it's still not justice."

Marcus asked, "What are you doing next?"

Vorpagel shaded his eyes, looking at the setting sun. There was a half circle of golden glow filling the western sky. "What else? A new class."

Marcus said, "Thanks for the education."

"Remember, the world is constantly changing and so is the field of law enforcement and criminal behavior. In order to keep up with the law and criminals we have to constantly keep ourselves updated on these fields. Just as the medical profession is dramatically changing, so it is with the criminal justice system."

"I'll remember."

Vorpagel smiled slightly. "Also, remember, take up

our quarrel with the foe. To you from failing hands we throw the torch."

The rookie said softly, "In Flanders field the poppies grow."

"And you are the next wave that fights the war. Fought by that incredibly thin blue line."

Why was this book written?

Why another book about profiling?

It is important for the citizens of a nation to know how their criminal justice system works. It is important for a citizen to understand new concepts and advances in law enforcement.

This book is a plea from one representative of the thin blue line. A plea to the public from a person who has spent almost a half-century teaching law enforcement personnel and investigation over one thousand *equivocal* death cases.

In that half-century I have learned a few things.

Over fifty years ago, I was given a month's training course in medical technique to be a corpsman in World War II, and five years later I was sent to the frontline in Korea and attached to a Marine rifle company.

I was horrified. Horrified at the chaos racked on the bodies of men. Horrified because the tiny amount of training wasn't enough. I performed amputations and plugged sucking chest wounds, but still knew those men would die.

I vowed then that should I survive, I would learn everything I could about any job I was in, so that I would never have these feelings of incompetence, inadequacy, and loss of self-worth.

What a terrible state our criminal justice system was in. Training was pathetic.

I joined the ranks of the FBI. I was placed in the training of local police officers and in assisting in investigation of unusual and bizarre crimes.

Police training in this country is woefully inadequate. The average hours of training are four hundred to six hundred. The cops are being shortchanged. To become a beautician in California, the law requires 1,600 to 1,800 hours of training.

Do we really think that giving a person a gun requires less training than giving a person a license to wield a pair of scissors?

And coroner departments across the country are in even worse shape. There are over three thousand coroner jobs in the United States. Every county has one. Only about two hundred coroners countrywide are forensic pathologists. All are entitled to pronounce the "cause of death." Most of them have little or no training. The job of coroner is, for the most part, an elected position.

Why are so many hours of education required to become any kind of professional, yet someone who happens to be related to the sheriff can become a coroner or a coroner's deputy and know absolutely nothing about forensics or pathology?

I've seen cases in which small animals were mistaken for babies by the attending coroner. I've seen homicides pronounced as suicides and vice versa. The havoc this wreaks on the minds of the victims' relatives is horrific.

The solution is easy. Pass a law requiring that coroners must receive training in forensics and pathology. Bartenders have mixology schools. Cooks have chef schools. Do we really care more about how our drinks and food are prepared than the cause of death of loved ones?

The public should know how depressing it is for police officers to solve a case and then watch as juries are swayed by legal histrionics. The cops know that most DA's offices are staffed by poorly paid prosecutors with small staffs, who cannot compete against the public funding for defense attorneys. And even when the defense attorneys lose, they drum up excuses for years to come, basing appeals on new decisions.

Jurors, for the most part, are poorly informed of the law and are barred from having or seeing important evidence on some tiny technicality. A possible solution? We need professional juries, just like we have professional judges. How often can we get unanimous juries, and why are 2–1 or 3–2 or 6–5 good enough for judges?

The cases in this book are frightening. But they are not all that unusual. There are some very bad people roaming around. The criminal system needs overhauling, it needs more education, and it needs more money to perform its role.

The next time a bond issue comes up for financial aid to your local police department, stop a moment before flagging the "no" card on your ballot. Stop and think about the guy down the street, or the gardener mowing your neighbor's lawn, or your barber. Stop and think that any one of these ordinary citizens could be a psychotic.

One-half of one percent of the country is psychotic. Doesn't sound like many people. But there are over two hundred and sixty million Americans. One-half of one percent of that figure is over one and a quarter million people.

One and a quarter million psychotics roaming free and waiting to explode should scare everyone into giving their police department the funds they so desperately need.

Think about it the next election.

INDEX

ABOUT THE AUTHOR

RUSSELL VORPAGEL, during thirty-two years of law enforcement, has become a legend at the FBI. He, along with Robert Ressler and others, helped put the FBI Behavioral Science Profiling Unit on the map—the psychological profiling unit immortalized in *The Silence of the Lambs*. Having served as a special agent in Quantico, New York, Detroit, Sacramento, Baltimore, and Monterey, he, as Ann Rule states, *"is not a television or movie detective who is teaching you; he is the real thing."* Featured on CBS's *60 Minutes*, he has trained FBI personnel around the world, and has taught courses in law enforcement to local and federal officers in thirty states. He obtained his law degree from Marquette University. He is currently a consultant and expert witness in criminal cases for his students, law enforcement, and prosecutors. He resides with his wife, Nancy, in Loomis, California.

JOSEPH HARRINGTON has been writing full-time since 1986. Born and raised in San Francisco, he, like his father and grandfather before him, was for many years the proprietor of a bar and grill under his own name in the city. He now lives with his wife, Lorraine, and family in the Mother Lode country of northern California.